ROCK & ROLL WAR STORIES

BY
GORDON G.G. GEBERT
LYNN RAMAGÉ

PITBULL
PUBLISHING LLC
2004

Rock & Roll War Stories
ISBN 0-9658794-2-9
Copyright © 2004 Pitbull Publishing LLC
All Rights Reserved

FIRST EDITION published by:
Pitbull Publishing LLC
P.O. Box 350
Fleetwood, New York 10552-0350

E-mail: PitbullPublishing@yahoo.com
GordonGebert2004@yahoo.com
www.GordonGebert.com

Edited by: Marcie X., Chris Decker, Ron Rogell, Warren G. and Craven Moorehead

Cover Concept and Design: Gordon G. G. Gebert, Geraldo Mercado, Marcie X, Mike A.
Cover Model: Sunni McKay
Cover Photo: Bobbye Medina

Grateful acknowledgement is made to the following for permission to reprint previously published Internet material:
Metal Sludge - www.Metal-Sludge.com - All other acknowledgements are enclosed

Special thank you to my brother Warren for making me funny - because "he's funny!"
Thanks to all those who contributed and encouraged:
The Gebert Family, Marcie X, Warren G., Bob McAdams, Mr. and Mrs. Chops, Slick Pelt, Sharlon S. (for helping famous people do laundry), Frankie Hudak, Craig L., Paul H., Pat Reale, Frank D'Amico, Joe Renda, Hane S., Danny Cheng, Geri R., MaryAnn Pierro, Mike Annechiarico, Mike Kakos, Mike Sciotto and family, Wendy Moore, Paula A., Dr. Pam, Dr. Steve and Dr. Dorline, Joe and Margie Grepo, Fani, JJ, Doug B., Gary H., Anthony D'Allesandro, John Cleary, Robin Irvine, Will Alexander, Keith Emerson, Greg Lake, ELP, Ralph Gatton, KORG (Jack and Ted), Nikki Tyler, St. Louis, Steve Altman, Nick Fakouri, Junko, Chris and Beth at www.KISSasylum.com, Judge Falcone, Janet Reno, Billy Reno, Joe Mulv., Downtown Gerry Brown, Shea Stadium Gang (Tony C., Jimmy, Frankie, Icky, Steven, Eddie, Cabo Bill, Angel, Mike Piazza and everyone else), Melissa St. Jude (www.MelissaStJude.com), WYSP, Drew and Mike in Detroit (You rock!), Tabitha Cash and all the girls that took the time to be creative and contribute. To Gene S. - I bet the cover fucked you up. I don't KISS and tell EVERYTHING! When is the bowling match? Good luck.

Lynn Ramagé would like to thank: Mike Vagnoni, Chip Ruggieri, Maggie Wang, Deb Scarpell, Steve Trager, Sherry Gretzula, all at Roadrunner, Dave Weakley, A.G. Automotive for keeping her car going, Drs. Luber and O'Reilly for keeping her going, George Eliassen for being there.

Gordon would like to
Dedicate to the Memory of:

Gene Russo
Manny Ford
Manny Berlingo
Denise Faranda
Vincenzo L.
Bill Mooney
Benjamin Orzechowski
Paul Agosta
Armand Gonzaga
Eric Carr
Mike Katz
Linda Susebach
Lisa Del Conte
Kim Rowe
Victims of The Station Fire - West Warwick, Rhode Island
&
The Innocent Victims of the September 11th Terrorist Attacks

The Disclaimer (Thank You METAL SLUDGE)
ROCK & ROLL WAR STORIES DISCLAIMER!

Nothing on these pages should be taken seriously.
Any resemblance to real persons living or dead is purely coincidental.
ROCK & ROLL WAR STORIES is meant for educational purposes only.
Void where prohibited.
ROCK & ROLL WAR STORIES may be too intense for some viewers.
Parental discretion is advised.
All models over 18 years of age.
Do not try this at home.
Some assembly required.
For recreational use only.
Batteries not included.
No HAZMATS.
No other warranty expressed or implied.
List each check separately by bank number.
Contents may settle during shipment.
Use only as directed.
Do not use while operating a motor vehicle or heavy equipment.
Postage will be paid by addressee.
Subject to CAB approval.
This is not an offer to sell securities.
Apply only to affected area.
Do not stamp.
Use other side for additional listings.
Do not disturb.
If condition persists, consult your physician.
No user-serviceable parts inside.
Freshest if eaten before date on carton.
Subject to change without notice.
Times approximate.
Simulated picture.
No postage necessary if mailed in the United States.
Please remain seated until the ride has come to a complete stop.
Breaking seal constitutes acceptance of agreement.
For off-road use only.
As seen on TV.
One size fits all.
Many suitcases look alike.
Contains a substantial amount of non-tobacco ingredients.
Colors may fade.
Slippery when wet.
For office use only.
Not affiliated with the American Red Cross.
Drop in any mailbox.
Edited for television.
Keep cool; process promptly.
Post office will not deliver without postage.
List was current at time of printing.
Return to sender, no forwarding order on file, unable to forward.
Not responsible for direct, indirect, incidental or consequential damages resulting from any defect, error or failure to perform.
At participating locations only.
Not the Beatles.
Penalty for private use.
See label for sequence.
Substantial penalty for early withdrawal.
Do not write below this line.
Falling rock.
Lost ticket pays maximum rate.
Your canceled check is your receipt.
Add toner.
Place stamp here.

Avoid contact with skin.
Sanitized for your protection.
Be sure each item is properly endorsed.
Sign here without admitting guilt.
Slightly higher west of the Mississippi.
Employees and their families are not eligible.
Beware of dog.
No shoes, no shirt, no service.
Contestants have been briefed on some questions before the show.
Limited time offer, call now to ensure prompt delivery.
You must be present to win.
No passes accepted for this engagement.
No purchase necessary.
Processed at location stamped in code at top of carton.
Shading within a garment may occur.
Use only in a well-ventilated area.
Keep away from fire or flames.
Replace with same type.
Approved for veterans.
Booths for two or more.
Check here if tax deductible.
Some equipment shown is optional.
Price does not include taxes.
No Canadian coins.
Not recommended for children.
Pre-recorded for this time zone.
Reproduction strictly prohibited.
No solicitors.
No alcohol, dogs or horses.
No anchovies unless otherwise specified.
Restaurant package, not for resale.
List at least two alternate dates.
First pull up, then pull down.
Call toll free number before digging.
Driver does not carry cash.
Some of the trademarks mentioned in this product appear for identification purposes only.
Objects in mirror may be closer than they appear.
For promotional use only.
Record additional transactions on back of previous stub.
Unix is a registered trademark of AT&T.
Do not fold, spindle or mutilate.
No transfers issued until the bus comes to a complete stop.
Package sold by weight, not volume.
Your mileage may vary.
Shake well before opening.
Contents may explode under pressure.
Objects in mirror are closer than they appear.
Warning: Choking hazard.
Unplug before removing back.
Contains sulfides.
ROCK & ROLL WAR STORIES has been modified to suit your intelligence.
ROCK & ROLL WAR STORIES does not reflect the opinions of network management.
This supersedes all previous notices.
Lather, rinse, repeat.

No dumping.

CONTENTS

INTRODUCTION

FOREWORD

COMMENTARY

CHAPTERS

INTRODUCTION

This book is a collection of the wildest stories from musicians, managers, radio personalities, photographers, groupies and anyone else connected to the music business, along with first-hand experiences by yours truly. These accounts will have you saying, "No way that's true." But everyone in the music industry knows that anything is possible. Some stories are already legendary; the other stories deserve to be.

How did I come up with the idea for the book? It all came about after my first book *KISS & Tell*. As soon as that book took off, I received calls from people in the "biz" that loved all the insane stories in *KISS & Tell*. The conversations were hilarious and my ego was stroked as they repeated their favorite anecdotes from the book. But, in true cocktail party fashion, they always seemed to come up with a story that would top their favorite story from my book. It was a running theme with every conversation. After the umpteenth story was told to me I decided I had to document their insanity along with my experiences. Everyone agreed it was a great idea. Hence ROCK & ROLL WAR STORIES was born.

I have to profusely thank Philadelphia's own Rock Journalist, Lynn Ramagé, for her invaluable contribution. THANK YOU LYNN.

To add to the appeal of this book I had to get hot babes involved somehow (who da man?). After *KISS & Tell* came out, my e-mail address went public and I was getting unsolicited pics of naked girls wanting to meet me. I was impressed. The question came to me... "How could I share this with my beloved readers?" I came up with the brilliant idea of having girls submit "creative" photos that had a military theme. In between each chapter a babe is featured - like a "ring girl" at a boxing match. With these great anecdotes I also give you... THE GIRLS OF ROCK & ROLL WAR STORIES! They have nothing to do with the stories themselves, but who the hell cares? Be sure to pick up The Girls of Rock & Roll War Stories Calendar.

Thank you for all your support. Keep the cards and letters coming. Let's put that in 21st century terms; Keep the e-mails and attached files cumming! ENJOY!!!

Thank you,
Gordon G. G. Gebert
GordonGebert2004@yahoo.com
www.GordonGebert.com

FOREWORD from Lynn Ramagé

I interview rock stars for Philadelphia's *Out on the Town* entertainment newspaper and *Ironworx* metal magazine. To me it's a glorified hobby. Freelance writers are right up there with the starving artists because most of us have to work "real jobs" to support ourselves. Back in the day, I also booked bands for the last dinosaur rock club in Philly called the Cellblock. The "Cell" has since burned down. I was there for two and half years and worked with over 36 national acts. I really enjoyed the production end of the business. I've had a fun ten years, the only thing I want written on my tombstone is, "but she had a good time!"

When Gordon discovered my contacts and connections he immediately sent me his first book *KISS and Tell* and I was rather amused by it. I have A.D.D. My attention span is worth shit, but I have to admit I read that book in one night! I just couldn't put it down! Well, I sent him some of my work and he asked me to collaborate with him on his latest book project. I thought, "Sure, why not?" I really appreciated the opportunity he was sharing with me.

We talked everyday online and eventually met at this cute little Rockabilly bar in Glenside, PA called The Blue Comet. He drove down with his friend Chops, the bass player from the band *Slick Pelt*. When I first saw Gordon I liked the way he carried himself, very self-assured. I also liked his personality. He is a rather blunt individual. I enjoyed working with him.

So here it is, I hope you enjoy. If any of the language or subject matter offends anyone, I'm not apologizing. If you offend easily, I suggest you read a lighter book.

COMMENTARY from Gordon

I called my publisher and put a halt to publishing this book after September 11th, 2001 because I wanted to add this one page commentary and allow time to heal. I felt this was important since the title of the book has a war connotation and I do not want readers to think I am making light or taking advantage of the difficult time the world is in. This book and working title was in the making since early 1999. Before we get to some inane comic relief I offer the following:

In the wake of the September 11th terrorist attack on the United States, I've had very interesting political conversations with friends and adversaries around the world via phone and Internet. Topics included how the world looks upon the United States and how they feel about us. I've traveled the world. I've seen first-hand how other cultures look upon us. They see us as "cocky" - that we are self-important. We do believe we are the number one country in the world. But let me explain to all our foreign neighbors around the world that you are mistaking our "cockiness" for what is extreme pride!

When I travel to other countries I am aware that I represent the U.S. I am extremely APOLOGETIC for not speaking native languages. Other Americans are seen as arrogant assholes when they EXPECT others to speak English in a foreign country. When I travel I am well aware of respecting other cultures and customs (as much as I want people to have the same respect when in the U.S.). We are looked upon as being the loud, ugly, spoiled Americans. I am one that wants to dispel that stereotype.

Human beings have an internal conflict with feelings of jealousy and prejudice. We all feel jealousy or prejudice at one time or another, sometimes to the extremity of hatred. Since the release of my two books on *KISS* and Ace Frehley I know full well the receiving end of hatred. I've personally experienced both ends of the spectrum of kindness and jealousy. The difference in good people and bad is how they handle their negative feelings. When someone feeds upon their hate and anger and acts upon it in a totally irrational manner (which in their own mind is rational and justified) that's when the line is crossed amongst a civilized and uncivilized human being.

September 11th is indelibly etched into my memory, as I live in New York only twenty miles from Ground Zero. It has affected me directly. I still have moments of disbelief. How can jealous scum come to our free country and use this country's very freedom against us? Anyone in the world can come to the U.S. and better their life and yet, there are people in the world that want to destroy a free country and even die to reach that goal. It is unfathomable.

The United States must choose (by the time you read this a decision might have been made already) from an array of very horrible choices. Whatever decision the United States makes I hope it's the best of all the ugly choices we have. We are in a war now. Unfortunately there will be more innocent civilian casualties in the United States and the rest of the world. Hopefully the whole world can get past this ugliness and move towards a more harmonious state. I hope and pray for world peace.

Back to unimportant matters:

For the overzealous, fanatical critics of my work... it's only entertainment. In the immortal words of Bill Murray in the movie *Meatballs*, "It just doesn't matter." If you don't agree with me, feel free to convey it to me in a civilized manner. To the people that support my work, I sincerely thank you.

To the men and women who serve our country - I SALUTE YOU and THANK YOU!

GOD BLESS AMERICA
GOD BLESS THE WORLD

CHAPTER 1
KISS AND HELL

At every book signing, radio show, concert, pretty much every appearance I make, I always get the same question - "Did you ever run into Ace or the *KISS* guys after the book *KISS & Tell* came out?"

Ace and I haven't run into each other physically, which is amazing because we run in the same circle of friends and industry people. We also live very close to each other. I do, however, see mutual friends that are always updating me on the latest gossip, whether I want to hear about it or not.

One friend ran into Ace in a restaurant in the Jefferson Valley Mall in New York. My friend was sitting with a buddy waiting for their food when Ace and a female companion walked in to get a table. He didn't recognize Ace at first. He said he was wearing a leather jacket and looked terrible. He was with some skanky bimbo (his words, not mine). When he finally realized it was Ace Frehley, he asked his buddy to come with him to approach Ace at his table.

He went up to Ace, extended his hand and said, "Ace Frehley! Do you know who I am?"

Ace said, "No," as he gladly shook hands, smiling and undoubtedly trying to impress his companion as a recognized celebrity.

My friend proceeded, "I'm Gordon Gebert's friend."

Ace quickly pulled his hand away as his smile quickly transformed into anger, "I hate that motherfucker!"

My friend laughed as he left the table obviously ruining Ace's dinner that night.

I heard one of Ace's reactions to the book, firsthand, when *KISS* was on the New York radio show Opie and Anthony. I was in my car when they were taking calls. One fan called in and asked about the validity of the *KISS & Tell* stories. Ace went ballistic. There was yelling and confusion in the studio.

Paul Stanley said on the air, "Ace just blew a gasket." I wonder why Ace reacted like that? The truth still haunts him.

I confronted Ace when he was a guest on Eddie Trunk's radio show (102.7 WNEW FM in New York), and Eddie has not forgiven me since.

KISS & Tell co-author Bob McAdams called me and said, "Ace is on the radio! Turn it on and listen to all the bullshit he's feeding the fans."

Towards the end of the show, fans were allowed to call in and stroke their idol's ego. One fan called in and asked about the book. Ace answered politely but still seemed perturbed by the question. The only thing that got me pissed off was when he tried to dismiss Bob and I as two mooks that hung out with him, and that the book was all bullshit. I went right to the phone and I called the station. I lucked out. They were at the very end of the show and they stopped screening calls and let me directly through. Ace had been beating the death out of Austin Powers' references because the sequel was just released and Ace is a movie fanatic who always seems to latch onto the catch phrase of the moment. When the movie *Scent of a Woman* came out, Ace was "hoo-ha"ing 24 hours a day. If he ever went for communion the priest would've said, "body and blood of Christ" and Ace would've responded "hoo-ha."

So, to not identify myself right away and get cut off, I did my stupid attempt of an Austin Powers impression. Of course Ace took the bait and they let me continue.

Then I ambushed him, "Hey Ace, it's your old buddy Gordon Gebert, author of the book *KISS & Tell*." I assumed Eddie thought it was just a caller kidding around but Ace immediately recognized my voice and I heard the start of pandemonium in the studio. Eddie let me continue but Ace was obviously trying to get him to cut me off the show.

"Yeah - it's me, Gordon. So Ace, you think my book is..." and they cut me off in mid sentence. In their panic they knocked the show off the air. There was dead air in the New York tri-state area as Ace and I spewed out explicatives at each other on the phone. "Fuck you!" "No - fuck you!!" That went back and forth for about half a minute and then he hung up. When they finally got back on the air, you could hear Eddie and Ace trying to compose themselves as they were prematurely wrapping up the show. Eddie did most of the talking trying to console Ace and re-focus his legendary guest.

Ace would never even consider publicly debating me on the truthfulness of my books, as he knows better. (Howard, are you listening?)

The majority of *KISS* fans I meet at *KISS* conventions and book signings are, for the most part, reasonable people. They keep a level head about the *KISS & Tell* book controversy. Most fans keep it in perspective and don't take the band's frailties to heart. But there is that one-percent minority that are assholes. They take the book as a personal insult.

One such person was Christopher Napolitano who writes for Playboy magazine. Bob McAdams and I were painted as being "two hanger-ons" by Christopher in the March '99 Playboy issue article on *KISS*. I called him at the Playboy office to have a civil conversation to defend myself and it got really ugly, real fast. You would think that the guy would be an intelligent, sophisticated man working for a respected, sophisticated adult magazine. But he turned out to be among the one percent. He couldn't get his puckered lips any farther up Gene, Paul, Ace and Peter's collective asses. Here is a married man (with child) working at Playboy pretending to be a bachelor and writing articles like "How to Pick Up a Super Model." And he called Bob and I shams? What a friggin' hypocrite. I guess that's being a hanger-on in the Playboy Enterprise.

Editorial Director, Arthur Kretchmer apologized profusely and offered me response space in a future issue of Playboy. I think they were afraid of lawsuits because Pitbull Publishing paid a nice chunk of change for a full-page advertise-

ment in that same issue. I asked him what good that would do? What *KISS* fan is going to read the update in a later issue? The target audience is gone, the damage is done.

Keeping with the tradition of *KISS & Tell MORE*, Christopher Napolitano not only receives the Kiss My Ass Award but he's been upgraded to the Kiss My Hairy Asshole Award.

KMHA Award

On September 29th, 2001 the Friar's Club and Comedy Central held a "roast" honoring Hugh Hefner at the New York Hilton. Ace was in attendance and was supposed to sit on the dais at this black tie affair. It turned into such a mess for Ace that it made the media. Here is a press release of what supposedly happened:

From: Kayos Productions (Carol Kaye - Ace's Publicist)
You may have read elsewhere on the web what supposedly happened to Ace at the Hugh Hefner roast in New York City, well right from the source here is what really happened...

When Ace got up to go to the bathroom Jackie Martling took his seat. When Ace returned, he decided to sit with his daughter rather than make a big scene getting back into his seat. That is it - simply put.

Nice try Carole. I feel your pain. A publicist for Ace Frehley is like being Pavarotti's dietician. Your story is bullshit! How do I know? Read on, this is what REALLY HAPPENED.

I received a frantic call on my answering machine the night of Hef's Roast, "Yo, pickup! It's Frankie, PICK UP THE PHONE!"

I had no previous knowledge of this event. One of my comedian friends is a member of the Friar's club (and, no, it wasn't my friend Frank D'Amico, star of stage and screen.)

"Wassup Frank?" I answered calmly.

"I'm down at the Friar's Club roast for Hugh Hefner and you'll never fucking believe who is on the dais!" with all excitement in his voice.

I'm figuring Hugh Hefner... Playboy, I thought, "Hmmmmm... who could it be? Candy Loving? She's gotta be fifty by now... who cares about her?"

Not having the patience to go into a guessing game, I impatiently asked, "Who?"

"Ace Frehley," Frank said with excitement.

"That's nice Frank. Have a good time," I said as I hung up the phone unenthused. He must have had nitro redial, by the time I let go of the phone it rang again.

"Yo, don't hang up. I want to fuck with him," he said with a scheming tone.

I wasn't into it but I humored him, "What do you want to do?"

"I don't know. I'll think of something," he said... a true improvisational comedian.

"Frank, I don't care. Go bust his balls if you have to. I don't want anything to do with him," I hung up again, not giving him a chance to talk me into whatever he was plotting. Frank knew me well enough to know all the "Ace" crap was behind me.

Fifteen minutes later the phone rang again, my answering machine kicked in with my terse message, "you have reached me, leave a message, beeeeeeeep."

"Yo, Gordon, pick up the fucking phone, pick it up now," with a sense of urgency from Frankie.

I picked up the phone, "Whaaaaaaaaat?" knowing what this was all about but not really interested.

"He's in the bathroom," Frank said excitedly. I could feel the wheels turning. He's hatching his own immature MTV show right on the spot.

"Frank, I'm really not..." he cut me off.

"Here he comes. I'm going to say a fan is on the phone. You talk to him," he rushed his words out as he began his friendly, charming spiel, "Ace! Ace! I have a friend on the phone that wants to talk to you real quick," I heard Frankie keeping pace with Ace, "He's a big fan and it would really make his day if you just said hello." I didn't want to talk to him.

Then I heard Ace stop and say to Frankie, in his very distinctive voice that sounds like Kermit The Frog on downers, "If I had to say hello to every fan on a cell phone..." and as if he couldn't finish the thought, all of a sudden he grabbed the phone and quickly blurted out, "Rock and roll." The "roll" part swiftly faded as he quickly handed the phone back to Frankie thinking he appeased him.

"Are you still there?" he was checking if I had hung up by now.

I continued humoring him with a half-hearted, "Yeah Frankie?" Not giving up, he tried to pull at Ace's heartstrings.

He pleaded, "Ace! Don't be like that. You really do want to talk to this guy. He's a big fan. C'mon, here, just say hello." I was literally rolling my eyes. I couldn't believe he said that! It sounded like I was the poor little sick kid in Bangladesh who needs your e-mails. Ace finally gave in. He took the cell phone and as he drew it near his ear.

Frankie said, "Just say hello. His name is Gordon."

The bomb was dropped. All of a sudden I heard Ace go ballistic, "Gordon? Gordon Gebert? That MOTHERFUCKER! (Seems I am the only 'Gordon' in Ace's world.) Tell that fuck to go fuck himself!"

Frankie was in hysterics as he got on the phone, "Did you hear that? He's still freaking out. Oh, shit," as he narrated the scene.

"Frank, why'd you go and do that?" but I was half laughing at Ace's over-the-top reaction. It amused me but not to the extent Frankie thought it would. "You're lucky he didn't destroy your cell phone!" I said.

"He's freaking out like a bum on the street muttering to himself. He's walking in circles," Frank said as he was enjoying the havoc he created.

"Talk to you later Frank. Say hello to some Bunnies for me," as I hung up in mid play-by-play hopefully for the last time. I didn't hear from Frankie the rest of that night.

I received several phone calls and e-mails the following Wednesday night from many friends. They all had the same theme. "Did you see the New York Post?"

Little did the New York Post know what started his "rough night."

New York Post, Wednesday, October 3, 2001

Page Six.com

Frehley's fury

ACE Frehley had a rough night Saturday. First, the KISS guitarist showed up minus makeup at the Friars Roast of **Hugh Hefner** with a black eye (given to him by his soon-to-be ex-girlfriend). Frehley then suffered the indignity of having his coveted seat on the dais stolen by **Jackie** "The Joke Man" **Martling**, forcing him to sit in the audience. Later, Frehley and his daughter **Monique**, 21, joined Hef, his harem of hotties, and **Rob Schneider** at Spa, where a drunken clubgoer groped and tried to kiss Monique. Frehley, his patience shot, responded by punching the guy in the face.

To add insult to injury comedian Jeffrey Ross, at Hugh Hefner's Friars Roast, pointed out Ace in the audience and was quoted as saying, "My childhood hero is here tonight - Ace Frehley from *KISS*."

He then continued, "Ace Frehley without the makeup looks like Dr. Joyce Brothers with makeup." The broadcast of the event panned on a gratuitously laughing Ace and then panned to - yes, a chuckling Dr. Joyce Brothers.

My favorite Jeffrey Ross line of all time was said about Penny Marshall; "I wouldn't fuck her with Bea Arthur's dick!" And he said that with both Penny Marshall and Bea Arthur present. He also authored the legendary quip to this question, "Hey Jeff, did you see the Pamela Anderson issue of Playboy?"

Jeff replied, "See it!?! I ruined it!!

Another event had Scott Ian, from the band *Anthrax*, talking to Ace before he went on stage for the New York Steel Benefit in New York City. He asked Ace if there was eventually going to be a final *KISS* show in New York. Ace said, "I hope so, so I can finally get them out of my fuckin' life."

Ace's most recent fuckup happened (I'm sure there are plenty more) when he was hired to play and schmooze at the 3rd Rock and Roll Fantasy Camp held in New York City the week of June 19th, 2003. RRFC is the brainchild of David Fishof and Harry Javer.

If you had the cash, $5,995.00 to be exact, you could've lived your fantasy of being a rock musician for 5 days and 4 nights and jam with the likes of *The Who*'s Roger Daltrey, Ace Frehley of *Kiss*, Markie Ramone of *The Ramones*, Leslie West of *Mountain*, Simon Kirke of *Bad Company*, Joe Lynn Turner of *Deep Purple*, Ricky Byrd of *Joan Jett and the Blackhearts*, Mark Farner of *Grand Funk Railroad*, Bob Mayo of *Hall & Oates*, Liberty Devito of Billy Joel's band, Jack Blades of *Night Ranger* and Rod Price of *Foghat*.

The itinerary included 6 hours of daily jamming including group lessons and jam sessions, small group instruction from celebrity rock n' roll musicians, record and bring home a music demo and video, celebrity seminars with industry celebrity artists and top industry music executives, an opportunity to do a Vh1 Classic promo, daily meals with other campers and celebrity musicians, plenty of photo and autograph opportunities, perform a Battle of the Bands at The Bottom Line night club and travel to and from camp events. Their cancellation policy is no refunds available.

Ace was scheduled to do an "Up Close and Personal" and talk to the "campers" about life on the road with "one of the greatest rock bands ever" for an hour and a half. Obviously, they did not know Ace's track record on commitments.

Newsday ran the following article:

Headbanging Guitarist Ace Frehley has taken head-banging to dizzying new heights.

Frehley, from the makeup-wearing heavy- metal band Kiss, reportedly fell down a flight of stairs and suffered a concussion, according to organizers of the Rock and Roll Fantasy Camp, a training session for amateur musicians that was held June 18-22 in Manhattan.

Frehley was scheduled to appear at the event June 19 and speak about his 30 years in the business, but he failed to show up.

He was taken to a hospital, where he remained for at least two days, according to a camp official. Calls to Frehley's publicist and management company were not returned.

Frehley, whose silver face paint and matching guitar and outfit made him one of Kiss' most popular members, is scheduled to tour with the band in August.*
*not confirmed by KISS or Ace's management.

Having known Ace, let me speculate on this one here. Ace either received half or maybe all of his fee before his scheduled appearance and didn't feel like following through with his commitment, beating the organizers out of their money and disappointing all those poor campers. Can we say un-happy campers?

Ace now says he's going into acting. ACTING??? When is he going to start acting like a human being?!

A final ironic note to all the Ace insanity from the die-hard *KISS* fans. I was recently informed that the mention of my name or Bob McAdams' name, as well as our books, were banned from the Ace Frehley List (Bulletin Board) on the Internet. I went to see it for myself and sure enough (amongst a few pages of rules) I found the following:

There is one topic that is off limits on The Ace List. The book KISS & Tell or its Authors. The topic was discussed on the list a long time ago and quite frankly everyone got just plain pissed off over it and later it was decided by the majority of the list that it was not worth discussing. And why talk about a book that runs down our favorite guitarist in the world anyway?

My question to the Board's operator; Now that Gene Simmons corroborates much of my book *KISS & Tell* in his book *KISS & Makeup* and endorsed my book as truth on his web site, are you going to apply the same rule and ban the mention of Gene Simmons?

CHAPTER 2
ROCK & ROLL BOOT CAMP

I began playing keyboards at the late age of fifteen. I don't know what the attraction of playing rock music was.... yes I do. Who am I fucking kidding? It was a great way to meet girls and get laid. But I was still passionate about the music. As the years went by, my circle of musician friends dwindled as they got "real" jobs. They found their soulmates (or so they thought) and I continued with my musical career and banging broads; so to speak. I guess I didn't mature. I should've been in a bad marriage by now instead of still having bad dates.

The insanity of rock can happen to any band, famous or not. The first band that I played in, at the age of sixteen, was a restaurant act called *Moods*. We played easy listening music and we sucked, plain and simple. The highlight of the night was my disco version of the *Star Wars* theme. This was way before Bill Murray spoofed it on *Saturday Night Live*. I was into *ELP* and *Deep Purple* and here I was stuck in Italian restaurants playing *Misty* and Burt Bacharach tunes. I wanted to make noise and play loud and proud. I wanted to smash the reverb and beat the crap out of my organ (the instrument).

So, at the age of 18, I joined *Legend*. I think every city in the United States had a garage band named *Legend*. This "*Legend*" had three brothers in the band. The oldest brother, Mike, played guitar and was into southern rock. The middle brother, Eddie, played a little of everything and took the bass duties. He was into melodic rock like the *Moody Blues*. The youngest, Steve played the drums and was into anything that grooved - it didn't matter to him as long as he was banging on drums (or pots and pans for that matter). The band was rounded out by myself and Tony, the singer. Tony and I were the only non-blood in the band. Tony was into glam rock - *T-Rex*, *Rocky Horror Show*, *David Bowie*; anything that allowed him to dress in drag was alright with Tony. My contribution was progressive rock. You can imagine our rehearsals when we had to pick songs. Surprisingly, the band was quite democratic in choosing material. We all got a chance to play our favorite stuff, to the pain and suffering of our audience. We should've called the band SYBIL.

I did insane shit in the band and didn't even warn the other members. One of our first shows was at Roosevelt High School in Yonkers, New York, famous for alumnus Steven Tyler. We presented one of our Sybil-like shows playing the entire aforementioned repertoire. When it came time for my choice of music I opened up with Keith Emerson's rendition of *Fanfare For The Common Man* as a segue into a version of *Rondo* (ala *The Nice* - goes way back kids - try to find it on Morpheus). As the bass and drums broke into the intro, carefully placed flash pots (well - we thought they were carefully placed) went off. The rest of the band didn't know about the planned pyrotechnics. One of my best friends, Bobby, and I, along with my brother, built the flash pots from scratch. I don't want to give the details of how they were built and give some delinquent ideas to experiment with, but they were very ingenious if I say so myself. The only problem was we got just a "tad" too carried away with the amount of powder and their mixtures. We had two kinds of flash pots, each with a specific explosive powder. One was for explosions and was loaded with flash powder. The other used gunpowder and was for shooting huge flames six to ten feet high.

Well the "shooting flame" pots worked perfectly. They were un-strategically positioned right next to huge stage curtains that could've instantly gone up in

Flash pot can

Mimicking my influence, Keith Emerson

flames. One disaster luckily avoided. The explosive pots were placed in front of the stage. As I was rocking and beating up a Hammond L100 organ an excited audience member rushed toward the stage and my brother tackled him right before he got to the front. For an instant the surprised fan was going to throw a punch at my brother until a loud explosion (to put it mildly) diverted his attention. This guy came within a foot of getting his head blown off. That night we could've easily been wrapping a headless corpse in burnt curtains.

The next week we played at our local Lemko Hall. Since I couldn't afford to buy the real deal, Bobby and I had built this big giant box to emulate Keith Emerson's modular Moog Synthesizer. The actual big Moog's went for upwards of $30,000. That was in 1978. This home-made one was about four feet high, two feet wide and a foot in depth and cost me about $30 in wood. The "front panel" was made out of plywood and painted black. The sides had

10

simulated wood contact paper glued to them. The back had barn-styled doors so you could pretend to "work on the guts". Housed in this monstrosity were a flanger, a spring reverb and a PAIA sequencer kit that didn't work - in other words, nothing of usefulness. The most ridiculous thing we added were Christmas tree lights to simulate LEDs (Light Emitting Diode). The rest of the "synthesizer" was filled with bogus labeling of wishful oscillators, filters, amps and appropriate inputs so a shitload of wires could be plugged in to look cool. Old keyboard players know about the tech descriptions. Don't worry if you don't understand. All you have to know is this giant piece of shit we built looked mighty impressive from far away. To carry around this friggin' thing we installed 1966 Lincoln Continental door handles on the sides. Instead of "borrowing" the Moog logo, we had to come up with our own name for this thing. The famed illustrator Robert Pizzo, also the guitarist in the New York band *The Treble Boys*, ended up painting big white letters across the front labeling it "MARZBOX". It sounded cool considering it was a monstrous empty box. This faux "synth" sat on top of an Eminent organ, which included (for all you gearheads out there) two Arp String Solinas built into a home organ cabinet bigger than a Hammond console organ. Like I said before, it LOOKED impressive. It was the last piece of equipment to be placed on the stage, and the first piece to be loaded out the door so nobody could get a good look at it. So many people would come up to me asking to look at this one-of-a-kind "instrument". Friends that were in on the joke would tell curious on-lookers that the Marzbox cost twice as much as the most expensive Moog synthesizer as we quickly whisked it away. It was so "expensive" you weren't even allowed to look at it up close.

Rick Wakeman eat your heart out!
Don't you wish you had a MARZBOX?!

During my encore performance at Lemko Hall, I jumped on top of the Hammond organ and proceeded to play the keys backwards. I then rocked it to make the organ make wailing sounds that only come out of a Hammond organ when you abuse it. As

I was giving the crowd a great show, the organ cracked a few planks on the stage floor. I felt it give way but nobody else noticed it. I moved away from the damaged floor and continued the show. I was gearing up for the last chords when the final flash pot was about to go off. The can was sitting very high up on top of the Marzbox. Big crescendo ending, drummer smashing away at crash cymbals and then BOOOOM! I was friggin' stunned as I was prepared for the explosion ducked under the organ and I still felt the concussion. It knocked me on my ass. I heard screams from the audience and while still stunned, I wobbled off the stage. I couldn't remember much. One part adrenaline and one part shell shock put me into a dream-like state. People were surrounding me congratulating me on a great show. I finally heard the audience applauding. I looked up at the Marzbox and the top was BLOWN UP. The fucking pot went off like a grenade. My brother got hit with metal shrapnel from the can. I looked up at the ceiling and it had a mushroom burn-mark on it. I was freaking out.

Apparently, we all knew we ran low on flash powder so we made up the mix with gunpowder. But everybody kept adding more powder to the pot without each other's knowledge. Hence the HUGE EXPLOSION.

While backstage, Pete Agosta (the promoter) was looking for me. I was shitting in my pants. Here we go, I'm thinking lawsuits, all kinds of problems.

Mr. Agosta, as we all respectfully called him, was a promoter from the Bronx and had big connections, like Pete Bennett (Pete Bennett is most known for his work with the Beatles. Check out his web site www.PeteBennett.com). Mr. Agosta "discovered" Steven Tyler and is featured in *Aerosmith*'s book, *Walk This Way*. This was one guy you did not want to get on your bad side, especially if you were trying to make it in the music biz.

Meanwhile, the fire department eventually showed up as the residual smoke poured out the front doors. Mr. Agosta finally cornered me.

I remember saying to myself, "Here it comes."

"Aur you rethponthible for de show?" he sternly asked with a foreign accent that I still wouldn't be able to identify to this day.

I meekly said, "Yes," as I couldn't blame anyone else. Believe me, it crossed my mind to just lay it on some unsuspecting bystander.

He grabbed my hand, and firmly shook it and said, "Dat waz ab-to-lute-ly dee moist a-maz-ing fuck-eenk show I eveer saw." This was a huge compliment coming from a guy who handled name acts. In the few years I had known him, I never heard the word "fuck" or any other curse words come out of this guy's mouth. He was blown away, no pun intended.

I was stuttering, "What about the ceiling?"

12

You don't know the instant relief I had when he acknowledged the damage with, "Noooo praa-bleem," sounding like Dustin Hoffman in *Wag the Dog*. All he talked about was having us back as soon as possible. Meanwhile, my brother's face was bleeding, the Marzbox was blown up and the ceiling had a mushroom bomb mark on it. I didn't even bother to mention the stage floor, which became even more ironic the next evening...

The next night Mr. Agosta's sons, Peter Harlow, Ricky Riff and Paul (I forgot his stage name) were about to take the stage. They were collectively known as *Fastball* (not the same *Fastball* as the one that did *The Way*). They were an energetic, melodic, pseudo punk band. As local musicians did back then, we all attended each other's shows whether we liked the music or not, as a show of support.

A group of us watched from the back of the hall as the initial chords began for their performance. Lead singer Peter Harlow dramatically ran out onto the stage, leapt into the air with a beautiful Air Jordan split and came slamming down. It was a beautiful rock and roll move, except he landed right on the spot I broke the night before. He went crashing right through the fucking stage. He was waist deep in stage - the audience was stunned. I was slinking down in the back as all my friends and I were cracking up as Peter crawled out of his humility pit. Sorry Peter!

Marzbox logo creator, Robert Pizzo, had a band called *Gracie* and they were booked to play at Lemko Hall on Halloween night. Bobby and I extended our pyro services to them as we proposed a brilliant idea. We would place flashpots inside ghoulishly carved pumpkins and strategically place them all over the stage. One pumpkin was placed on Robert's Marshall amplifier.

The band was haunted that night as the power kept blowing out on them. As they went on to their final chord to end the night, Robert turned toward his Marshall to get that trademark feedback out of his guitar. He had forgotten about the flashpot inside the pumpkin. His face was about two feet away when suddenly, BAM!, the flash pot went off. This time, luckily, with almost the right amount of powder. We managed to blow the tops of the Jack-O-Lanterns off. Instead of smoke on the ceiling, there were pumpkin bits all over the place. Robert said he saw the flashed imprint of the carved pumpkin face burnt into his retinas for days. The explosion was captured on audio tape. I have a copy. I still flinch whenever the explosion comes. It gets me every time.

CHAPTER 3
BANG A GONG

It's hard to believe that back in the 70's, before August 1st, 1981, when MTV was born, we only had seven television stations. And none of them had 24-hour music videos. In fact, any worthwhile rock 'n roll was airing on weekends after 11:30 p.m. The two main programs were *Don Kirshners Rock Concert* and *The Midnight Special*. And even those shows had their share of crap. You had to wade through many weeks of *Maria Muldaur* and *Leon Redbone* to get to *David Bowie* or *Jethro Tull*. We were so desperate for anything that rocked, we would find our-selves delicately fine tuning the UHF knob to try and catch some fuzzy, weak audioed British show that might be airing something like *T-Rex*. And if you actu-ally found something, you'd call your friends no matter what time of night it was. If the wind was blowing right, maybe he would be able to tune it in too. This might sound pretty pathetic, but actually all this deprivation gave every morsel of rock a real impact.

I remember the first time I saw *Queen's Bohemian Rhapsody* video. Until then, I had never seen them play, let alone, seen a moving image of them. I knew every second of their first three albums (yes - the big round black vinyl things) but had only seen still pictures of them. By today's standards, that seems absurd. But it did give the broadcast a real eventful feeling. The next day, everyone would talk about it and analyze it. We didn't even have VCR's to record it. It thundered into our living rooms for a few minutes and then it was gone. You relied on memory if you wanted to re-live it. Sometimes they'd broadcast the show "simulcast" on the radio. Then you would check with all your buddies to see who got the best audio recording of it off the radio. It took a little more work to be a music fan in the 70's. You had to seek it out; it did not come looking for you.

Another great source that we would constantly keep our eyes and ears on was a radio show called *The King Biscuit Flower Hour*. They would broadcast record-ings of live concerts from all around the world. The wide variety of bands spanned from *The Beach Boys* to *Motorhead*; from *Elvis Costello* and *The Police* to *Linda Ronstadt* and *Elton John*; from *John Lennon*, *The Stones* and *The Who* to *Blondie* and *Adam Ant*. Not to mention *Clapton, Peter Gabriel, Bowie, Zappa, U2* and countless others.

"The Biscuit", as we affectionately called it, debuted on February 18th, 1973 with an odd mix of bands that included *Blood, Sweat and Tears* (check out the David Clayton Thomas story later in the book), the *Mahavishnu Orchestra* (fea-turing fusion greats John McLaughlin, Billy Cobham and Jan Hammer) and, then

unknown singer/songwriter, *Bruce Springsteen*. Like any other show it had its share of clunkers. But over the 22 years, the "*Biscuit*" has covered virtually every band worth it's salt. Over 450 artists had been recorded, including the band *Angel*, who I currently play keyboards for.

I never, to this day, understood how a flour company (King Biscuit flour company) became involved with recording and broadcasting live concerts over the radio. For years, I always thought the *King Biscuit Flower Hour* was actually the King Biscuit Flour Hour. Check out their web site: www.king-biscuit.com.

One really top-notch act was broadcast on a Sunday night in March, 1974, on WNEW radio. It was a *Who* concert, and it turned out to be one that the *Who* probably wishes I never listened to. During one of the breaks the DJ said to stay tuned for a "special announcement for New York area fans." I could almost guess what it was going to be. Sure enough, they announced tickets would go on sale the following morning for four Madison Square Garden shows on June 10th, 11th, 13th and 14th for the *Quadrophenia* tour. I immediately called my friend, Del, who was a huge *Who* fan. He immediately called our other friend, Claude, who wasn't such a huge fan, but jumped at the chance of sitting in a huge arena filled with pot smoke. Claude had an older brother who worked in Manhattan and could go to the Garden to pick up the tickets. (This was way before the days of Ticketron or Ticketmaster. You had to actually go to the venue to buy the tixs.) He bought four tickets.

The Who sold out all four nights in New York on the strength of a single 60-second radio spot! It was their first appearance in New York in three years. It was their first appearance at the Garden ever, and all 80,000 seats sold out in record time.

Del and Claude each took a ticket, leaving one for me and the extra one for my younger brother. The only problem we had now was convincing our parents to let us go. We were about a cab ride, a subway ride and another cab ride away from the Garden. We would be out till at least one a.m. And, oh, we were age fifteen and thirteen. It would be sorta like a *Leave It To Beaver* episode, except this episode would have a lot of urine stained hobos and deranged panhandlers in it. We had about three months to wear down our parents with lots of screaming, crying and yelling. I don't remember how we did it, but somehow we did.

Early one June night (Thursday, June 13th, 1974 to be exact) we headed out to our first big time rock concert (Except for my younger brother. He actually went to the Fillmore East when he was nine years old and saw *Alice Cooper* and

Bloodrock. My oldest brother took him as sort of a goof. You know the hippies who had the cool dog with the bandanna? My brother went a step further. He brought a little tiny human being with a bandanna.)

I'm not sure anyone of us really knew where we were going, but no one had the balls enough to admit it. So we all sorta headed out, secretly hoping the other guys would find the Garden. Thank God the streets in Manhattan are numbered. You really have to be a total idiot to get lost in Midtown. And we weren't "total" idiots. Finally, we spotted Madison Square Garden. It was like finding Mecca.

We made it to the concert early enough to "check out our seats" before the show started. With the lights on, our seats didn't look too bad. We were in the upper deck, but we could see the stage pretty good. The arena looked friggin' huge and it was already filled with smoke. Every stoner from every high school in the tri-state area seemed to be there including the king of all stoners, our friend Claude. He smoked more weed than John Hurt in *Midnight Express*. And he was well equipped for this evening's festivities.

While Claude rolled enough joints for section J, the three of us decided to get some food. While we were on line for our jumbo salty pretzels, we heard loud music blasting through the outer hallways of the Garden. The warm-up act had started without us. As we ran back into the arena a totally new atmosphere struck us. It was pitch black and the stage suddenly looked a lot smaller. Only specks of colored lights lit up the stage. We also realized that we were much more behind the band than we first thought. The sound was loud; but really distorted and echoey. For a few moments, I really couldn't tell who the hell was on stage. I could see that the lead singer was holding a flute. That was the first clue that this was indeed the warm-up band, *Golden Earring*. They were a Dutch band who had a smash hit at the time called *Radar Love*. After getting used to the acoustics and the nose bleed seats, it became apparent that this band was there to really kick ass. They tore the roof off the place and the crowd really responded to them. During the finale, the Drummer (Cesar Zuiderwijk) jumped clear over his kit as his seat exploded with several huge flash pots. This was like stealing a page right out of the Keith Moon playbook. We couldn't wait to see how the *Who* was going to follow this show. It was going to be spectacular, we were sure of it.

After the lights came back on for intermission, we could hardly see the other side of the Garden because the amount of pot smoke had quintupled since the beginning of the show. At this rate we would be in cardiac arrest before the *Who* played *Baba O'Reilly*. We headed out to the snack bar lines for a few sodas while Claude went to the bathroom to pull another ounce of pot out of his colon (I'm speculating on that one). Just as we were getting to the front of the line, it happened again. The music started blaring. The *Who* started without us. They were pounding out *Can't Explain*. Within seconds the snack bar became a ghost town as everyone rushed back to his or her seats.

There they were. It was a little unreal. Keith Moon was attacking his drums like a Beni Hanna Chef having a seizure. Townsend was wind-milling his power chords. Entwistle was frozen solid like a stuffed.... Entwistle. And Daltrey had his mic swinging out to the tenth row. We were in awe that he swung the microphone so haphazardly and didn't hit anyone including himself. It was like seeing Mount Rushmore. Except for one important thing... it sounded like shit. *Golden Earring* sounded much better. Don't get me wrong. The *Who* were playing great. The sound system was heinous. Daltrey's mic kept cutting in and out and the monitors were crackling and feeding back. You could tell Daltrey was getting more and more frustrated. You could feel the tension even in the nosebleed section. You could see him kicking the monitors around. He knocked one into the first row. He slammed one microphone into the stage floor as his roadie handed him a new one. Between songs he complained to the soundman and techs that were set up around the 40th row. The other three band members never outwardly complained. It seemed to be Daltrey who was getting the most fed up. And then in an instant, it all came to a head. Daltrey's mic cut out during the first encore, *Punk and the Godfather* and he walked over to a stack of P.A. speakers and toppled them over mid-song. He slammed his mic down and left the stage as the *Who* finished up the remaining chords, with Townsend feebly supplying the last few vocals. After the song, the remaining members of the *Who* left the stage. The crowd was stunned. They weren't done playing all their greatest hits. There were at least a couple of standard encore songs yet to be performed.

After a few minutes some roadies came out onto the stage. Everyone was sure that they would make some minor equipment adjustments and the *Who* would return. Not so. As the roadies hit the stage, the house lights came on and they began to break down the equipment. The people in the audience were booing and cursing. The gentle hippies stood on their seats holding lit matches in quiet protest. As for the four of us, we didn't know what to do. For all we knew this happened all the time. We were disappointed, but we weren't as mad as a lot of the people around us. We stood up and booed to feel included with the crowd. But we were sort of smiling as we did it.

As we stood there my brother put on his jacket to get ready to leave. He hadn't worn it till then, only carrying it since it was a warm summer day. In his pocket he found a heavy wooden spool of thread. It must have been put there to remind my mother to sew some tear in the armpit or something. As he stood there feeling the weight of this oversized spool in his hand, he nudged me and said, "Betcha I can hit Moon's gong from here."

"Huh?" I said back.

"How much you wanna make a five dollar bet I can hit that gong with this spool?" my brother challenged.

"Are you friggin' nuts? You know how far that is? You won't even reach the stage, let alone hit the friggin' gong. And besides, we're at a weird angle."

Claude chimed in, "What are you fuckin' high?" Which was a joke because he was the one wrecked off his ass all the time.

"Make it ten," he said.

Claude and Del started goading him on, "Yeah, go ahead, you can do it," all the time knowing for sure he wouldn't make it. They just wanted to see some poor schmuck in the lower section get smacked in the cranium. All around us, while we were involved in this stupid little banter, the crowd was still booing the *Who*. My brother took off his jacket, cracked his knuckles and stepped out into the aisle so he could get a little more leg into it. With two quick crow hops he whipped it into the pot filled air. It was like slow motion as it hurled its way down toward the stage. Right away we realized that it had the distance. This little spool was gonna

Gordon with the John Entwistle Band: Gordon on the left, guitarist Godfrey Townshend in the middle, drummer Steve Luongo in the back, John Entwistle right front. R.I.P. John Entwistle

19

make it. But did it have the accuracy. We kinda lost sight of it for a second, and then cutting through the droning boos of the crowd you heard it... dunggggggggggggggg!!!!

He hit the fucking gong. We couldn't fucking believe it. It was clearer than Daltrey had been all night. The spool ricocheted off a few more things and came spinning out into the middle of the stage. The crowd heard it and responded. They let out a mock cheer. One of the roadies walked by and kicked it into the orchestra pit. A second later it was thrown back up on the stage. The audience cheered again. And then it started happening. First there was a beer cup thrown, then a beer bottle, then a shoe. It just started building up like a *Who* song. A roadie stood out at the foot of the stage and implored the crowd to stop. He was pelted with everything from Good 'n Plenty to hash pipes. He took cover in a nest of amplifiers. Another roadie built a foxhole out of trap cases. They were locked down under fire. Shit was flying in from everywhere. The gong was the main target. It had more dents in it than Roseanne's ass. It was pandemonium. People started jumping up on the stage and actually smashing equipment. We stood above the ongoing carnage with our mouths open. My brother was scared that they would somehow trace the spool of thread back to him. Del and I were scraping together ten bucks and Claude, with eyes like slits, sat there and said, "cool," as he sucked in another joint.

Back at home, my parents were watching the riot "live" on Channel 7 Eyewitness News. They were there to do a fluff piece on the *Who*'s first appearance at the Garden and ended up with a reporter with his finger in his ear, crouching around like he was in Vietnam. My parents were freaking out. Little did they know, Mom's spool started it. We got home around midnight.

Well, we got the spectacular finale we anticipated. We heard that the *Who*'s equipment would end up smashed to bits at the end of the show. We just never figured we would play such a huge part in getting it done.

CHAPTER 4
ROCK & ROLL CADET

In 1979, *Spoiled Rotten* was my first real local gig in New York. It was a cover band, but they worked for the number one booking agency at the time, Creative Talents Associated, or as they were known back then by the acronym, C.T.A.. The band had a real P.A., lights, a truck and a road crew and we worked practically every night in every club in the New York, Connecticut, New Jersey area.

I was excited as we headed out to do our first gig at a club in Long Island called Beggar's Opera. All my friends made the trek to see the debut of *Spoiled Rotten*. I was impressed as the road crew professionally loaded in my equipment, set it up perfectly and tuned my synthesizers. We had the biggest, baddest road crew in C.T.A.'s entire roster. They had names like Orca, Grizzly, Rhino and Lucifer. You get the idea. The club was packed, psyched to hear a new band. The band was in the dressing room (an actual dressing room - I hit the big time) all trying on last minute wardrobe decisions. The previous day I went out and bought a rock and roll "outfit" (for the time) of a few tight pants and glittery shirts, etc... I decided on the white "inhale to get them on" *Sassoon* jeans. You had to put your body in a horizontal position to begin the war between body and pants. I tried the jeans on the night before at my parent's house.

My mother screamed, "You are going to wear THOSE? You can see that you are circumcised!" That's the point Ma.

In stereotypical rock fashion of the time, I opened the first set with a solo keyboard intro. With strings, synthesizer, organ, piano I began the set with a mutated version of the *Angel Theme* from the band *Angel* (little did I know then that I would be playing with that very band today). I gave the signal to the rest of the band to hit the opening dramatic chord to begin *Spoiled Rotten*'s rock and roll legacy. I jumped up ala Pete Townsend to come down dramatically on the keyboards and impress that crowd with showmanship right out of the gate. The huge spotlights, along with a dramatic flash pot explosion, were going to blind everybody.

Instead, the only thing I heard was sssshhhhhhhhhhrrrriiiippppppp. My fucking pants split. Not a little crotch split. Not a little ass sticking out split. The pants almost split in half off of me. The only thing that held the fucking thing from completely disintegrating was the waist band. Zipper and all, from waistband to waistband, my pants were flapping like a flag in the wind. Now I'm playing with one hand covering my privates, trying to face into the keyboards, like it was a bathroom stall with somebody trying to sneak a peak next to me.

My mind is reeling, "Wow! The lights couldn't have been any better. That spotlight is really on the mark. I shouldn't have complained at sound check that I'm not getting enough spotlight."

Now I'm yelling at my brother trying to get his attention. He comes over to the side, by the keyboards, and I'm yelling, "Get my green Rick Wakeman shirt." This particular shirt fit really long, down to my thighs, almost like a skirt, with big huge bell sleeves. He ran into the dressing room and came back with a white short midriff type of shirt.

I yell again, "I want the green, Rick Wakeman shirt."

He yells back, "But it won't match the rest of what you're wearing. This is better!"

I yell back, "I'm losing the rest of what I'm wearing. I split my fucking pants you idiot!" I yelled "you idiot". Imagine - me calling him the idiot when I'm the one onstage with practically my fucking birthday suit on. Well, in your younger years you don't yell "you idiot" to a sibling when you are in a precarious predicament. It inadvertently gives them the upper hand. Of course that pisses him off and he takes his sweet time back to the dressing room and returns with the properly requested clothing, but dangles it just out of reach from me, asking for an apology about the "you idiot" remark. Meanwhile, I'm trying to play at a hundred decibels, look cool and also try to get the attention of the light guy to turn OFF the friggin' lights on me. Finally, between the second and third song, I got my green shirt on me and can resume normal rock moves as the shirt is long and acts as a skirt.

Playing in the clubs.

What a relief.

The stage was high and I rocked between two sets of keyboards on both sides of me. A crowd of girls congregated in front of my side of the stage. I was thinking this was really cool. This is what it's all about, rock chicks.

I noticed all the girls in front of me had Cheshire-like grins. My ego was swelling. I said to myself, "Self, I love this job." Towards the end of the set I figured out why all these girls congregated in front of me. They were all looking up under my "dress". Free peep show. By now I didn't give a fuck, it was our secret between me and the girls in the front row.

CHAPTER 5
YOU MAKE ME SO...

Joe Renda is one of the funniest guys I know and I wish I got to hang out with him more. He's a great guy to be around. When you got together with Joe you always knew it would be "good times, good times." "Crazy" Joe Renda owned a recording studio called NorthLake Sound in North White Plains, New York. A little side-note, Joe discovered the infamous Jerky Boys. I wish he would write a book on that whole experience.

The studio was in an A-frame house in the style of a European ski lodge, a very cool place. The clientele ranged from the local bands, to the guys in *KISS*, country western artists, etc... Joe was working on a project and had the great fortune of getting David Clayton Thomas, lead vocalist of *Blood, Sweat and Tears*. You might know him from old hit songs like *You Make Me So Very Happy*, *Spinning Wheel*, etc... etc... from the 70's.

At the time Joe was able to get David, he was on top of the charts. So this was a great honor to have a star of such magnitude in the presence of his studio. Joe called David's publicist and asked what he could do to make David's experience at his studio an enjoyable one. The publicist suggested having David's favorite food on hand, Mexican.

"Great, I'll call the Mexican caterers," Joe said happily. He was excited. This is going to be great.

The day of the recording session arrived and so did David with his entourage. Everybody entered the studio and David wanted to get right to work. He went directly to the vocal booth. All the musicians crowded into the room where the engineer was manning the huge sound mixing board. Everybody was in awe as David Clayton Thomas professionally belted out the song. The recording reels were spinning. The VU meters were jumping. Lots of nodding and thumbs up were given in salute of his talent.

After the song, David had both hands on his headphones and asked into the microphone, "How was that?" and waited for a reply as he looked through the soundproof glass. For those not familiar with a recording studio, communication is made through the studio speakers and the artists' headphones.

The engineer hit the "talk-back" button and looked around the room for opinions when someone said, "That was okay."

David took that as he could do better and said, "Let's do it again." Joe glowed with content that the recording process was under way and went up to his office.

After awhile, Joe went back down to check how it was going and David finished another "take" and asked the same question, "How was that?"

Instead of the engineer hitting the button, someone else hit the talk-back and said, "That sucked!"

Joe was shocked and astonished how honest and brutal the criticism was and David just said, "Okay, let's do it again."

Usually in a studio you must coddle fragile egos and always remain positive. Any criticism must be made in a positive way to keep the vibe of the recording process on an encouraging path to get the best performance out of an artist.

Joe thought, "Wow! David Clayton Thomas is so professional they cut out all the namby pamby bullshit and just cut to the brutal truth. Very impressive. His producer must have some incredible ear. It sounded great to me."

Joe went back upstairs to do paperwork and leave all the recording work to the industry's best of the best. An hour later Joe decided to peak in on the progress again. David was still singing the same song with incredible intensity. After the "take" David asked the same question but with a hint of impatience, "How was that?"

"That sucked," was the reply back into his headphones.

David spotted Joe and pointed at him, "You!"

Joe, half pantomiming the reply through the soundproof glass, "Me? Huh?"

"Yeah, you." the speakers in the studio boomed, "Do me a fucking favor! Get

From left to right: Tod Howarth, Crazy Joe Renda and John Regan at a Florida KISS Convention.

26

rid of your fucking producer! The guy who keeps telling me I suck!!"

Joe replied, "My producer?" Joe looked puzzled, "I thought he was your producer."

Joe turned to the critic, "Who the fuck are you?"

"I'm the caterer," the guy said with a hint of a Spanish accent that was now quite evident. Joe went ballistic, "THE CATERER?! WHAT THE FUCK ARE YOU DOING?"

Now the Spanish accent got thicker, "De guy ask how de singing. I dought he ask me. I don't like dis kind of mu-sic."

David Clayton Thomas stormed out of the studio pissed. Joe was mortified.

After a week of phone calls and apologies, Joe convinced David to come back to the studio and finish the project.

The day arrived and David made his reappearance and they half chuckled about the event of the past week. To make it up to David, one of the house musicians whipped out a big mound of coke. David took one look, turned around and left the studio to never return again.

CHAPTER 6
SOMETHING STUPID THIS WAY COMES

Before you read this, get a hold of the *Still Wicked CD* entitled *Something Wicked This Way Comes* (Amazon.com carries the CD) and play track five (entitled *SAM*). Listen to the lyrics very closely. Those lyrics are dedicated to this chapter!

After the *KISS & Tell* book came out my plan was to get back to the business of music. A lot of people wanted me to play with them while writing *KISS & Tell* but I was on a mission to finish the book.

My good friend, Vince Martell (*Vanilla Fudge* guitarist), introduced me to Ron Leejack. Gene Simmons and Paul Stanley had a band called *Wicked Lester*. Ron was their guitarist before Gene and Paul decided to break up the band and move on to form a new band called *KISS*. Ron was also infamous for briefly playing with an old classic band called *Cactus* which featured Tim Bogert, Carmine Appice, Jim McCarty, and Rusty Day. Ron and I became friends and every conversation ended with Ron saying, "we gotta get together and play."

During my book writing period, I had an idea on the backburner to take the unreleased *Wicked Lester* material and re-record them with a celebrity-filled roster of musicians. It would be a fun project and *KISS* related. So when the book was finally done I called up one of my best friends, drummer Michael Sciotto, and I asked him if he wanted to do this recording project with me. Mike agreed. I would center this undertaking around the original recording artist, Ron Leejack. It would finally bring that "we should play together" idea to fruition. We would recruit other celeb-friends and come out with something really cool. I actually spoke to the original producer, Ron Johnsen and he thought it was a brilliant idea.

Our first song to be recorded would be *She* (*She* was written by Gene Simmons and Stephen Coronel. The song was recorded by both, *Wicked Lester* and *KISS*.) Mike laid down a great rhythm track and our endeavor was under way. Ron laid down the rhythm guitar tracks and scratch vocals. I wanted to bring in Joe Lynn Turner to belt out the final vocals. We got sidetracked from doing the whole "*Wicked Lester*" cover project by recording an idea Ron had. It turned into a song entitled *Cajun Rain*.

Then I brought in a song penned by another friend, Kerry Scott, called *Bodies Talking*. The project was going off in all different directions and taking an extremely long time to finish. I wanted to get something complete before a May '98 European *KISS* Convention tour so we would have product to sell. Unfortunately, all communications broke down between Ron and I. I will spare the people involved and avoid the ugly details - I know, I know, I'm letting some of you people down. You expect more from me. To make a real long, ugly story short, Ron and I went our separate ways with duplicate master tapes. I went on to Europe and just plugged my books. Ron went on to Europe selling unfinished, rough-mix cassettes of the material we worked on. When I got back from Europe, Mike and I went into the studio and finished the cuts we began. I wanted to put out some representation of the music we worked so hard on. So the CD entitled *Still Wicked -*

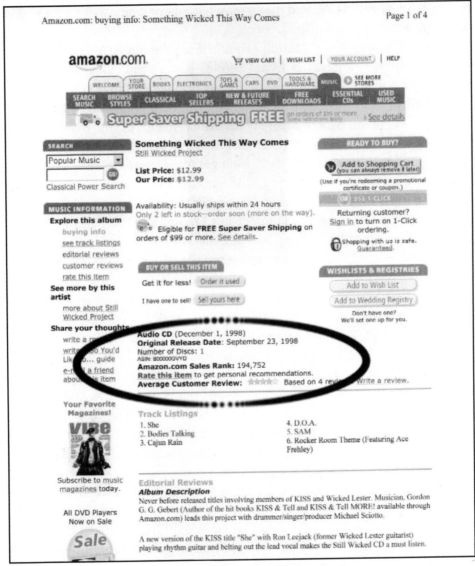

Circled: Amazon.com Sales Rank

Something Wicked This Way Comes was finally released. Not what was originally intended, but at least something was done.

Here is where the insanity begins. Actually the insanity began when we started the project but I am being extremely benevolent in this chapter.

Amazon.com distributes the CD. I received a letter from a lawyer, hired by Ron, to send an accounting of all CDs sold and demanding a residual payment as per their calculations. Ron AND his lawyer estimated over 194,752 CDs sold by Amazon.com. I wanted to know where the hell they got that figure. Ron's lawyer said Amazon.com has a sales count right on their web site. I wanted to know where does it state over 194,752 CDs have been sold? Their reply again, right on the Amazon.com web site.

I kept wondering where the fuck were they getting the idea that over 194,752 CDs had been sold through Amazon.com? If that were the case, they wouldn't even be able to find me as I would be in Tahiti sandwiched between several naked girls drinking some concoction with an umbrella in it.

I looked on the Amazon web site to see where they could possibly get this idea. As I looked around I started laughing hysterically out loud. Amazon.com Sales Rank number 194,752. What fucking morons! The number meant how many CD's were OUTSELLING ours. There were 194,752 CD titles that were ahead of the *Still Wicked* CD title in sales, NOT the number of CD's sold. I could see a musician making the mistake but a supposed educated lawyer. This fucking guy hounded me for months threatening to take me to court. I blew them off on purpose because I was waiting for the subpoena. I wanted to go to court so bad just to see them look like complete fools. I think they eventually figured it out. I never received the court papers.

Another lawsuit that finally did go to court was from Lydia Criss. The following blurb is what was covered by the press.

NEW YORK (NY) - Professional photographer, Lydia Criss (ex-wife of *KISS* drummer, Peter Criss) has filed an "unauthorized use/failure to give credit of copyrighted photos" infringement lawsuit against Musician/Author Gordon G.G. Gebert. Lydia Criss is claiming that photos she took have appeared in the book *KISS & TELL MORE* without her consent. Lydia Criss of New York, NY, filed the lawsuit Tuesday, March 26th in small claims court. Gebert has not filed a counter-claim. Ms. Criss is seeking damages that include the usage of two photos in the book, *KISS & Tell MORE* on page 213, Chapter 13, in the section entitled *The Photo Gallery* (ISBN # 0-9658794-1-0 Pitbull Publishing Company). She is also seeking damages for "lack of photo credit" and "unauthorized use." The total in damages equals $1500.

Ralph Edwards/Stu Billett Television production offered the two parties to settle their case on the television show *The People's Court*.

Mr. Gebert comments, "I would love to do this case on *The People's Court*." Mr. Gebert continues, "This is the third legal action brought against me. The last two cases I won. I'm very confident I will win this case also. I'm tired of playing mister nice guy and not counter-suing... but all this makes great material for my new book *ROCK & ROLL WAR STORIES*!"

The Court Case is scheduled for a date in May, 2002.

It all started in mid-November, 2001 I received an "invoice" from Lydia for $1500.00. It was for two photos in my second book. First of all, I was wondering how Lydia got the idea that these were her photos to begin with. At the time, all New Yorkers were pretty much still stunned about the 9/11 attacks. I didn't think much of the "invoice" and I filed it under "stupid things I need not worry about".

Lydia Criss

New York, New York ▓▓▓▓

Invoice

Invoice #: 00062501
Date: 11/11/01
Ship Via:
Page: 1

Bill To:

Gordon Gebert

Ship To:

Description	Amount	Tx
1 Photo of MARK NORMAN and TWO UNIDENTIFIED GROUPIES by Lydia Criss	$250.00	
Additional Fee For UNAUTHORIZED USE of above photo	$250.00	
Additional Fee For LACK OF PHOTO CREDIT for above photo	$250.00	
1 Photo of MARK NORMAN, MANNY FORD, JOHN OSTROSKY, LYDIA CRISS AND TWO UNIDENTIFIED GROUPIES by Lydia Criss	$250.00	
Additional Fee for UNAUTHORIZED USE of Above Photo	$250.00	
Additional Fee For LACK OF PHOTO CREDIT for above photo	$250.00	

These photos were used on Page 213, Chapter 13, in The Section entitled THE PHOTO GALLERY of "KISS & TELL MORE!" ISBN #0-9658794-1-0

Thank you!

Freight:	$0.00
Sales Tax:	$0.00
Total Amount:	$1,500.00
Amount:	$0.00
Balance Due:	$1,500.00

A month later I received another invoice. This time it was stamped "Past Due / Please Remit". I knew Lydia did not think kindly of my books or me for that matter. We used to be very good friends before Ace turned into an asshole. Like I said before in *KISS & Tell MORE*, some mutual friends of Ace and I were mature enough not to take sides and remained good friends with me. I held great respect for those people. The people, like Lydia Criss, I just shrugged off as not worth having as a friend if they were going to be immature and take sides. I took these invoices as just a way to try and bust my balls. It wasn't working. Either that or she needed money.

In late March of 2002 I received a Fed-Ex letter from Warner Brother's-People's Court Producer Alicia Justin. It stated that The People's Court wanted to hear the case that was filed against me by Lydia Criss. At the time I received this I was not aware of any lawsuit. I didn't receive any subpoena and I had no clue what it was about.

I called the Producer, Ms. Justin and asked her what the letter was all about. She told me that her staff sifts through thousands of pending court cases around the nation and they chose our case. I thought Lydia Criss asked The People's Court to take her case. Ms. Justin assured me it's just luck or whatever you want to consider it that the case was chosen. She said I should be receiving the regular subpoena in the mail to appear at local court within the next few days. I then asked her if she knew who I was or what the case was about. She did not know and I practically heard her smile when I explained I was the author of the controversial *KISS* books and Lydia Criss was the ex-wife of a member of *KISS*. I heard her contain her excitement as she wanted this case to air. She explained to me that she had to contact Lydia and get her to agree to do the show along with me. She asked me if I had any questions. I looked over the letter and asked her about stipulation number two. *Should the Judge rule in your favor, The People's Court will award you a nice sum of money for your time. (In regular small claims court, you would not win anything.)* I asked her what the "nice sum" was. She said two hundred dollars. I just laughed and said nothing. She said she would get back to me on that. She asked if I was interested and not wasting her time. I said I was definitely interested if I could use the show for publicity purposes for my books. She said it would not be a problem at all. We ended our conversation with her telling me she would get back to me with Lydia's decision.

A few days passed and I received the regular subpoena in the mail. The court case was scheduled for May 8th, 2002 in New Rochelle, NY.

Ms. Justin called me the day I received the official notice. She was happy to tell me that Lydia was interested in having the case tried on *The People's Court*. I was surprised. Alicia (we were now on a first name basis) provided more details for me for the televised court date. They would provide limo transportation to and from the show. I was allowed as many "guests" as I wanted to come and be on the show as spectators in the court room. I asked Alicia if I could bring down a bunch of girls in *KISS* makeup to fill the court room gallery. I was half-joking but she said that was a fantastic idea. I think she was bucking for a raise after this show aired. She also told me my sum of money would be considerably higher if I won the case.

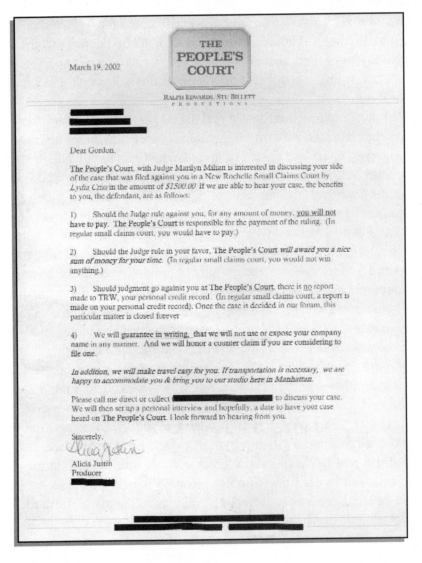

March 19, 2002

THE PEOPLE'S COURT

RALPH EDWARDS / STU BILLETT
PRODUCTIONS

Dear Gordon,

The People's Court, with Judge Marilyn Milian is interested in discussing your side of the case that was filed against you in a New Rochelle Small Claims Court by *Lydia Criss* in the amount of $1500.00 If we are able to hear your case, the benefits to you, the defendant, are as follows:

1)   Should the Judge rule against you, for any amount of money, <u>you will not</u> have to pay. The People's Court is responsible for the payment of the ruling. (In regular small claims court, you would have to pay.)

2)   Should the Judge rule in your favor, The People's Court *will award you a nice sum of money for your time*. (In regular small claims court, you would not win anything.)

3)   Should judgment go against you at The People's Court, there is <u>no</u> report made to TRW, your personal credit record. (In regular small claims court, a report is made on your personal credit record). Once the case is decided in our forum, this particular matter is closed forever

4)   We will guarantee in writing, that we will not use or expose your company name in any manner. And we will honor a counter claim if you are considering to file one.

In addition, we will make travel easy for you. If transportation is necessary, we are happy to accommodate you & bring you to our studio here in Manhattan.

Please call me direct or collect ▮▮▮▮▮▮▮▮▮▮▮ to discuss your case. We will then set up a personal interview and hopefully, a date to have your case heard on The People's Court. I look forward to hearing from you.

Sincerely,

Alicia Justin

Alicia Justin
Producer

I assured her that I was going to win and I also told her that she should be prepared for Lydia's temper. I could sense she was playing dumb when she asked why I said that. I just told her Lydia could be unpredictable. Alicia 'fessed up that Lydia was a little difficult on the phone with her but assured that she was interested in doing the show. She could not discuss anything further than that. I understood. She told me she would call in a few days with more instructions.

I was prepared for the show. I had a bunch of girls lined up to dress up in sexy outfits with *KISS* make-up on. They were all going to get copies of my books to hold up in the court room. I was going to put my books on the podium. I wasn't even worried about the case. I knew what my defense was. Even if I turned it into a circus and lost I didn't care. Lydia would win and so would I.

A few days later Alicia called, Lydia backed out of doing the show. I was so disappointed. So was Alicia. I asked her what the problem was. She said that Lydia was all high-strung on the phone and said she wanted to pursue this in regular court.

I said, "Didn't you reiterate the advantages to her?"

Alicia said that they went beyond show policy and assured her that she would be paid for her appearance whether she won or not. If Lydia won, she would be awarded $1500 plus appearance money. They offered her extra perks that Alicia wasn't about to disclose to me. I got the picture. Lydia was being vindictive and wanted to beat me in regular court so the money would come directly out of my pocket. *The People's Court* was guaranteeing her money even if she lost. Lydia was cock-sure that she was going to win.

We ended up going to regular court on May 8th. I walked into small claims court. It was packed with litigants. I spotted Lydia sitting alone in the third row. I sat in the last row and awaited role call. As they called out my name, I belted out a loud "here!" and I saw Lydia turn around. I smiled and waved. She had a puss on her face. The court instructed that our case would be heard by an arbitrator and all the legal mumbo jumbo that it was a final decision and no appeals could be made, etc...

I was in a good mood and I made a conscious effort to make this confrontation as amicable as possible. A woman judge led us to a room where our case would be heard. The gentleman that I am, I let the ladies go first through the door. Lydia was ahead of me and let the door close on me.

I laughed, "So this is how it's going to be." I kept my composure. The Judge sat us at a table and explained the rules. Lydia was going to go first and state her case. I felt bad for her, she was nervous. The Judge gave the floor to Lydia, Lydia started explaining her side. I watched enough Judge Judy to know not to interrupt Lydia on any of her points even if they were outright lies. I didn't have to anyway. Lydia pulled my book out of her briefcase and threw it on the table. She explained that the book (she referred to it as "trash") was written about a highly revered, respectable rock star. I quietly chuckled to myself. Revered? Respectable rock star? I then thought Lydia must be hitting the sauce a little too hard lately. I quietly listened.

She then went on how she didn't want her likeness in my trash book. She said that she wasn't a celebrity and that she never gave permission, etc... She was trying to drive that fact home when I raised my hand to speak.

I was actually waiting for the Judge to say this but I interjected, "She's not suing me for her likeness in the book. The suit is about ownership of the photos. Why is this an issue?" The Judge agreed an instructed Lydia to continue with just the facts. If the Judge sided on Lydia I could've poked holes immediately on the celeb issue. Lydia has been re-married and divorced and continues to call herself Lydia "Criss". She books herself as a celebrity guest at *KISS* conventions and has been writing a book that was supposed to be released years ago entitled *Sealed With a KISS*. With celebdom (my word!) comes the good and the bad. You can't have it all good.

Lydia then went onto the issue at hand. She opened up the *KISS & Tell MORE* book and pointed out the photos. She stated she took the photos, they were hers and I was unauthorized to use them and I did not provide photo credit to her. She was pretty nasty in tone about the whole thing.

The Judge then handed the book to me and asked if these were the photos in question. I said yes and I placed the book down in front of me. Lydia was full of contradictions and I was just about to point out the pertinent ones. It now became my turn to speak. Before my first sentence was complete Lydia interrupted me. I didn't need the Judge to reprimand her.

I quietly turned to Lydia and said, "I politely gave you your turn to speak. It is now my turn. I'd appreciate it if you did not interrupt me." The Judge looked impressed and probably happy that there was one cool head in this case. It could have easily turned into a direct pissing match if I responded to Lydia's scathing remarks.

The Judge repeated, "If you'd like to interject, feel free to raise your hand and speak when you are told to speak."

I pointed out that Lydia contradicted herself when she wanted photo credit but on the other hand, she wanted nothing to do with that "TRASH!" I also pointed out that Lydia was in the photo, how could she be in the photo and be the photographer at the same time?

Lydia screamed out, "Ever hear of a timer, asshole?" Whoaa, the Judge was getting nervous as Lydia was getting agitated.

"There is no need for that kind of language here," reprimanded the Judge. Lydia ignored her and sneered at me. It was getting ugly. I kept my cool.

I replied, "These photos were taken with a disposable camera." I asked Lydia but looked at the Judge, "Why would you want photo credit, as a professional photographer, for a candid photo of poor quality from a disposable camera? It's not even a concert shot! It's a candid shot of a bunch of friends hanging out in a hotel room."

It was a rhetorical question as I did not care about the answer. I was building up to my real point. I stated Lydia Criss has obvious animosity towards me for whatever reason and she was wasting my time and the court's time. "This lawsuit is ridiculous," as I pulled out the negative and placed it on the table, "I own the negative, I own the photos."

Lydia reached in her bag, excited once again, and threw her copies of the photos on the table as if it were her ace in the hole so to speak.

"Then how the hell do I have these?" Lydia stated.

"I took the photos, you were in the pictures. I sent you copies and you never thanked me," I replied.

She yelled, "My friend Manny is in those photos! He died recently!"

"Lydia," I replied, "You didn't even go to his funeral. Manny became friends with you through me. I went to High School with Manny."

Lydia started yelling about how they were her negatives and she sent them to me so I could print the photos in Ace's Rock Soldier Magazine. The Judge listened to her points but got annoyed that it was becoming an argument. I could see she let it continue as I wasn't getting agitated and it wasn't about to escalate on my end. It takes two people to fight. I just quietly rebutted all the points Lydia was excitedly trying to make.

I turned to the Judge to finalize my side, "Lydia claims she is a professional photographer and I do not refute that. I've dealt with many professional photographers in my time. Number one - professional photographers almost NEVER lend out their negatives. They will send copies of prints for you to work with. Number two - if a professional photographer does have to part with their negatives or slides they will ask that you sign for them. They keep it on record so nothing like this happens. Number three - I have all the negatives from my disposable camera. If

Lydia was going to 'lend' me her negative to print photos from, like she claims, why would she send me ALL the negatives? The two photos in question are on one strip. There are six strips of negatives. They are my negatives, my photos. Thank you."

The Judge cut off Lydia and said she heard enough. She told us that we would be informed of her decision by mail.

After we were dismissed Lydia pointed at the book in front of me, "That's my copy." I handed it to her. I was going to ask her if she wanted me to sign it but I knew better not to antagonize her. I thanked the Judge and even said to Lydia that it was good to see her, to keep the day a happy one despite the confrontation. Lydia kept her puss on. Why be so fucking miserable?

Ten days later I received the judgment. I opened the letter. Blah, blah blah, claim dismissed, no monetary award. Judgment in favor of defendant. Total judgment: $.00.

Lydia fucked herself. She would have at least received money from *The People's Court*. After all that, I still felt bad for her. I'm waiting for her new book to come out. Should be interesting. Here's a title suggestion, "Criss and Tell".

Kinder, Gentler Ways to Say Someone is Stupid.
An experiment in Artificial Stupidity.
The wheel's spinning, but the hamster's dead.
Warning: Objects in mirror are dumber than they appear.
Couldn't pour water out of a boot with instructions on the heel.
Chimney's clogged.
Elevator doesn't go all the way to the top floor.
If he had another brain, it would be lonely.
Slinky's kinked.

The photos in question

CHAPTER 7
DOUBLE TAKE!
BY MICHAEL SCIOTTO

Years ago I went to a real cool club called Stringfellows in Manhattan. Before it became an upscale, ahem, "Gentlemen's Club" it was an upscale celebrity club. You had to dress nice to get into this place.

One night I dressed all rocked out and went with the members of my band. As we walked in I was impressed that Cher was going in ahead of us. We didn't make a big deal of it but we thought it was pretty cool. Later on that night I realized it was not Cher, but a Cher look-a-like.

All I kept saying to my bandmates was "what kind of asshole dresses up and tries to look like a celebrity? What kind of cheap vicarious thrill does it give them? What kind of life must you have where the only thing that gives you a thrill is dressing up and acting like somebody you are not? I understand a fan is a fan but don't try to impersonate that person. Is it their thrill to feel like a celebrity for a moment? I just don't get it."

Well, from that day on I can't help but notice "celeb-a-likes." Sometimes it's subtle, sometimes it's blatant. Look around, you'll spot them. You see them everywhere. The guy who sorta looks like Bond but just can't contain his douche bag tendencies and wears some ridiculous Bond-like sunglasses. I hate these people.

Years later, my band *From The Fire* was doing a showcase at the China Club in New York City. We only played three songs that night but we kicked ass. In fact, we got our record deal that night. I felt really good coming off the stage. As I walked off I saw this guy walking towards the stage. He looked like Slash from *Guns 'n Roses*.

I immediately said to myself, "Look at this douche look-a-like. Who's he trying to fool? What a dope." He came up to me and sincerely complimented me on my drumming. The guy was genuine with his compliments but I totally blew off this moron for trying to come off as a celebrity.

In my head I was saying, "Yeah, right! What a Slash look-a-like DICK! Yeah, you really fooled me. Why don't you buy a top-hat... DUFUS!"

Outwardly, I just shrugged and walked quickly past him as I gave him the half-hearted "yeah, thanks," not even fully acknowledging his presence.

As he walked past me towards the stage I heard the host, Richie Canata (Sax player from Billy Joel's band and *The Beach Boys*) announce, "We have a real surprise here tonight... SLASH from *Guns 'n Roses*!" In mid-stride, walking away from the stage, I did a Homer "DOH!" Then I thought, "Was that Bond in the rest room?"

41

CHAPTER 8
ROCK AND ROLL POLITICS

Here's a letter that was supposedly written by Ted Nugent, the rock singer and hunter/naturalist, upon hearing that California Senators Barbara Boxer and Diane Feinstein denounced him for being a "gun owner" and a "Rock Star." It was passed around the Internet as his supposed response after supposedly telling the Senators about his past contributions to children's charities and scholarship foundations which have totaled more than $13.7 million in the last 5 years. Ted denies writing the letter although he admits he wish he did. It was a very believable hoax.

I'm a bad American - this pretty much sums it up for me.

I like big trucks, big boats, big houses, and naturally, pretty women.

I believe the money I make belongs to me and my family, not some midlevel governmental functionary with a bad comb-over who wants to give it away to crack addicts squirting out babies.

I don't care about appearing compassionate.

I think playing with toy guns doesn't make you a killer. I believe ignoring your kids and giving them Prozac might.

I think I'm doing better than the homeless.

I don't think being a minority makes you noble or victimized.

I have the right not to be tolerant of others because they are different, weird or make me mad.

This is my life to live, and not necessarily up to others expectations.

I know what SEX is and there are not varying degrees of it.

I don't celebrate Kwanzaa. But if you want to that's fine; I just don't feel like everyone else should have to.

I believe that if you are selling me a Dairy Queen shake, a pack of cigarettes, or hotel room you do it in English. As a matter of fact, if you are an American citizen you should speak English.

My uncles and forefathers shouldn't have had to die in vain so you can leave the countries you were born in to come disrespect ours, and make us bend to your will. Get over it.

I think the cops have every right to shoot your sorry butt if you're running from them after they tell you to stop. If you can't understand the word 'freeze' or 'stop' in English, see the previous line.

I don't use the excuse "it's for the children" as a shield for unpopular opinions or actions.

I know how to count votes and I feel much safer letting a machine with no political affiliation do a recount when needed.

I know what the definition of lying is, and it isn't based on the word "is" - ever.

I don't think just because you were not born in this country, you qualify for any special loan programs, government sponsored bank loans, etc..., so you can open a hotel, 7-Eleven, trinket shop, or anything else, while the indigenous people can't get past a high school education because they can't afford it.

I didn't take the initiative in inventing the Internet.

I thought the Taco Bell dog was funny.

I want them to bring back safe and sane fireworks.

I believe no one ever died because of something Ozzy Osbourne, Ice-T or Marilyn Manson sang, but that doesn't mean I want to listen to that crap from someone else's car when I'm stopped at a red light. But I respect your right to.

I think that being a student doesn't give you any more enlightenment than working at Blockbuster or Jack in the Box.

I don't want to eat or drink anything with the words light, lite or fat-free on the package.

Our soldiers did not go to some foreign country and risk their lives in vain and defend our Constitution so that decades later you can tell me it's a living document, ever changing and is open to interpretation. The guys who wrote it were light years ahead of anyone today, and they meant what they said - now leave the document alone, or there's going to be trouble.

I don't hate the rich. I help the poor.

I know wrestling is fake.

I've never owned, or was a slave, and a large percentage of our forefathers weren't wealthy enough to own one either. Please stop blaming me because some prior white people were idiots - and remember, tons of White, Indian, Chinese, and other races have been enslaved too - it was wrong for everyone of them.

I believe a self-righteous liberal Democrat with a cause is more dangerous than a Hell's Angel with an attitude.

I want to know exactly which church is it where the "Reverend" Jessie Jackson preaches; and, what exactly is his job function.

I own a gun, you can own a gun, and any red blooded American should be allowed to own a gun, but if you use it in a crime, then you will serve the time.

I think Bill Gates has every right to keep every penny he made and continue to make more. If it makes you mad, then invent the next operating system that's bet-

ter and put your name on the building. Ask your buddy that invented the Internet to help you.

I don't believe in hate crime legislation. Even suggesting it makes me mad. You're telling me that someone who is a minority, gay, disabled, another nationality, or otherwise different from the mainstream of this country has more value as a human being than I do as a white male? If someone kills anyone, I'd say that it's a hate crime.

We don't need more laws! Let's enforce the ones we already have.

I think turkey bacon, turkey beef, turkey fake anything sucks.

I believe that it doesn't take a village to raise a child-it takes a parent with the guts to stand up to the kid and spank his butt and say "NO!" when it's necessary to do so.

I'll admit that the only movie that ever made me cry was Ole Yeller.

I didn't realize Dr. Seuss was a genius until I had a kid.

I will not be frowned upon or be looked down upon or be made to keep silent because I have these beliefs and opinions. I thought this country allowed me that right. I will not conform or compromise just to keep from hurting somebody's feelings.

I'm neither angry nor disenfranchised, no matter how desperately the mainstream media would like the world to believe otherwise.

Yes, I guess by some people's definition, I may be a bad American.

But that's tough.

Ted Nugent

Yngwie & Derek's Verbal War To End All Wars

Yngwie Malmsteen's band toured Brazil. The first show took place October 2, 2001 in Porto Alegre, to be followed by Curitiba on the 4th and Sao Paulo on the 5th. There was a "situation" during the Porto Alegre show, and keyboardist Derek Sherinian posted this message about it at his personal site, DerekSherinian.com:

First of all, I would like to preface this letter by saying that I am not a fan of one using their musical status to promote religious or political beliefs. I am also not one to post on message boards, but something happened to me on stage last night that I feel compelled to write this letter.

I am currently the only American in Yngwie Malmsteen's touring band. What happened at last night's gig in Porte Allegre, Brazil was shocking. Midway through the set, Yngwie finished his guitar solo spot with the 'Star Spangled Banner.' The crowd of about 1500 people started immediately booing very loudly, and throwing shit on stage. The crowd started chanting, 'O S A M A !!, O S A M A !!!' To see the Anti-American rallies on CNN is bad enough, but to be in the middle of one is scary beyond words.

So after Yngwie's solo we had about 5 more songs to play. All of my spirit was gone. I finished the set disgusted, and without looking at the crowd for the rest of the show. After the final song, the band went to the dressing room. I told Yngwie, 'I refuse to go out for the encore under any circumstances, FUCK THESE PEOPLE.

Yngwie went back on stage by himself and played the Star Spangled Banner again to a choir of loud boos.

He then said on the microphone, 'God Bless America, and FUCK YOU ALL' and walked off stage. Again, the crowd went into a riot and started throwing shit on stage again. We immediately were rushed back to our hotel. I have no idea of the status of our gear.

I want to thank Yngwie for backing me up, and for standing up for the U.S.A.

To the people in Porte Allegre, you should be ashamed of yourselves. I don't give a fuck if I ever play your peasant infested third world city again.

God Bless America,
Derek Sherinian

A different version from Brazilian Journalists:

Yesterday, Y. Malmsteen started his Brazilian tour in Porto Alegre, and based on what people who were there said, it was one of the funniest concerts ever, a complete freakshow.

It all started when Malmsteen decided to play *The Star-Spangled Banner* on one of his million solos. Of course, even given the context, etc..., it does not make sense to play it in Brazil. People went "booo" and started screaming "Brazil, Brazil."

From this point on, the concert went on a little tense. So, he played *The Star-Spangled Banner* again and again, even putting it in the middle of his songs. So the crowd reacted louder and louder.

In the meantime, unhappy with the negative reaction of the audience, keyboardist Derek Sherinian started doing obscene gestures (middle fingers and stuff). Vocalist Doogie White saved his dignity and didn't do anything.

So, the provocative session stopped, and the concert went well. The break before the encore was getting long, people thought he would not return.

He did, and then he said, "Do you want some more?" Some went "boo" again, some didn't say anything, some screamed "fuck you!" and some wanted more. Then he said, "If I play *The Star-Spangled Banner* will you boo? If you boo me, we won't play anymore. It's up to you."

Most of the people didn't react to this, and the show went on. They played two songs, and *The Star-Spangled Banner* as the closing act.

Then, the most magic moment of the night. He turned to the audience at the end and says: "GOD BLESS AMERICA AND FUCK YOU!!!!!!!!"

And so he left the stage under a rain of beer cups, sandwiches, snacks, plastic bottles and everything people could throw at him.

We'll never know what really happened, you decide...

CHAPTER 9
GET UP AND ROCK YOU MOTHERFUCKERS!

I grew up seeing *Twisted Sister* every other weekend in a club. Not by choice. They just played every frickin' night in the New York tri-state area. Always great entertainment and you knew they would draw a crowd so you wouldn't end up in a femaleless club.

Lead singer, Dee Snider, was and still is a great showman, singer, frontman, and entertainer. His stage persona sucks you into the moment. If you never witnessed a *Twisted Sister*, *Widowmaker* or Dee Snider solo show, you are missing out on a true rock performance. Dee is very cool, intelligent and I'm going to sound like Bill Murray from the movie *Stripes* when I say, "I want to party with you!" But the difference between Bill and I is, I'm being sincere. I do have to explain how Dee is onstage for you to get the full understanding of the story.

Dee explodes onto a stage as if he snorted half of Columbia and drank all of its coffee crops. Wallflowers, posers and non-participants in Dee's rock and roll party are not allowed. They are the enemy. If you are at a Dee show and you stare at him with your arms crossed with no approval, Dee will spot you and berate you with an endless barrage of banter until you finally submit with some sort of reaction! You cannot hide from his radar. He will pick you out of a crowd. His non-stop rap will have you giving him the thumbs up, just to shut him up and get on with the show. Once in awhile a heckler would get on him and it would eventually end up in a brawl.

One particular concert, Dee was in his usual "I need feedback people" performance. "Let's have some audience participation out there." In between songs Dee would chatter and pump up the crowd every chance he got. Dee would point to sections of the crowd with one hand, his other to his ear, and then wave both his hands in true rock star fashion. Well, this particular night, this one section of the crowd was not as exuberant as the rest

DEE SNIDER

of the audience. Dee noticed this and began to get on their case.

"This section here... Do you know how to rock?" shouting like Sgt. R. Lee Ermey. "HELLLLLLLOOOOOOO people - I said DO YOU KNOW HOW TO FUCKING ROCK?" The response was not up to Dee Snider standard.

"Look people - if you can't join the rock and roll party then just get the fuck out," as the rest of the audience started booing this section.

Dee began berating these non-participants, "You fucking people don't belong here. I never saw the lamest bunch of fucks in all my life, get the fuck up and rock, etc..., etc..."

This continued all throughout the performance, pointing at the rest of the crowd with approval and thumbs down to this "lame" section. At one point Dee had one section yelling, "you suck" to this section. As the show ended Dee trotted off into the wings waiting to be greeted by his manager and get the ego boosting show review. Instead, the manager greeted him with a smack in the head and screamed, "What the fuck is wrong with you?"

Dee all shocked and stunned, "Whoa... What's going on? What happened? What did I do?"

Dee's manager replied again, "What the fuck is wrong with you? You know that section you ranked on all night?"

"Yeah," Dee still stunned by getting smacked in the head.

"That was the HANDICAPPED SECTION you ASSHOLE!"

Dee said his dick shrunk when he heard that.

CHAPTER 10
THE FINGER

Everyone has that one sick fuck in your group of friends. You know the guy. The one who always got in trouble with the cops, defied society and the establishment. They did the dares without blinking. They'd jump off a wall that you would easily break your leg if you tried. They laid on the railroad track and let a train pass over them. They ate the worm at the bottom of the bottle of tequila, took the hit of blotter acid and then camped out all night at the cemetery. You were scared of them. You knew they belonged in an institution but deep down you wish you had their balls (in a warped way). Along with their sort of admirable unflappable balls to the wall personality they also had the one thing that turned everybody off. It ruined the Steve McQueen image they could have achieved if it wasn't for that one trait. They were GROSS. In our little group of high school friends, that guy was Charlie. I could easily write a whole book on Charlie, but we'll just stick to this brief chapter (I couldn't stomach writing a whole tome on him anyway).

Charlie played drums, became a roadie, and eventually drove a truck as adult Charlie. (Saying adult Charlie is an oxymoron. You know what? Let's just drop the oxy if you know what I mean). He is smart in his own way, but constantly works on perfecting immaturity. He knew things that scholars didn't, like the term "felching." It is so gross I don't want to be blamed for letting you know what the term

means, so you are on your own. I thought he made it up until Kirstie Alley made a reference to it in a Playboy interview. I can't believe she made reference to it. But she's sort of a down to earth slob anyway and maybe she's a female version of Charlie.

Let me preface this story by saying that I am totally turned off by scatological humor. I don't even like to say the word "fart" in front of women. Yeah, I'm weird like that. I'm the first one in the audience to give the disapproving frown if a comedian resorts to bathroom humor. If you are like me, then skip the rest of this story. If you are a pretty woman, please skip this chapter so I can keep some sort of dignity. MOM - STOP READING THIS BOOK! PUT THE BOOK DOWN!!

Okay, now that we only have the

Charlie in High School

Rotten.com fans left let me start off with Charlie's farts. He can annihilate with his anal expulsions. Howard Stern's Fartman has nothing over on Charlie. Charlie is the King of all Kings in the gastric intestinal world. The real sick thing about it is that he's shamelessly proud of it. With this fact in mind, we will digress for a moment before we go on to the main story.

A few years back one of our best friends was getting married. We had to do something special for Bob before he took the big plunge. The bride-to-be told us that Bob didn't want a bachelor party and we should all take him out to a nice dinner. Let's get this straight... Bob didn't want a bachelor party? I don't think sooooo. More like SHE didn't want Bob to have a bachelor party! So what do you do when this situation presents itself? Oh we took him to dinner... in Canada! She didn't tell us where to take him or how long.

So we concocted this huge Mission Impossible plan to kidnap him from New York and lead him into his last days of decadence in Montreal. The plan included Charlie, Frank, Warren, Tom, yours truly and the victim, Bob. The big day arrived and both Bob and his fiancée had no clue. We picked Bob up and left a note on her pillow.

The note said, "We have your boyfriend. He won't be back for a few days, signed 'The Breakfast Club'." Meanwhile, Bob dressed up in his formal restaurant attire and we were all in sneakers and jeans. This should have been a clue.

We got in the car and put a wrapped present on Bob's lap and instructed him not to open it until we told him to.

After two hours on the road Bob began to get a little perturbed because we wouldn't give a straight answer to the question, "Where the fuck are we going?" I think he was just anxious to get to "the restaurant" to eat. As we continued the drive Bob saw a sign that said "Montreal, 300 miles."

"Hey Gordon, remember that time we got trashed and we ended up in Montreal? We had a blast. We should do that again," Bob innocently said. Everybody in the car looked at each other and simultaneously instructed him to open the box on his lap. Bob opened it and pulled out socks, shaving cream, razors, etc... with a clueless look on his face. It was a travel care package. We all started screaming, "YOU'RE GOING TO FUCKING MONTREAL!!!" He was mortified. We didn't know that his fiancée had her parents flying in from San Francisco to meet their new son-in-law-to-be the next day. How was he going to explain this? (Life is a movie. Quote Goodfellas scene: "What's wrong with you? Henry! You're not normal, she's right. What's wrong with you Henry? What kind of person are you? What is the matter with you? What the fuck kind of people are they?")

Well we got to Montreal and our mission was to drink, party and search for women twenty-four/seven. I could digress much more on what happened that whole trip but I will keep it on the subject of Charlie. Plus I have to keep the code of honor amongst men (again, I don't *KISS & Tell* everything). We ended up in "the" happening nightclub of Montreal and started a good rap with a whole bunch of girls. We were doing real well when fucking Charlie issued the most heinous gas bomb. He literally cleared the fucking room out. I never smelt anything so horrible in my life. This evil vapor seeped and hovered. He absolutely ruined all our chances with any females. He pretty much ruined everybody's sex drive in the whole club. All he did was laugh like a fucking mental patient. We wanted to kill him. This is just one example of the strength of his colonic capabilities. There should be a yellow and black "Danger Radiation" sign tattooed on his ass.

Well that leads us back to the main story. One time we were bantering about women, as all guys do… when alone… with no women around. We began discussing dates and experiences with various women in explicit detail. Charlie's turn came around and this was his story:

"This one time (I expected to hear next, "at band camp"), after a gig, I met this girl. She was a Russian nanny. I got her to go back to my place and we were making out and stuff. After about ten minutes I pushed her head down and she gave me really lousy head. Halfway through she started shifting around, trying to get her legs over my head. I had a clue what she was trying to do but I pretended not to know what she wanted. There was no way I was going to eat this bitch. I didn't even know her. After about three attempts she finally just asked me to eat her.

I said, "No way!" Besides I already blew my load. She said it wasn't fair and she started whining. It was getting pretty annoying, as she was relentless.

I said, "Alright, alright. I'll go down on you." I started diddling around down there trying to avoid the inevitable. She was getting impatient waiting for my tongue to touch her fish hole. As I made believe I was going to dive in, I took my free hand and stuck my finger up my own ass.

We all looked at Charlie like, "Why would you do that?"

Then he winks at us and says, "I gave her the Stinky Sanchez. I put my ass finger under her nose and said, 'C'mon Honey, smell that! Would you fucking eat that?' She started apologizing and crying. I got out of eating her. She was probably douching for days after that."

Then Charlie leaned to the side, farted and cackled like a loon.

She's probably still in therapy!

CHAPTER 11
JUST SAY... YES

I'm not one of those who remember dates well, but this account was easy to track down as it happened the night before a huge event, the Atlantic Records 40th Anniversary Concert/Party held at Madison Square Garden. Next to Live Aid and Woodstock, the Atlantic Records 40th Anniversary has to rank as possibly one of the biggest concerts of its kind. For almost 13 hours, the music never stopped. On May 14, 1988, *Led Zeppelin*, *Yes*, Keith Emerson, Carl Palmer, *Genesis*, *Iron Butterfly*, *The Rascals*, *Crosby, Stills & Nash*, *Foreigner*, Paul Rodgers, Bob Geldof, Booker T. Jones, Wilson Pickett, *The Coasters*, *The Spinners*, Peabo Bryson, Dan Aykroyd, Roberta Flack, *Manhattan Transfer*, Debbie Gibson, *The Bee Gees*, Ruth Brown, LaVern Baker, Ben E. King, *Average White Band*, *Vanilla Fudge* and more - were all on the same stage, the same night.

The previous evening was both memorable and not so memorable at the same time. I'll try and recall as much as possible.

The night began at the China Club in New York City. I ran into my friend Domenique that worked at the Atlantic record company. We ended up hanging out with each other at the bar. As the night progressed we introduced mutual friends to each other. One tall "chap" was very excited to see Domenique. I say "chap" as he was obviously English by his accent.

Domenique's social graces were excellent as she immediately introduced me, "Chris, I would like you to meet my friend, Gordon. Gordon, Chris."

We shook hands and I remember thinking, "Holy shit! This guy's hands are fucking huge! What the fuck?"

Anyway, the three of us grabbed a table and ordered drinks. Domenique ordered a beer, I the same, and Chris ordered a bottle of Stolies (Stolichnaya). I looked at him with surprise as he ordered a whole bottle. The waitress didn't even blink. We went back to our conversation. Domenique asked Chris if he was excited about the next evening's show.

He shrugged and replied, "Just another show."

All of a sudden I finally realized who this guy was. It was Chris Squire, the bassist in the band *Yes*. I felt like an idiot not recognizing him. *Yes* was one of my favorite bands growing up and I've seen them a few times in concert. The waitress came back with our beers, the bottle of Stolies and three glasses. Domenique and I immediately pulled money out. I told her to put her money away and I would buy. Chris waved both of us off and handed the waitress a hundred and told her to keep the drinks coming.

I must explain that I am not a drinker at all. Two, three beers in a social situation and I am good for the night. Anything beyond that I am an incoherent, inebriated fool (as opposed to a sober one). I could count on one hand the amount of times I've been intoxicated to the point of passing out. This particular incident I wish I had one less finger to count.

We continued enjoying each other's company and drinking. I nursed my beer. Chris poured his Stolies and drank it like water. He poured glassfuls for Domenique and I and we politely sipped at them every time he raised a "cheer." At one point in our conversation Chris asked us if we were together, as in "romantically" together.

Domenique and I both laughed and said at the same time, "Not at all... We are just very good friends." I wouldn't have minded at all to get "involved" with Domenique as she was (still is) extremely attractive, and she has a wonderful personality. Our "relationship" just never went in that direction, and I always respected our friendship. In other words, she wasn't interested in me that way!

After Chris heard this information he began to aggressively hit on her in front of me. This made me uncomfortable. Maybe I was getting in the way. I wasn't about to be a third wheel. My body language signaled that I was about to announce my farewell when Domenique gave me a look of, "Don't leave me alone with a drunken Chris Squire!"

Then she raised a glass for a subtle toast, "Here's to good friends! CHEERS!" All three of us downed the vodka. Chris patted me on the back like a drunken Russian, "Drink!" After a few initial hard shots the rest were going down way too easy. Chris and I were now going at it - drink for drink. Only difference was his body mass was much bigger than mine. The fucking drinks were probably going to his big hands. And he more than likely had done this before... BEFORE BREAKFAST! An amateur drinker like me going toe to toe with a professional! Something had to give... probably my liver.

Let's flash forward to closing time at the China Club. Four in the morning and time to leave. I couldn't get up from the table. I was obliterated. My legs wouldn't work. My head was spinning. Chris made a last drunken effort to hook up with Domenique. She politely refused. She asked if he was alright. He said his salutations and headed back to his hotel. Domenique's concern turned towards me.

I slurred, "I'll be fine," and I pulled out my car keys. Domenique realized I drove into Manhattan. Most people that live in Manhattan assume everyone gets around by cab in the city.

Domenique's common sense took over, "You are in no condition to drive.

You are staying at my place. I'm only a few blocks away."

"...can't leave my car...where it is ...have to move it. It'll get ...towed," I slurred. The rest was a blur to me. All I knew was I had to get my white 1959 Cadillac in a spot that would be legal the next morning... preferably near Domenique's apartment. I don't remember moving the car. I think Domenique drove the monstrosity. I barely remember passing out in Domenique's apartment on the living room floor. I was out for about four hours. It came to about nine in the morning, and I was still drunk! I do remember that I was extremely embarrassed that I got so intoxicated in front of her and she had to babysit me. My only thought was to get out of there as quickly and quietly as possible. As if this was going to regain some sort of dignity the next time we would run into each other.

I finally found the front door. This was after I walked into a closet door thinking it would lead the way out. I went down stairs out into the sobering morning sun. Now I had to find my car. Fortunately, a white 1959 Cadillac was not a hard car to find. My head was still spinning when I saw big white Caddy fins down the street. Every little accomplishment was a feeling of brief relief. The next step, however, seemed preposterous. I had to get home.

I started the car and pulled out of the spot. I had to get my bearings on where the hell I was. I found the West Side Highway and headed north. As I drove I literally saw double! I put one hand on the wheel and I used my other hand to cover

Chris Squire and Gordon G. G. Gebert

57

one eye so I could see straight. The thirty-minute drive seemed like hours. All I wanted was to be in my bed. I had one major worry the whole ride home. Suppose I got pulled over? What the fuck was I going to do? Maybe pull a label off a beer bottle and stick it to my forehead and explain that I wasn't drinking, that I was on the patch? I finally made it home.

Today, I wouldn't even think of getting behind the wheel even if I only sipped a beer. My friends think I'm a little overboard with my stubbornness. I always answer the "one beer is not going to hurt ya" logic with "I do not want to give any cop a reason to bust my balls. I don't want alcohol from a mouthwash on my breath when I drive."

This story does not end as a casual drinking story with the Bassist of *Yes* and my quest to get home. Noooooo, I wish! I now had to deal with the hangover. And this was no ordinary hangover. This was the hangover of all hangovers! The God of hangovers. A new definition of hangovers that would never be beat in my lifetime or Chris Squire's. Whichever comes first.

The crawl up the stairs seemed as long as the ride home. And I did crawl. Of course, my house was built on a huge hill. It had to have over one hundred stairs to reach my front door. It was like the stairs of Montezuma.

The biggest feeling of relief was when I finally made it to my bed safe. That feeling lasted maybe a minute when the sudden nausea and stomachache overtook me. I felt too fucking weak to get out of the bed! I just wanted to throw up over the side of the bed and get it over with. But other urges implored me to attempt to get out of the bed and crawl to the bathroom. In other words, I didn't want to clean a disgusting mess. Amongst having a low tolerance for booze, I also have a weak stomach. If I even have a thought of someone wretching to throw up - I WILL THROW UP! So if I threw up in bed and passed out, I'd wake up to puke and I'd immediately add to it. It would become a vicious cycle.

I crawled towards the bathroom. Of course, I had to have a huge house and the bathroom was a long trek down a huge hallway. I thought the ride home and climbing stairs was an eternity. The crawl to the bathroom was like the movie *Andromeda Strain* when the guy was hit with the laser crawling up the ladder trying to reach another substation to stop a nuclear explosion. I was so fucking weak. I was trying to psychologically speak to my stomach and bowels (yes - I had to do that too!) to hold off. They didn't want to listen. My brain tried to do several commands at once... move the arms and legs towards the bathroom and argue with the stomach and bowels at the same time. My brain was yelling at the stomach and bowels to hold on till we reach the toilet. All this conflict was just making the struggle impossible. The porcelain throne was within reach. I was too weak to sit up on it. I proceeded to regurgitate into the bowl. The putrid alcohol smell was overwhelming. The upheaval was so strong that all of a sudden my bowels let go. It was disgusting. I might as well have been two years old, sitting up and shitting myself. Somehow, I mustered enough energy to teeter onto the bowl.

I sat with my legs apart, elbows on my knees, my head held weakly in my hands and proceeded to puke between my thighs into the bowl. As I was performing this feat, the worst case of diarrhea was now exploding. I know what your thinking, "Drink story. Hangover of all hangovers! Puke and shit. No big deal!" Some of you might even be saying, "Been there! Done that! Bought the t-shirt." No my friends. It gets worse! "How could it possibly get worse?" you ask. Read on.

Back to the bowl, sitting there with every orifice exploding or I thought every orifice was exploding until I had to... sneeze. A sneeze just snuck up on me. You would think you couldn't sneeze with all this going on. This was not an orgasmic sneeze. The kind that builds up and finally releases. This was a sneak-up, exploding sneeze to go along with my stomach and bowels. I sneezed amidst the shitting and puking. When I sneezed, neither my mind nor my body was prepared for it, and I just passed out. I didn't know what hit me. I felt like I got kicked in the stomach. The pain was excruciating. I was on the cold tiled floor when I regained some kind of consciousness. I was doubled over in pain. I couldn't move. I didn't know what the fuck happened to me. I had to get to the phone and call for help. The closest person that I could call lived only ten minutes away. Unfortunately that was my father! But now I was desperate. I crawled to the phone (the longest journey of my friggin' life!)

I got a hold of my father and tried to explain what happened. I just needed help getting to the doctor doubled over in pain in my weakened state. I didn't explain to my father the drinking part. I just said I was sick, throwing up, etc... and I needed help to get to a doctor. Well, outwardly, my father is not the most compassionate man. I'll put it to you this way, once I broke my thumb working on a car at my parent's house. The bone was clearly sticking out through the skin. I ran into the house and placed my hand under cold running water, spewing assorted profanities to help cope with the pain.

My father walked over to me and asked, "What happened?"

My answer, "I broke my fucking thumb!"

My father said, "Let me see." I uncovered the injury. He didn't even flinch.

"Yup, you broke it you idiot!" There was nothing worse than getting humiliated while you're injured. It just simply made the pain worse. After the remark my father walked away. I wondered where the hell he went? Was he going to help me out? Within a minute he came back with the car keys jingling.

"Cool," I thought, "he'll take me to the hospital."

He tossed the keys to my good hand. "Here, take the car." I drove myself to the hospital. So, I wasn't expecting much compassion in my current situation. I just needed to get to the doctor.

My father arrived and walked in to find me on the floor in an extremely weak state. As he got closer he smelled the alcohol.

"Your fucking drunk! You called me over because you 'tied one on' and now your sick," he headed out the door.

"No, wait! Dad, something happened. I'm hurt. I need a doctor!" I implored him. I knew I shouldn't have called him. I got anti-compassion which made my suffering much worse. I convinced my dad to help me to the doctor's office.

Once there, I explained what happened to the doctor.

"Doc, this is embarrassing but I got drunk last night...," he cut me off.

"No, really?" he sarcastically replied. He wasn't compassionate but at least he didn't yell at me.

I looked at him with the look of, "I'm in no condition for sarcasm."

"This is not just a hang-over case. Let me explain. I got sick, deservedly so, and I was throwing up and diarrhea..."

He cut me off again, "If I could cure hang-overs I'd be richer than ..."

I cut him off, "Doc, amidst throwing up and diarrhea, I sneezed really hard and I passed out with pain in my lower abdomen," I was proud that I could use a medical term, "lower abdomen", for the Doc. The doctor started laughing.

"Okay, let me check," and he proceeded to poke around with his fingers in my lower stomach. Then he said, "I have to check you for a hernia."

I knew what that meant! He immediately got professional on me and grabbed my balls.

"Cough," he requested several times. "Well, you got lucky. You almost gave yourself a hernia."

"What!? How?" I asked.

He then explained that when I sneezed, unprepared, my muscles were caught off guard and my intestines pushed through the muscles. I fortunately did not rip the muscle, only strained them. If these muscles ripped it would result in a hernia. The strain and the weakened condition that I was in just made it feel like I was punched in the stomach. In reality, I punched myself from the inside out!

The Docs parting words were, "You strained yourself. You'll be alright. Take it easy. Don't drink so hard." You didn't have to tell me that Doc. I'm going to hear it for the rest of my life from my parents.

That day *Yes* played at the 40th Anniversary Party at Madison Square Garden. They performed four songs; *Owner of a Lonely Heart, Hold On, I've Seen All Good People* and *Roundabout*. Chris Squire looked and played fine. Prick!

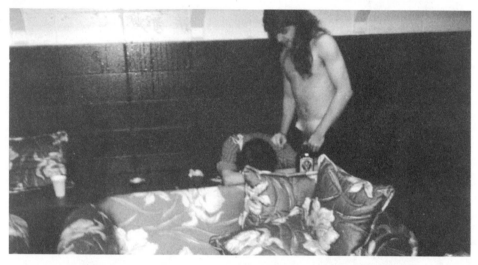

This photo has nothing to do with the *Yes* story but for the only fact that it's one of my best friends (who shall remain nameless) passed out in a drunken stupor and being abused by Metallica's Lars Ulrich. Lars whipped out his dick and basically pulled a "cow cunt" on my passed out, inebriated friend.
Thank you nameless friend for being a great sport and submitting this photo.

CHAPTER 12
WELCOME BACK MY FRIENDS TO THE SHOW THAT...
ALMOST ENDS IN DISASTER

If you read my past books, you would know one of my absolute all-time favorite band is *Emerson, Lake and Palmer*. And if you have followed the band throughout the years like I have, you would know that they had their share of mishaps. A few I have witnessed, and once almost became a victim.

ELP's second gig was at the Isle of Wight Festival in 1970 (as opposed to the Isle of Lucy - long live Spinal Tap) and it, literally, exploded them on to the music scene. According to Carl Palmer they were scheduled to play at 3:30 in the afternoon for one hour. Keyboardist, Keith Emerson, recalls the festival band roster was very competitive and they had to come up with something to get noticed. They found two antique cannons at an antique store and had the idea of firing them off at the end of their final classical cover piece, *Pictures at an Exhibition*.

Before the day of the show, Emerson and his roadie, Rocky, brought the cannons to Heathrow Airport to test them out. They chose Heathrow so the incoming and outgoing plane engines would mask the explosions. These days you would instantly be arrested for terrorism if you ever tried that. They checked them out and they worked "wonderfully" (Emerson's own word). Emerson told Rocky, "when it comes to show time, double the charges."

At the show, they performed their classical adaptation of "*Pictures*", as *ELP* fans now affectionately call it. Towards the end of the piece, Emerson spotted an Italian photographer leaning over the barrel of one of the cannons trying to take pictures of the band. While playing the keyboard, he tried to get the photographer's attention to warn him to get away from the cannon. Foot switches would ignite the cannons which both, Keith Emerson and Greg Lake (bassist) controlled on each of their respective sides of the stage. When Emerson triggered his cannon, this eight hundred-pound piece of wrought iron leapt into the air and the photographer was thrown into the pit in front of the first row of the audience. Emerson recalled a look of horror on Greg's face when he saw the force of the explosion. For a second, Emerson thought Greg would chicken out on igniting the cannon on his side of the stage. Greg stepped on the switch, the second cannon went off and rock history was made.

About the Isle Of Wight, Greg Lake recalls, "I remember driving down there and getting passed by Keith Moon in a pink Rolls Royce. As he went by, there were legs flapping out the window. They were lady's legs with stockings and sus-

Jones Beach
Keith realizes something's wrong

Jones Beach
Ribbon controller after it goes off in my face

Photos by Marc Eisenoff

penders on. What he had done was he got one of these blow-up dollies and put nylons and suspenders and then put the window up, trapped the legs in the window and was driving down towards the Isle of Wight with these things hanging out."

In 1974, performing at the Cow Palace in San Francisco, Keith Emerson blew his fingernail off during Tarkus, it was the third song in the set. During his solo, Keith would come out with an instrument called a ribbon controller. It is a strange instrument, very hard to describe. It connected to a Moog synthesizer and you can tap along the length of the ribbon to get steps or swooshes or other wild dive-bomb sound effects. It allowed him to move away from his stationery position at the keyboard and take center stage to further his showmanship. To visually punctuate the sound effects, Keith would shoot pyrotechnics from the underside of the instrument. This night the pyrotechnic blew his fingernail off. He threw the ribbon controller down to the stage and stomped on it! He continued playing the complete concert while wiping blood off all of the keyboards.

A more recent concert that I attended at Jones Beach, New York, had my friend, Marc wishing he didn't have the premium front row seat. Keith came out with the Ribbon Controller and the pyro effect did not trigger. As he hit the

A successful firing.

64

instrument to get it to fire, it suddenly went off pointed accidentally towards the first row. The roman candle type flame thrower made a direct hit on Marc. He escaped unscathed but shaken up. After the concert, drummer, Carl Palmer was very concerned with lawsuits. The band was quite lucky it hit their number one fan and he just took it in stride.

Keith Emerson's famous act included mauling a Hammond L100 organ. He would take this instrument (which was like a piece of furniture) and rock it, throw it, jump over it, stab it with daggers and play the keyboard backwards. The organ was built in such a way that when you abused it, the way Keith Emerson did, all sorts of wailing and whining sounds emanated from it. The famous comparison was "Keith Emerson is to the organ, what Jimi Hendrix was to the guitar".

One particular concert I witnessed (and this has happened on several occasions), Keith was doing his "act" on top of the keyboard, bronco bucking the instrument across the stage. Keith is reckless. He got a little too close to the front of the stage and the organ tipped over into the audience with him on it. He rode it down like Slim Pickens riding the bomb in the movie, *Dr. Strangelove*. It was a big drop. Greg and Carl continued playing but were craning their necks to see where he disappeared to and if he was all right. The audience in the front helped Keith get back on the stage. Once on the stage, he held up his hands to show he was alright and gave a playful motion to the arena that he couldn't continue with that particular instrument as it fell into the front row. All of a sudden the organ magically rose up. The crowd in front lifted the heavy instrument and threw it back onto the stage. The organ miraculously reappeared and Keith was astonished, as was the rest of the audience. The show went on.

One show that didn't go on was at Roosevelt Stadium in Jersey City, New Jersey. It was an outdoor concert that was scheduled in the summer of 1975. This place held great concerts but it was a dump. As in all outdoor concerts, you are at the mercy of Mother Nature.

The day was overcast and the weather reports called for a slight chance of rain. The promoter decided to gamble and go ahead with the concert. The crew set up *ELP*'s elaborate stage; three tractor-trailers full of equipment including a state-of-the-art quadraphonic (four-channel) P.A. system. Early birds were allowed to enter the stadium to grab the best spot to camp out and wait for the show. The stage was set up resembling a circus with a large red and white striped tent in the middle hovering over Carl Palmer's immense drum kit. Looking at the stage, to the left, was Keith Emerson's towering Moog synthesizer, organs, and other keyboard instruments. Center stage was covered with Greg Lake's fancy imported Persian rug.

The sky started to threaten again so the crew covered all the equipment with plastic tarpaulins. Then the rain started and it came down hard. It immediately made the field a muddy mess. The crowd began running for shelter under the bleachers. A few of them helped *ELP*'s crew as they began to frantically take down the P.A. because the tarp did not protect the cabinets. The wind kicked up. To make things even worse, lightning hit the stadium. People began to panic. A bolt hit the outfield light tower and the thunder immediately boomed through the stadium. Any hope of a concert was dashed. Just when you thought nothing could get worse, it did! The relentless gusting wind formed a funnel cloud in the middle of the stadium. A friggin' mini-tornado formed right before everyone's eyes. It began to hail. The twister sucked up everything. There were flying blankets, plastic knives, soda cups, empty beer cans, all kinds of trash. It plowed through the remaining crowd, towards the stage, like it had a mission. The whirlwind hit the center of the stage, knocking down the tent, and knocking over most of Carl's drum kit. It then turned stage right directly hitting Emerson's setup and knocking over his huge, expensive Moog Series III Synthesizer face down into the pool of mud and water on the stage.

As quickly as the mayhem began, it subsided. An eerie calm settled over the stadium. The weather just became a steady, dreary, summer rain, but the

ELP CAUGHT IN NATURAL WHIRLWIND

"It was like a scene from Captain's Courageous. There was no visibility, the stage was shaking, Keith's Moog fell into three feet of water and broke apart." With these astounding words Roosevelt Stadium stage manager, Eddie Carlin, attempted to recapture the scene of the biggest natural disaster in the four year history of nature's awesome trio, Emerson, Lake and Palmer.

At Roosevelt Stadium, sometimes called the biggest outdoor pigsty in New Jersey, ELP set up their massive equipment on the Buckminster Fuller-esque "Mobius" unit turntable stage.

The morning sky was hazy, but by two PM the stadium field was drenched by the first of a series of thunderstorms. The stadium doors opened anyway, and by four, blanket-covered ELP-waiters were drenched by another torrent.

Undaunted by the overcast sky, however, the merry Moogsters began their set promptly. Suddenly a terrific gale with winds up to 60 and 70 mph) rose up, and according to photo ace, Chuck Pulin, barricades toppled over, P.A. stacks were knocked onto the stage and one youth, caught up in the mini-tornado, was wrenched skyward. "I never

saw him come back down, either," added Mobius expert George Honchar. "And then the whole side of the stage collapsed."

Much of ELP's priceless equipment was soaked and nearly ruined. The next gig at Saratoga, N. Y. was cancelled and the Manticore electronics experts spent three days and nights drying out and fixing the delicate solid state connections. "Weather," commented one journalist, "is the last thing rock stars can't control."

Emerson, Lake and Palmer: "It was like a tempest in a teacup," quoted an ELP roadman, "a 30,000 person teacup."

stage looked like a train just passed through it. The water in the parking lot was up to everyone's waist. Cars were submerged to the door handles. The water was swirling bright orange colors from a friggin dye factory next to the stadium. It stained everything.

Keith Emerson named it the "worst show" in Keyboard Magazine some years ago. According to him, the Moog was immediately shipped off to Moog experts where it was carefully worked on with hair dryers until the components were back in working order. As a testament to 1960's technology, once dry, the synth worked like new.

Two weeks later, as if to defy Mother Nature, *ELP* played Roosevelt Stadium on a perfect summer evening. The opening act was a group ironically called *SNAFU*.

One of the wildest moments in rock history was a stunt Keith Emerson dreamed up for a show called the California Jam. A grand piano was to magically rise up twenty feet in the air and spin, end over end, WHILE EMERSON PLAYED IT.

Keith stated, "We tried it first at the California Jam. There were about 400,000 people, I think, were there. Basically this was a grand piano that I sat on and the piano was hoisted up to a certain height and then was rotated with me playing. And getting quite dizzy."

When they tested the "flying piano," it was lifted up on hydraulic lifts and the *ELP* crew manually spun the piano with Emerson sitting on a custom designed piano bench that was attached to the piano. As it was spinning, Emerson tried to get the attention of the crew to stop it. They obviously didn't have the stopping part well thought-out. Keith yelled several times to stop the piano. When they finally heard the frantic command, they abruptly stopped the spinning piano, and, as the laws of physics applied themselves, Keith Emerson slammed his nose into the piano like Wile E. Coyote. His nose went from A Sharp to B Flat. The crew took note: Stop spinning piano graaa-duuu-aaal-ly.

Greg recalls another haphazard show; "This (particular) show was in Bologna Stadium (Italy). Francesco (Italian Promoter - Francesco Sanavio), bless his heart, said to us, 'you needn't bother to bring your own stage and your own lights. We'll supply them. All you need to bring is your backline equipment and everything will be here.' We show up at two o'clock in the afternoon in Bologna. It's an empty stadium. There's just grass and there's nothing. There's no stage.

There's no lights. There's no nothing and there's no Francesco."

Francesco's account in his Italian accent, "I think I forgot lights but I didn't forget the people pay the ticket."

Greg paraphrasing what he was thinking that day, "He's got the day wrong! He's got the day wrong! So, now he's got to find a stage and lights. By now this is three o'clock in the afternoon and there's already thousands of kids starting to clamor around the stadium. Inside nothing!"

Francesco recalls, "He's (Greg Lake) asking for lights. Twenty five thousand people, everyone with one match, was plenty of lights."

Somehow, someway, Francesco pulled it off. The show was a go. But the actual show didn't go as smoothly as everyone wished.

Greg recants, "Carl does his cue (for the encore), we come back on stage, we start to play, whoooosh, this skyrocket goes between my legs. I'm not talking about one of those you get in a news agency. I'm talking about a mortar. And it shoots between my legs and goes straight into the audience and explodes. Then the whole stage exploded with fireworks. And what he had done during the show, he erected a fireworks display behind the group. But a big one, on a wooden scaffold and then he lit it and it fell over. So when it went off, instead of going up into the

Gordon G. G. Gebert, Keith Emerson, Jerry Kovarsky, Jack Hotop, Jordan Rudess

sky and being like a firework display, it just blew straight through the stage. The whole thing. And there was stuff spinning around. It was a nightmare. Nobody got hurt, I don't know how, but nobody got hurt. At the end of the day, it was all right. And that's Italy. At the end of the day it's always all right. And what do you do, it's simple? You go to the restaurant, right? That's it! Ayyyyyy!"

Carl Palmer on his famous custom-made drum kit, "The dream really was to build this stainless steel drum set. I just figured that this material, stainless steel, would be perfect for the sound projection. Well, by the time we assembled all of those drums, we found we could not lift the bass drum. It was too heavy; one man couldn't do it. I didn't think of transport at the time, that it would be costly to move around, or staging. In Roanoke, West Virginia we had to cancel a concert because the stage collapsed because the drum set was too heavy. I think, packed in the road cases, it came to a ton and a half. It was unreal.

I was in Los Angeles and I met Ringo Star.

He came up to me and said, 'I've got it, I've got it, I've got it.' He'd actually bought the drum set from the lady that had bought it off me. I didn't want to keep it in storage because it was such a beautiful thing. Anyway she ended up moving it on, putting it back into some auction and Ringo went along and bought it. Apparently, he wanted it the first time but he got there late. So he managed to pick it up. He's got it now. And Ringo, you're welcome to it."

Rock star excess reached a new height when the press reported Greg Lake's extravagant Persian rug for the stage. The tour manager at the time was Andrew Lane.

His take on the whole thing; "No, he (Greg Lake) never had a carpet roadie. He did have a carpet. And it was actually quite practical, I think. If you can visualize every night, a different gig, a different venue, Greg liked the stability of one thing that was the same. He'd walk on stage and his carpet was there. He'd feel at home."

Greg: "It actually started when I got electrocuted in Germany off the microphone. About 240 volts, bang straight in the head. Passed out. (After the incident) What I said was you have to get me a rubber mat to stand on. So they got this rubber mat and it looked dreadful. So I said, look, get some carpet and cover it up, thinking they'd get some black carpet or other. Well, anyway, up turns this Persian rug. Looked quite nice, so it stayed.

Andrew Lane: "It was blown up out of all proportion. Was an expensive carpet though (laughing)."

In September of 1997, yours truly almost became a casualty of Keith Emerson's recklessness at their Beacon Theater show in New York City. While performing their encore, Keith jumped over the Hammond Organ and laid it on top of himself and whipped out some daggers to stab the organ's keys. I happened to be at the edge of the stage enjoying the show. I had my camera with me and as I snapped a photo of the act directly in front of me, Keith went to stab the

The moment after this photo was taken the knife in his hand slipped and almost hit me.

organ and the knife slipped and landed directly in front of me. Luckily it stuck into the floor and did not bounce any further.

Emerson commenting on his accidents, "... not only that. I've broken my nose; I've broken ribs. You name it. In fact, we just got back from South America and I fell over a monitor speaker on the stage and almost ended up in the front row of the audience. I managed to sprain my wrist on that one but luckily nothing was broken."

Capping off the injuries of *ELP*, Keith has had major nerve transposition surgery to correct a hand problem. Carl Palmer has also had surgery for carpal tunnel syndrome.

My message to the guys, "Be careful and thank you for the years of great music."

I am impatiently waiting for Keith Emerson's book to come out. It's called *Pictures of an Exhibitionist*. Should be a good one.

ELP FACT: Since 1977, *ELP* still holds the attendance record (over 78,000 people) at Olympic Stadium in Montreal, Canada.

CHAPTER 13
HAIR BANDS OF THE 80 S
BY LYNN RAMAGE

The Stowaway

One of the nicest people I had the opportunity of meeting was Chip from the band, *Enuff Z'nuff*. I told Gordon I was interviewing him and he told me how nice Chip would be. Gordon also requested that I try and get the full Madonna story off Chip. After I heard basically what it was about, there was no way I was going there. I hope the "Material Girl" appreciates my discretion. Gordon, however, probably would have gone right for the jugular, who knows?

{Chip told some of the story on Howard Stern's radio show. Basically, he claims he fucked Madonna and after he came, he pissed while still inside her.}

I prodded Chip's memory banks for a few minutes and got him comfortable for a good story.

Finally the synapses fired up; "I know one! Okay, we were in Council Bluffs, Iowa. We had just played and we were driving to the next show. At the show that night, there was this promiscuous girl that made an obvious impression on all of us. We all wanted to bang her but we didn't get the chance. We were expressing ourselves quite bluntly. It was typical 'three in the morning on the road guy talk.'

While we were all partly fantasizing and partly recalling what went on at the venue, I looked in the back of the bus and THERE SHE WAS hiding in a big speaker cabinet. I could see her beady little eyes glowing in the darkness! We were an hour into the trip. We all freaked out. We pulled over into a truck stop and she was scared to death because she overheard us talking about her, saying all sorts of terrible things. After trying to convince her that we weren't the monsters she thought we were, she finally was coaxed out of the cabinet. We called her family, gave her some money and left her at a truck stop for her family to come pick her up. We could have gotten in a lot of trouble because she was underage. We were almost out of the state too, which would've added

Enuff Z'nuff - Chip is the one wearing the hat.

more legal problems.

She snuck right in a P.A. speaker cabinet. That was pretty scary. I bet she'll never hook up with another band again after overhearing what we had to say about her."

Website: www.enuffznuff.com

Super Angus

I chatted with guitarist Angus Young of *AC/DC* while they were on their world tour for the *Ballbreaker* release in the summer of 1996. I found him to be a very happy, even-keeled sort of guy. He liked to laugh a lot. He found me as amusing, as I was amused with his thick Scottish accent.

We talked about all sorts of things and I recall asking him, "Angus, in your history, what perhaps is the funniest or the coolest thing that may have happened to you?"

He responded, "The coolest or funniest thing? Hmmm, gees, well there are a lot of them. I think probably the funniest thing was, once, somebody came up with the bright idea of putting me in a telephone box in a Superman suit and they wanted me to spring out of it with a cued explosion, ya know? But apparently what happened was; the explosion went off, the door on the telephone booth got stuck and I was stuck in there. They thought it was going to go on fire and they had to lift the box off me! (laughter) Yes, that was on stage.

Angus Young

No I wasn't hurt. But I was sure laughing a lot!" {Derek Smalls called... he feels your pain.}

Fire In The Sky!

I got to interview *Aerosmith* guitarist, Brad Whitford on the second leg of *The South Of Sanity* tour.

Lynn: Finally, what, in over 25 years of all this craziness, is a moment that particularly stands out in your memory?

Brad Whitford: "Well, I suppose there certainly was quite a few of them...let me think...off the top of my head...there was a time when we had started to move up in the world of travel. I think it was one of the very first planes we had used to tour on. It was an older plane. I recall like a DC-3... I remember sitting in the back of the plane thinking 'Wow! This is great! Wow! We have our own plane! I can go talk to the pilot,' which is what I decided to do. We were up in the air not even a minute and we could see from the cockpit that the left engine exploded into flames! Oil was pouring on the engine which was burning which made it look real bad with tons of smoke pouring out. We had to make an emergency landing in Washington D.C. Well, that was certainly an 'exciting moment' that has stuck in my memory... (laughter)"

Lynn: Did this story make your book?

Brad Whitford: "No! That didn't make the book!" {And it shouldn't have made this one either! Saving the good ones for your book, eh Brad!? Prick!}

Brad Whitford

Stuart Smith/Heaven & Earth Road Story

"Years ago, back in the early 80's I was in a band in England called *Sidewinder*, which toured extensively around England & Europe. It was in the early days, and we had the whole band, with two crew members, in a Ford Transit van with all the equipment."

"One night we were travelling through the British countryside and in the middle of nowhere, we got a flat tire. To fit all the gear in, we'd left the spare at home. So we had to rough it in the van. We broke out the beers and had a few drinks to pass the time till the repair shops opened in the morning. A few of us got out to have a piss and after a minute, a great big scream came from behind this bush. Our drummer had pissed on an electric fence meant to keep cattle in. He was leaping about like a kangaroo. Although it must have been very painful, we were in hysterics for the rest of the night."

"Wacky" Weed

Fear Factory's Guitarist, Dino Cazares, explained to me, "We have this really big underground cult following. You have to be very special to like the band. It's funny, the old school fans call the new school fans 'newbies.'"

I asked if there was anything really funny, weird or bizarre that ever happened to him. I also asked him to totally forget that he was talking to a woman because nothing would offend me.

He coyly replied, "You're actually gonna put this book together? There are a few things that have happened to me... where do I begin? Now you don't care how sick it is? Okay, I'll tell you a good story then. We were on an American tour in 1995. We had this one tour manager, I can't give names, who was a complete asshole. And I mean a COM-PLETE asshole, ya know? Every day you woke up, you just wanted to hit him. But the bad thing about it was he did an amazing job. He was one of the best tour managers we ever had. I guess you take the good with the bad, you know what I mean? The whole tour I was like, 'Goddamn, I just want to hit this fucking guy, Goddamn...' but if I hit him I'll kill him 'cause he was small and I'm a big guy."

"So, one day we were playing in Seattle and this kid comes up to me and says, 'Hey man, I'll give you some bud if you get me in the show.' I'm like alright. So he gave me some pot and I got him into the show. Now the funny thing is, I don't smoke pot but I got some just so I could give it to whoever else wanted to smoke it. It turned out it was this really, really killer pot, because I showed other people who were like, 'Oh my god! That's great shit. Oh my god, smell it. I want it, I want it.' I wasn't about to just give away this killer pot. I was gonna keep it for a special occasion. I didn't know what it was quite yet."

"The asshole tour manager was a really big pothead. A REALLY BIG pothead, right? So one day after a

Fear Factory

74

show, I was with a girl and an idea popped into my head. Oh my god! This is great. I had this girl give me a blow job, right? And I got the pot, right? You guessed it. Right when I came, I came all over the pot. I let it dry. The next day I gave it to my tour manager and he smoked it. He said it was the best pot he ever smoked (laughter)! So there you go, my revenge. So maybe if he reads this, it'll be even better (more laughter)!"

"Another time we were playing this show in Los Angeles. We have a lot of friends in L.A., so when we were done playing I did what I usually do, that is throw guitar picks out into the crowd, shake hands and stuff like that. Usually the singer will shake some hands and leave the stage while I'm still throwing picks. I'm usually the last one to get to the dressing room. This one particular night I stayed out on the stage for a really long time. When I finally got back I was dying of thirst. I looked around for something to drink and by then everybody had drank everything. All the liquids were gone! No Gatorade, no water, no beer, nothing. I saw an ice tray full of melted ice. I'm dying of thirst so I thought, 'You know what? I'm gonna drink this tray of melted ice water out of the tray.' So I picked up the tray and I started drinking it. I took a couple of big gulps. All of a sudden my singer got up out of his seat and pushed me, making me drop the tray."

He yells, 'Don't drink that water!'

I say, 'Why? It's just melted ice.'

He yelled back at me, 'I just washed my feet in it!' (laughter)

"I just went, 'Oh my god!' I didn't throw up or nothing."

"I just got reminded of another story from that last one. One time I was really into this girl. I used to use this one come-on line. I told this girl, 'You are so fine that I would drink your bath water.' She arrived at the next show with a jar full of bath water. She called my bluff, 'Here you go now, you got to drink it.' I drank it. That one I got sick. It was because of the soap. I was put on the spot in front of a bunch of people. But it was funny at the time. I don't use that line anymore because I didn't get laid after I drank the bath water."

Website: www.FearFactory.com

Emergency Delivery off the Audubon

I got to meet up with Rudy Schenker, guitarist for the *Scorpions*, during the *Scorpions/Motley Crue* 1999 summer tour. The *Scorpions* always put on a great show. This tour was promoting the release of *Eye II Eye*, which is really a wonderful extension of the *Scorpion's* sound.

I asked Rudy for a funny story and he replied in his thick German accent, "The point is we always have a funny story. And, as always, when people ask us about them, we forget."

"I remember a few years ago we were driving on the Audubon in Germany and we had to get petrol. We were all dressed up on our way to a formal dinner in a Mercedes limousine. We stopped at the petrol station and the driver got the fuel. After pumping the fuel, he started driving through the parking lot to find our way back onto the motorway. All of a sudden somebody ran in front of the limo with his hands in the air!"

Lynn Ramagé and Rudy Schenker

"Our driver stopped the car and the guy pleaded breathlessly, 'Hey…! You guys… have to… help me! You have… to help me…, please!' He was panicking and couldn't complete his sentences, 'I have to... get this... cow..!' We all got out of the limo and tried to calm him down so he could catch his breath. We were telling him to slow down but he was still panicking."

"Still out of breath he tried to get the words out, 'I have... to get... this... young cow...' Now we were getting back into the limo thinking the guy was crazy."

"Finally he caught his breath and yelled, 'I have to get the young cow out of the old cow.' Now we had to see what the hell this guy was talking about. We got back out of the car and we followed him to a little truck. Out of the back of the truck we saw the back end of this cow WITH A PAIR OF LITTLE HOOVES sticking out of her. There was a thick long rope tied around the little legs."

"This guy was still very upset, 'Guys!! You have to help me, you have to help me! We have to get this baby cow out right away!' Five of us, in Tuxedos, grabbed onto this rope and we pulled and pulled. It was hard. We didn't think we could do it until, finally, the baby cow came out! We actually got it out! When it came out it wasn't moving. Then all of a sudden it started wobbling around. We helped this guy get the newborn cow into his truck. I'll tell you one thing, it was unbelievable! It was an amazing experience. Both cows were fine, yes. Moooooo!"

CHAPTER 14
BATTLE WOUNDS
BY LYNN RAMAGE

Security Guard Gets "God Smacked"

Ozzfest '99 was hot as hell and more crowded at the Camden E-Center then I can ever recall. I expected a total zoo that day and my expectations weren't too far off. If I had to guess, it seemed like 40,000 people. You name it and it was going on... the big thing that day was the girls were going topless and getting their boobs air-brushed with designs, smiley faces, etc..... Then there were those who would just flash for the hell of it... and you could hear the primal chant of "hooters, hooters, hooters" everywhere!

My interview with Sully Erna, lead singer of *Godsmack*, was scheduled for four p.m. sharp. They were on stage while I was sent to the wrong door which, from experience with that venue, is par for the course. Thank God for cell phones. I sent my partner around the building to see if their tour manager, Bob Dallas, might be waiting to let me in. Sure enough, my partner Sherry phoned me, "Get your ass over here."

We really didn't have to wait on the back patio too long when Sully came right over with hugs and kisses (ya gotta just love him).

I jokingly asked him if he was married and he said, "Naww."

So I said, "Ya wanna be?"

He stopped, tipped his sunglasses and said, "Darlin', I'm not looking for Mrs. Right, I'm looking for Miss Right Now!"

I asked him what was the weirdest or funniest thing that has happened so far.

His response was; "Ahhh, man to pinpoint something? Hmmm....I guess the weirdest thing to happen to me so far is when we played Fort Myers, Florida. It was like 20,000 people outdoors, and a couple of songs

Sully Erna, lead singer of *Godsmack*

into the set I jumped down into the crowd. When I came back up on stage, one of the bouncers didn't realize it was me and he started chasing me! He caught up to me and put me in this bear hug. I didn't know who the fuck he was so I punched him and knocked him out! There was a big fight on stage between our people and the security people. Then later on, we apologized to each other because he didn't know it was me and I didn't know he was a security guard. The word 'security' was written on the back of his shirt and I never saw the back of him! The band however never missed a beat. It was really, really strange. It made the news."

www.Godsmack.com

Buck Cherry

Buck Cherry was opening for *Fuel* on this night down at the Electric Factory in Center City, Philly. There hit *Lit Up* was lighting up the airwaves at a very rapid rate of speed. Their live performances kick major ass and frontman Josh Todd reminds me of a cross between Tommy Lee and Sid Vicious. His stage antics really struck me as another Axle Rose. He has this tattoo of "CHAOS" tatted in huge letters across his stomach.

He explained to me, "it kinda describes what goes on between my ears!" We had time to chat prior to the show and I asked Josh for a funny tale.

"Oh well... I can't really comment on the sexual stories but, in our first sold out show, which was in Dallas, Keith went on his back to do a guitar solo. As he tried to get up off the ground he pushed his guitar up. It caught on the strap locks and it whacked him right on the top of the nose. He broke his nose during the show. This was half way through our set, he was bleeding real bad. He had to get eight stitches after the show. His nose was broken but he finished the set. It was kind of a milestone moment for the band since it was our first sold out gig but Keith had to go and bust his nose during the show."

www.BuckCherry.com

{Hey Josh! Now do you wish you told us a sex story?}

Buck Cherry frontman Josh Todd

A Dog's Night Out!

by John A. Sepetys

Hair of the Dog is actually a band I discovered advertised in Metal Edge magazine. They seemed to have a cool hard rock look about them so I contacted their management to find out more about them. They immediately forwarded the self-titled CD out to me from the West Coast. I was the first in Philly to give them any press. This band is really good and I recommend checking them out. At the time of this story there was a dispute over the band name. It seems there is an Irish folk band of the same name.

(The Irish band, states on their web site: In 1998, *Hair Of The Dog* applied to The United States Patent And Trademark Office to protect our name and logo. On September 21st, 1999, *Hair Of The Dog* was granted a service trademark and patent. There are other bands out there using OUR name. We are sorry for any confusion that this might cause.)

John A. Sepetys was kind enough to write this story for me.

(The following incident took place during the second leg of a tour with *RATT*)

Historically, topless women and rock-n-roll have proved to be a combination as fool proof as peanut butter and jelly. Quite simply... they just fit. With this in mind; Ryan Cook (*HOTD* lead singer), Joe Anthony (*RATT* employee), and Eric Christian (Warren DiMartini's tech) embarked on a trip to the Dollhouse in Raleigh, NC for what promised to be an evening filled with booze, girls and innocent fun. I believe it was around the stroke of eleven when the three thrill seekers jumped in a cab and sped off anxiously under a warm Tuesday night sky. Somewhere in the distance a dog may have barked.

Upon arriving at the club, an overbuilt, muscle head jerked Ryan aside and informed him he could not enter because his sleeveless shirt was against dress code policy.

"You gotta be kidding me," Ryan replied. "Chicks show their fuckin' tits in here and I can't show my arms?" Joe Anthony was quick to intercede and suggested he buy Ryan a Dollhouse T-shirt for cover-up purposes. This counter offer seemed to appease the gorillas as they agreed to permit the three to enter. At this point I find myself thinking, perhaps one of them should have detected a hint of foreshadowing in this incident and thereby sensed the impending doom. Then again, hindsight is always 20/20.

Anyhow, the next three hours or so passed by quite pleasantly. A scantily clad waitress delivered a nonstop flow of alcohol to their table and lovely dancers provided top-notch entertainment. When closing time finally rolled around, Ryan and the boys had become best of friends with nearly all the Dollhouse daughters.

After bidding their farewells, they exited the club and moved outside into a sea of drunken testosterone.

Eric, dressed in his typically furry and flashy attire, went back to the door and knocked on the glass to see if he could use the restroom inside. Another muscle bound ape rudely denied his request. So Eric, perhaps overreacting, spit on the window and walked back to the cab where Ryan and Joe were waiting.

Before the cab could pull away, Mr. Muscle threw open the car door and leaned in to announce; "Why don't you do us a favor and don't ever come back!" At this point Joe Anthony pulled his sturdily built frame out of the cab and planted himself to exchange words with the overzealous bouncer. Ryan and Eric quickly joined Joe and launched into a verbal counter attack of their own as a squadron of eager bouncers streamed out of The Dollhouse doors.

Trapped in the middle of all this yelling was the poor cab driver. With tensions and tempers escalating, he panicked and frantically tried to flee the scene. The frightened little man punched down on the gas, but he had forgotten to take the car out of reverse. His automobile rocketed backwards and tore an open driver's side door off a dancer's jeep parked behind him. Now added to the thunderous bellows of arguing men, were the screams and shrieks of an angry stripper who's vehicle had become the first casualty in a war that had officially not yet begun.

Ironically, it wasn't The Dollhouse bouncers or Ryan and his boys who drew first blood. In fact, the altercation probably would have ended as nothing more than a shouting match had a small, stocky drunk not stepped out from the crowd and threw a wild punch at Joe Anthony. After absorbing the stranger's blow, Joe moved to defend himself, but he never got the chance. A swarm of bouncers pounced on him and wrestled him to the ground. Ryan and Eric tried to rescue their bleeding and completely outnumbered friend, but the attempt was immediately thwarted by another gang of gargantuan boneheads. Ryan was thrown to the ground alongside his buddy Joe, and Eric was tied up like a pretzel with both arms twisted around his back. Despite his elbows and shoulders being dangerously close to snapping, Eric refused to breakdown and instead continued to taunt their evermore frustrated bouncers.

"Come on you pussies... is that all you've got?" he exclaimed. Finally, however, Eric's voice rose to a panicked cry. "Wait..." he pleaded "Wait!!!" Ryan and Joe froze in a moment of frightening silence, suspecting the brutes had in fact broken Eric's arms. They soon realized their concerns were unfounded though when Eric finished his statement. "I've lost my shoe... somebody help me find my shoe," he yelled in reference to a clog, which had slipped off his foot during the melee. At this point, with tensions somewhat eased by Eric's concern over his naked foot, the episode momentarily appeared to be nearing a peaceful end. No such luck.

The three attempted for a second time to get into the cab and leave the whole mess behind, but they were suddenly ambushed from all sides. Burning streams of pepper spray rained down upon them and in a matter of seconds they could feel their faces catch fire and their lungs begin to implode. For Ryan and Joe the effects were immediately staggering. Eric, on the other hand, was wearing his wrap around, goggle style sunglasses and this provided a temporary protective shield against the liquid blitzkrieg. He walked directly into the burning blasts, all the while antagonizing his attackers until the paralyzing moment when the spray eventually leaked beneath his glasses. He, too, was then rendered blind and left gasping for air. The bouncers, now satisfied that they got the best of everyone, filed back into the club patting each other on the back for a job well done.

When we got got back to the hotel, the poor desk clerk working the late shift that night must have thought he was hallucinating when Ryan, Joe and Eric stumbled through the doors. Huddled together with their swollen tomato faces throbbing, they rambled across the lobby like three blind mice in a rugby scrum. Their first instinct was to run for the showers, but they soon discovered that was a painfully wrong decision as the pulsing water only intensified and deepened the burning sensation. Not until hours later did their dermatological fires subside and

even by morning they still wore red, puffy faces as a reminder of the previous night's misadventure.

What the preceding story offers, besides an interesting anecdote, is an insight into the popularly asked question, "What do musicians do on their days off?" I personally use the time to relax, regroup, and give my liver a much-

Management: Rata E. Sepertys
310 581-9909

Hair of the Dog

SEG

needed rest. As I've come to discover, however, I am part of the "wimpy" minority and most others share a wholly different philosophy as effectively evidenced by the characters in the story above. These differing philosophies can account for a lot of puzzling tour situations, including why on a Tuesday night in Raleigh I was tucked snuggly into my hotel bed while three others found themselves knee deep in exotic dancers, pepper spray and muscle bound jerks. Ahh...the ancient paradoxes of the road.

CHAPTER 15
PURPLE HEART
BY LYNN RAMAGE

The Rock & Roll War Stories Purple Heart Award goes to George Guidotti.

One of the last hair-bands in the late eighties to get signed out of Philadelphia was *Heaven's Edge* to CBS/Columbia Records. Their "deal" didn't seem to last too long, which in my opinion was a real shame. These guys really were worth more of a shot then they got. Bassist George Guidotti elaborated on a different kind of shot he experienced.

George: Thank you Lynn. Well, everything you said rings true. We didn't really get a fair shake. I always felt like, remember when *FireHouse* had that one big hit? That's all we needed... just a little more time. At least we would've made some money. We would have been done by now, maybe in the same spot, but maybe we could've made some cash. Who knows?

Lynn: How long were you signed to CBS before your story happened?

George: This is the kick in the ass! We had just announced it that night that we had just got signed.

Lynn: Now this was at the Empire Rock Room in Philadelphia? What happened that night?

George: Okay. Well there was some sort of scuffle, which is normal in any night club. That kind of stuff happens all the time. Somebody got tossed out and then apparently screamed, "I'm gonna come back and kill all you motherfuckers, blah, blah, blah." Nobody thought much of it. The usual stupid threats from a drunk.

Lynn: Did you see the guy?

George: No, I had never seen him until my trial. The fight happened while we were

Rock & Roll War Stories veterans, Heaven's Edge

85

playing. The guy was thrown out of the club while I was on stage. We finished our show and the club was pretty empty. A few of us just lingered around drinking while our equipment was being broken down. I told the rest of the band I was going to cut out early and said my goodbyes.

Robin Parry (wife of guitarist, Steve Parry): Everyone came to my house before the show as I was the hair teaser! We were all so pumped and we planned to come back to my house to celebrate after the Empire show.

During the show there was some drunk ass guy waving a heinekin bottle on his middle finger and threatening Steve and the band. He was getting way out of hand. As he looked like he was going to get violent, I leapt on top of him and threw him away from the stage. The next thing I knew the bouncers were all over him.

George: While I was walking out the front door, I immediately noticed a drunk girl sitting on the front of a van. She was pretty toasted because her dress was way up around her waist and she was swaying.

I remember thinking, "Look at that girl over there with her mini-skirt way up her ass (chuckling)" and then all of a sudden - BANG!

Robin: I was one of the first to leave the club with George right behind me. I was going to prepare for the party that we planned at my house. As I walked out the door I heard "I'm gonna fucking kill you!" and saw a guy in a rusty Chevy Nova with a shotgun pointed right at me. I freaked! I dove to the ground and rolled under a truck as I heard the shot.

George: I crouched down and I dropped whatever I was carrying. I just heard the bang. I felt an impact, it was almost... Lynn, it's so hard to describe... it was like an electric shock! I didn't see the gun but I felt something after the blast. It was tingling and it felt like an electrical shock throughout my whole body. The guy fired a shotgun with birdshot pellets, not buckshot. Thank God because buckshot is a lot bigger. The electric shock I felt was the pellets hitting nerves. Everything was tingling.

I said to the girl, "I got shot!" I could hardly talk. It must've taken my breath away.

The drunken bimbo slurred, "Noooo ya didn't. It was a firecracker!" It was ridiculous! I thought to myself, "I'm obviously not going to get any help here."

Robin: I tried to get the guys in the truck to let me in. They were so scared they wouldn't let me in! I was freaking out!!! I was still ducked under the truck when they said the guy with the shotgun drove off. I ran back to find George covered in buckshot and blood.

George: I limped back into the club and got to the stage and I go to the guys,

"I got shot!"

They're like, "What? Get the fuck out of here. Stop goofing around."

It was surreal. I had white pants on. They finally realized that I wasn't fucking around and realized it was real blood all over my crotch area. They freaked out. By now I started feeling weak. Billy Kaye grabbed me and threw me up on the stage. From there, my arm really hurt and swelled up as I looked at it. Then all of a sudden I got this horrendous groin pain. It was just like someone took a sledgehammer and smashed my nuts!

I'm talking to myself, trying to remain calm and assess the situation. "Alright, I got shot in the dick, I got shot in the balls, ughhhhhhhhh." It wasn't working. There were still a few remaining fans in the club and my bandmates pulled down my pants.

Ridiculous as it sounds, I was screaming, "I want to see my dick!" It wasn't a scream of pull my pants down, let me see my dick. It was a scream of hoping my dick was STILL THERE! That's all I kept hoping. Mark (the singer) basically sat on my head, at this point, to hold me down from moving. I guess he was also trying to stop me from seeing the damage. After they pulled my pants down, he got a clear view and said, "Oh no, no. It didn't hit your dick. But it came mighty fucking close." He didn't want to tell me I got hit in the balls. He didn't have to. I felt it. My balls were shot up really bad! My hip took some damage and my arm, but my nuts... that was just the most intense pain!

The difference between a gun and a shotgun is a gun fires only one bullet. A shotgun sprays hundreds of pellets. Birdshot are like bb's. I got hit with over one hundred seventy bb's. The cigarette machine in the foyer of the Empire was hit and it was just blown apart! And the asshole that owned the Empire never even changed the friggin' machine after it happened. He just left it there like a memento. It just gave me the willies every time I walked in that club after it happened... The sight of it reminded me of the pain. It was just unbelievable.

The ambulance took forever to get there. Once there, the attendant kept asking me questions. I didn't want to talk. I just wanted to moan because moaning made me feel better.

I got to the hospital and the emergency doctors said I needed to see a Urologist right away - that's the dick doctor and he wasn't on call that night. We had just had a storm and the Urologist's phone lines were down so the police had to go to his house to get him! In the meantime, they still wouldn't give me anything for pain. It was like an hour and a half wait. It was a really bad night.

The emergency nurse and doctor took my pants completely off. I sat as best

I could to finally see what was going on down there.

I said to myself, "Holy shit!" It looked like a couple of multi-colored base-balls down there. Everything was swollen. I was awake the whole time. I didn't go into shock and I remember everything!

As I was trying to estimate the damage, I have to get graphic, would you believe right where I pee... there was a pellet imbedded there! I pointed it out to the doctor.

The doctor took his thumb and said, "Just hold on George," and just flicked it out. You figured he would have gotten a complex surgical instrument and anaes-thetized the area to gently remove the invasive metal. The doctor flicked it out like it was an annoying booger, or as if he was playing marbles. That was my first instinct but I figured I'd let a professional handle it. All those years of schooling and he flicks it out! My mother and the band said it was the only time they heard me scream. No anesthesia, no numbing, no nothing!

The Urologist finally arrived. They didn't know what they were going to do about my balls. He told me, "You are probably going to lose your testicles. Most likely you will have a colostomy bag for peeing."

I thought right then and there, "It's over. Just let me die right here, right now. Here I am, the night we announce we get signed to Columbia records and it's already fucking over for me."

I remember as they were wheeling me in I said, "Oh noooo, I'll never fuck again!" I also kept saying, "I got shot in the fucking balls!" as the doctors were discussing my case.

My mother came in to see me prior to surgery and she was just white. By the look on her face I knew it wasn't good. They had told her I had a 50/50 chance of surviving because a lot of shotgun victims go into shock, plus the danger of the pellets traveling to main organs.

Lynn: Did you have your big hair that night?

George: I'm about to lose my dick and my balls and a 50/50 chance of los-ing my life and you're asking me if I had my big hair that night?! To answer your question - I was totally teased up that night! As a matter of fact, an old nurse was gonna cut all my hair off. I was in intensive care for I don't know how many days, all sweaty and the hairspray was just yuck!

When they wheeled me out of surgery, I was just in and out of it. Every time I awoke in my room there was a different person standing over me; my friends Reggie, Lisa and another time Dave and Mark. I thank everyone that cared.

But the first thing I remembered doing consciously was, and I don't remember who was in the room, I reached down, felt and thought, "Oh my God, I've got my dick and both my nuts!"

A Specialist was brought in, that my manager had called, and he was able to save them. He actually took my one nut out, took all the pellets out and put it back in. They had to give me a plastic urethra and they didn't have to cut my dick open for that. While recovering I had a tube coming out of my dick, out of my nose, out of my arm, and out of my throat. I opened the hospital gown and I had thirty-three staples all the way down my stomach. I was traumatized. It was unbelievable!

Lynn: Do you have scars now?

George: My thigh got it bad and I've got some holes there. I've got scars from above my navel all the way down to the groin because the doctors had to cut me open to get the pellets out. When the pellets go in you they're still moving around. They had to go into my organs because the pellets could have went to main organs, into my bloodline, anything to fuck me up. When they're in you, they're still circulating around your body. Even now, I still have some left in me that have settled.

Lynn: Are you ever going to get them out?

George: Nawww.... I'm not going to mess with them. Every time they do, they have to stick a needle where they are and that hurts worse than taking the pellets out. I hate needles. Good thing I have Italian leather skin.

All the doctors told me later that they thought it was a jealous husband thing. All I remember thinking, even as they were putting me under, "I'm losing my nuts and I'm gonna be a fucking cripple!"

I think the time that it took for me to recover really hurt the band. I was only in the hospital fourteen days and I played out about a month after I got out. But by then the record company's producer had gone on to another project and our studio time got delayed. If this hadn't happened we might have made it before the "grunge thing". It was just enough time for us not to become famous, ya know?

Lynn: Now did they catch this guy that did this to you?

George: Yeah, they finally got him. Somebody at the club, that had seen the fight, knew him and eventually gave his name. The investigators went to his house and found the shotgun.

Robin: I had to badger the cops for weeks to do anything about the shooting. It seemed like they really didn't give a shit about a crime at a rock club. I personally pounded the streets to get information. Finally, a groupie of the band that saw the shooting was pretty sure she knew who did it. She was afraid to come forward as a witness. Anyway, I gave the guy's name and address to the cops. They found the gun and bullets. We had three eye witnesses.

George: At the trial they tried to make me look like the criminal. I was cross-examined about being in a band and the type of music I played. I had long hair, this guy had short hair. I could tell by the head juror, the way she was looking at me, that the defense successfully made me look like I was dirt! I could just tell.

At the end of the trial I was trying to get my life back together and the band had to go on the road to support the new record. The defense attorney used it against me and said in his closing statement, "Oh, George is fine. He's not even present here in the court room now..." Another big mistake I made was not getting a lawyer. I'm the victim. I didn't think I would need a lawyer. I thought I had an open and shut case. This guy friggin' shot me. I had witnesses. They said my witnesses had been drinking that night. They even accused me of sleeping with my witnesses! I wanted to scream - WITH WHAT? A cock and balls full of BUCK-SHOT!!! It was a bunch of bullshit!

And would you believe he got acquitted!? Would you believe that shit? UN-FUCKING-BELIEVABLE!!!

Robin: His family had a real good lawyer who got the guy off. Seems the cops never fingerprinted the gun and a lot of other holes in the investigation didn't help.

George: Ya know what Lynn? I was going to give the shooters name for the book but it would probably get me, you and your publisher in trouble. All I have to say is that's our wonderful judicial system for us! It blows!

Lynn: Ya know what, George? With our luck the motherfucker would try and sue the both of us.

George: I said that to my wife, Judy. He'll hunt us down and finish the job, right? That guy got on with his life like nothing ever happened.

I'll tell you what... I always thought, no matter what, always tell the truth in life, right? I have always tried to be a pretty honest guy but you know when they questioned me in court, they asked me if I saw the guy? I told the truth. I honestly didn't see him. I figured there were three eyewitnesses. That should've been good enough to identify the guy. The cops found the shotgun in the guy's house for chrissakes.

But right now, if I had to do it over, I would lie so fucking fast to nail that guy! Obviously they want to protect the guilty and this is the way "our system works." So if I had to do it all over again? I'd say "Yeah, he looked me right in the eye." I'd lie under oath, yes I would and you can print that! That's our system for you! They made me what I am now and I would lie in a fucking heartbeat! That motherfucker spent one night in jail! I could kick myself!

Luckily most of my medical bills got paid by the local bands like *John Eddy*, a guy from the *Hooters*, *Robert Bush*, *Britny Fox*, *Cinderella*, *Gypsy Rose*, *Tommy Connwell*, *Tangier* and *Street Talk*. The list goes on. I couldn't name them all simply because so many friends and strangers came to my aid. I thank them all. They helped raise twenty nine thousand dollars for me...and the bills were thirty nine thousand. The band had a tough time getting insurance after that.

Lynn: Didn't you mention another deal?

George: We recently got a call from a label in Sweden that was wondering what we've been doing which led to the deal on Perris Records.

{In 1999 The band was asked to record a song for the *Motley Crue - Kickstart My Heart* tribute abum. The guys went into the studio and recorded *Don't Go Away Mad (Just Go Away)* from the *Dr. Feelgood* album. Proceeds of the CD sales are donated to the Skylar Neil Memorial Foundation. This was set up to help children in hospitals, after *Motley Crue* frontman Vince Neil lost his 4 year old daughter to cancer.}

Lynn: Now I have to ask this George?

George: Yes, I can still have kids! Everything works. I remember I got so excited in the hospital when I got a hard-on on the seventh day. It hurt like hell with the catheter in me but I was so happy to get one ya know?

Website: http://come.to/heavensedge

Rock & Roll War Stories
Purple Heart recipient:
George Guidotti

CHAPTER 16
BRITNY FOX
BY LYNN RAMAGE

I remember when I first actually met Dean Davidson. It was pretty much after his *Britny Fox* days and around the *Black Eyed Susan* era. He had come into the Cellblock club and I recall being very fascinated with this mystery man. Over the years we became very good friends (oh, we've had our yelling matches), and spent countless hours on the telephone late into the evening. In fact, I swore Dean never slept. He was always up all hours of the night. It was never uncommon for Dean to call me at three or four a.m. My nickname for him is Dracula. He used to always say something like "you have to always be up and prepared for battle." Whatever that meant? We shared a lot of stories over the years.

Britny Fox formed in Philadelphia, Pennsylvania in the summer of 1985 when founder "Dizzy" Dean Davidson hooked up with ex-*Cinderella* guitarist Michael Kelly Smith. With the addition of bassist Billy Childs and original drummer Tony "Stix" Destra, the band was complete. Tony was killed in a car accident and was replaced by Johnny Dee.

They named themselves *Britny Fox* because Dean had a family tree from Wales England and one of his relatives was named Brittney Fox and he thought it was a cool sounding name. "Dizzy" Dean got his nickname after a pro baseball player. They were signed by Columbia Records. *Britny Fox*'s self-titled debut was one of the most successful premieres of the 1988-89 season, selling about one million copies and bringing more than 625,000 fans to their 130+ shows. They also won Metal Edge Magazine's 1988 Reader's Choice Award for Best New Band.

In mid 2000, *Britny Fox* reunited under lead singer Tommy Paris for a mini-tour of some east coast clubs. They recorded these shows for a live album, *Long Way to LIVE*, released in February of 2001.

One evening, I was visiting Dean's house and we were in the great room on this huge black sofa. I was comfy and I'll never forget this story he shared with me. He is one of the best storytellers too. I had tears of laughter rolling down my face.

First off, you have to understand that Dean doesn't get close to many people. Even though he is known as a very nice guy and has done a lot over the years to help local musicians, he has his quirks and different ways about him. Dean doesn't like anyone to eat off his plate. It really sets him off.

While on tour with *Britny Fox* (and the band swore he never slept on the tour bus either) he had just about had it with this sound guy, nicknamed Ace. When they would stop to get a meal, Ace would constantly pick food off everyone's plate, including Dean's. Well, finally Dean had enough of this plate picking. He bought a box of Ex-Lax, the kind that comes in chocolate blocks. In his hotel room, he whittled a bunch of shavings and stuck it in his pocket. When dinnertime came, Ace did his usual annoying habit of picking food off of everyone else's plate. Dean ordered a chocolate cream pie for desert. When no one was looking Dean sprinkled the Ex-Lax shavings all over the top of the cream on the pie and naturally Ace dove in as Dean backed off. Everyone knew about it too, everyone but Ace!

About an hour later, back on the bus, Dean said he could see Ace holding his stomach. He had horrendous cramps. Well, the golden rule on any tour bus is "no shitting in the bathroom." Usually you learn to schedule your bowel movements before you leave the hotel, restaurant, wherever.

By the time they got to the hotel, Ace was blue! He was the first one off the bus. He bolted through the hotel lobby and all the way down the hall to his room. The bathroom was right there as you walked into the room. Everyone assembled by his door and listened. It sounded like a marching band warming up their tubas. Everyone was in hysterics. Unfortunately though, Ace hadn't quite made it in time. There was an explosion of diarrhea all over the back wall behind the toilet.

Dean said, "It was everywhere, just everywhere, like blood on a crime scene!"

Well after I wrote the account of this story, I mailed it off to Dean's house. He called me back and told me I left out some key parts of the story. Like the other conspirators and how he had loaded Ace with practically six pounds of food the day prior to slipping him the Ex-Lax. Also, for extra insurance, on the bus, Dean pulled out a chocolate bar and hid chunks of Ex-Lax under the chocolate bar. When Ace bugged him for some of the chocolate he got the Ex-Lax instead of the real chocolate!

Dean was always pulling some sort

"Dizzy" Dean Davidson

of stunt on tour. He's like a kid at heart. One time I stopped by his house after a heavy snowfall. He had made all these huge snow-forts and tunnels with flags and everything all over the front lawn. It looked like he was ready for an invasion.

In Dean's own words, "There's a lot of stuff I did. Bobby Buttons was our keyboard player in '*Britny*'. I did so much stuff to him his hair turned white on the tour. He wanted to leave! It wasn't as if I didn't like him. I loved the guy. He was just one of those guys I used to pull pranks on. I liked to pull stuff on Michael Kelly Smith too because he's a vegetarian. I use to cut pieces of ham into the shape of pizza triangles and lift the cheese up and put the meat underneath and pat the cheese back down. He would eat three pieces, while preaching, 'Oh you guys eating meat, it's so bad, it's wrong, yada yada yada,' and we'd be laughing."

"We had a road tech that wasn't a citizen of the United States. He was a great tech and we wanted to keep him here. One night, after a show, our manager said jokingly to this groupie, 'Hey, if ya marry our roadie, Goz, he'll get his green card and he can keep working for us here in the U.S.' and she said, 'Okay.' Just like that. We got him married to this strange girl and he got his green card. And check this out, when *Britny* left the tour they were still married another three years after that! That amazed me."

"While we were working on the *Boys in Heat* album, we were staying at the East Gate Towers building in New York City. Richie Weistenburg (our road manager) put us on the twenty-third floor. It is not a good idea to house a rock band on the twenty-third floor of a building. I loved it. It was exciting. You could see what was going on in all the other buildings around you, if you know what I mean? There were hotels across the way. That was entertainment in itself. At the time they were making *Jason Goes to Manhattan*, one of the *Friday the 13th sequels*, right on our block. That was very cool to watch."

"Now I'll explain why it's not a good idea to put a rock band on the twenty-third floor of a building. The first thing we did, innocently enough, was got into a contest on who could make the best paper airplane with producer, Neil Keirnan. We went through three tablets of paper. Billy held the record for the farthest distance as his plane sailed three blocks away! A few days of this and there were paper airplanes all over Manhattan. No one knew where they were coming from."

"As we got bored of paper airplanes, we moved on to even more insane things. We played bombardier. We took toilet paper and rolled them into big balls and soaked them with water. They had weight to them. Every time someone had to go out to the store to run their errands they were at risk of being bombarded with these toilet paper bombs. It was like, 'Oh shit, how am I going to get out the door to the corner?' Everyday we would do this. Our guys would run out the door and duck down behind cars to try and avoid being hit. These bombs would hit the ground like a sack of jello."

"We eventually graduated to filling gallon milk cartons and tossing them down. Billy and Bobby Buttons went out one time and we threw a jug of water and it just missed Billy. When this thing hit the ground it sounded like a stick of dynamite. Looking back we could've killed someone."

"But it got even more insane. Towards the end of our stay, I got into a fight with Michael Kelly Smith about the band van. I complained to the rest of the guys and our manager. Why does he have it? Why does he always get it? Why does he always get everything? Even after all my protesting, Michael kept the van and used it as if it was his own. We all paid into it, about five grand each. I was frustrated with the situation and nothing was being done about it. I would argue directly with Michael that he should reimburse my share. It was only fair. Michael would blow off our argument and just continued his selfish ways. I said, 'Okay, that's the way you're going to be?!' and Michael thought I dropped the issue."

Dean continued, "I bided my time and one day Michael left the van parked directly below the apartment. I don't know why he did that because he knew it would be in danger of getting hit with our 'bombing raids.' The only people in the apartment were Richie, Billy and our friend from Atlantic Records, Dave Feld. Dave was this really cool guy that used to hang out with Jonny Dee a lot. They were in the kitchen when my wheels started turning."

"I took a forty gallon green hefty trash bag and filled it with soap and water. They were looking at me like what the fuck is he doing? I sealed the bag and dragged it over to the window. It was real fucking heavy. I struggled with it and rolled it up to the ledge. None of the guys would help me. They just stood around and watched. They kept saying, 'You're crazy!' I saw the van twenty three floors down directly below the window. I heaved the bag full of soap and water out the window. The guys ran to the other windows when the bag went out. They didn't believe I would do it. There it went, down two floors, ten floors, twenty floors, then BAM!!! You think the gallon jugs made a loud explosion? This thing exploded right on target. It hit the roof of the van. The whole roof was caved in like a foot. The suds hit the windows of the building six, seven stories high. When Michael saw the damage I said, 'There! That's my piece of the van!' They all thought I was crazy when I did that."

Website: www.JarodDean.com

Billy Childs

Lynn: So tell me Billy, really, is it true Dean never slept? He told me that it used to drive you guys nuts?

Billy: Well, it didn't really drive us nuts, we used to think he was nuts...we couldn't figure out why he wouldn't sleep, ya know? When he did sleep, he would sleep sitting up a lot of times. I'm a bad sleeper myself. We used to hang in the back of the bus and play Nintendo or Sega. I remember I would come up to the front after a few hours and there would be Dizzy Dean at the front table watching a movie or whatever! You'd never catch him in a bunk. Dizzy and I are a lot alike in certain ways.

The "chocolate cream pie" stunt was definitely the best! That was pretty much Dean and I pulling that off. I remember pulling into the truck stop. We had talked about it before and it just got to the point where we were fed up with this guy, Ace, eating all our food. That is how we got him to eat so much Ex-Lax because of his natural gluttony. We put it all over the pie and he ate three pieces of it. When we got on the bus after the truck stop, we broke out the chocolate bar. Everyone was taking a piece and Ace just joined in. All of us ate the real chocolate, he got the Ex-Lax. That's how we got so much into him! He was a big guy and he ate a lot! Everyone but him knew what was happening. After about a half-hour, he started shifting on the bus... and we were all waiting to see what would happen next. We were pissing ourselves. It was a long ride too! It was during the *Ratt* tour. We had just left Texas. It was hilarious. He, for the longest time, thought it was from the Mexican water. By the time we finally got around to telling him, he was like "you muthafuckers!" He was surprisingly good-natured about it.

Dean was really good at playing jokes on people. We had this tour manager we called "Silky." He was a real pompous New York asshole; you know what I mean? We're a band that just wanted to have some fun. We didn't want to deal with this guy.

He had this hat that he loved, but we all thought it was a real stupid fuckin' hat. Someone blew their nose in it. We ended up destroying his hat and he got way fuckin' bent over this.

He complained, "I called your manager, and if this practical joke shit doesn't stop..."

He would whine about all our antics but he would pull shit, like never buy his own cigarettes. If there was a pack sitting on the table on the bus he would grab smokes out of it. We didn't know him too well and when you're touring that shit gets old really fast. Little things like that take on an added significance when you're an annoying prick on the road.

We set him up. We left a pack of cigarettes out but replaced them with exploding cigarettes with incredible loads. He came on the bus and started going off on us about our practical jokes and ended his rant, "and if one more thing happens I'm going home." The timing couldn't have been more perfect! He scoffed a cig out of the pack and we all looked at each other. He lit it and it went off, baboom! We were pissing ourselves. This guy was doing all kinds of shady shit. It was the end of him when we found out that this guy was robbing us blind.

Another time we had this roadie named Steve. He was a real drinker, big time. Some nights he would literally crawl back to his hotel room. He would get so fucked up he would always climb into the wrong bed. One time Ace and I were out fooling around with these girls and we went back to the hotel and there's Steve passed out in Ace's bed!

Ace was pissed; "Mutherfucker has done it again. He does this all the time, the son of a bitch is in my bed." So he goes; "I'm gonna piss on this motherfucker." I was laughing. I didn't believe he would do it. Ace whipped out his dick and pissed on Steve lying on his bed! Steve never woke up either.

I was never much into doing blow but we had a wardrobe girl that did. That's what kept our crew going... the riggers, the light guys, they were all up ridiculous hours on those big tours. We had a day off in Dallas. It was a gold record party that day. The wardrobe girl called me to come down and pick up my laundry. When I got there she asked, "Wanna do a line?" I thought, "Why not? I got the day off. What the fuck."

An hour and five or six huge lines later I went back to my room. As soon as I walked in the phone rang. It was my manager and he asked, "Yo, where ya been? We have the guy here from the life insurance company taking blood tests so you can get your policy. Get your ass over to my room."

I'm like, "Oh my God!" I'm all freaked out and high. I'm thinking maybe it's not in my system yet... maybe it takes a while... I don't know... So I went over to the room and they took my blood for the blood test. About a month later my manager called me and said, "What the fuck did you do? You'll never get life insurance. You set the thing off the meter!" Needless to say I didn't get the life insurance.

Did Dean ever tell you the Bobby Buttons stories? Bobby was our keyboard player when we recorded *Boys in Heat*. It was a sweltering summer up on the twenty-third floor of the East Gate Towers in Manhattan where we stayed. This was like in 1989. One day Bobby was sleeping in his bed and we just got this weird idea. We used rolls and rolls of duct tape and taped him into his bed. We turned off the air conditioner and we took everything we could find in this place... every sheet, every blanket, drapes and loaded it on top of him and covered him. Five of us did this and we just sat and watched him. He started sweating and after ten minutes he woke up yelling at us to get him out of the bed.

That was just some of the harmless stuff we used to do! Those were the fucking days.

CHAPTER 17
BECK AND BUCKINGHAM MAYHEM
(THE MEETING OF THE B BENDERS)
BY WENDY MOORE

It was a fateful Halloween night in 1997. If there weren't any parties to go to, the thing to do for me, besides trying to find Stevie Nicks' house, was to go to the famous Rainbow Bar and Grill on Sunset Boulevard in Hollywood, California. My friend Kathreen was dressed up like a beautiful renaissance wench. I, the perfect vampiress who wore custom-made porcelain fangs and a floor length velvet hooded cape that my mother made for me.

We went upstairs to where another small bar was that also had a small dance floor. The tiny dance floor area was filled with ghouls and goblins, and of course, the local bimbos wearing close to nothing. Sometimes I think Halloween is just another excuse for girls to show off their new plastic body parts for the drunk guys to drool over. During the course of the evening Kathreen and I got separated. Kathreen was hanging out downstairs while I was still upstairs on the dance floor. The downstairs is a dining area, famous for the pizza. Soon I found myself being yanked off of the dance floor by an out-of-breath Kathreen who was trying to yell something over the loud music.

As she dragged me down the narrow staircase, she asked, "Guess who's in the restaurant area?" Kathreen is famous for spotting celebrities a mile away. I waited for her to answer her own question as she pushed me gently forward. "Jeff Beck," she said with excitement! We both knew what we had to do. You see, Kathreen is an aspiring guitar player, (how else would a young girl in her 20's know who Jeff Beck was?), and I am a singer. But we leave the p.r. "work" up to me because I'm good at it. She left me alone to do my work. I approached the table that Jeff and three other men were sitting at. I find it's much easier to approach famous men when there aren't any women with them.

"A piece of cake," I thought. I politely got the attention of one of the guys at the table. I asked him if he had an address where I could send my demo. He turned to Jeff and whispered in his ear. They called me to come over closer while Jeff was writing something down on a napkin. At the same time, the guy I spoke to was also writing something down on a piece of paper. I introduced myself to all of them and, without invitation, slid into the booth next to Jeff and his friend. He handed me his napkin that had his London address on it. And his friend, whose name was Jed, handed me the phone number to a studio that he owns in L.A.

No one was eating, just drinking beer. I was offered a drink, but since I don't really drink, I just ordered a coke. Jeff seemed very pleased about my being there next to him in the booth, but a passing waitress wasn't so pleased. She kneeled down beside me and suggested that I stop bothering them. No one heard her say this to me, so I just ignored her. I'm sure she just thought of me as an uninvited groupie. Actually, at the time, I wasn't sure if she was right or wrong, but I wasn't going to let anyone ruin it for me. I felt that I was far from being a groupie, because I didn't necessarily want to have sex with a rock star as much as I wanted to BE a rock star!

As the night progressed, it seemed as if Jeff's nose was swelling larger and larger and got redder and redder, as he pounded down imported beer. It was a busy night. People were just about squeezing by, stuck in a slow moving current. As each new group of people neared our table, gawkers would lean in to get a look at Jeff.

Jeff finally yelled out loud, "I feel like a bloody museum piece!" It was funny, but he did seem a little annoyed. He turned to me and looked down at my lower half, noticing the very long slit that went all the way up to my waistline on my velvet skirt. He started to slide his hand up and down my thigh with delight.

He said, "Wow, I love a girl with long legs." I thought he was very cute from the start. I love older men, and I love large noses. Isn't that weird? But most of all, guitar players turn me on. So do British hair styles and British accents. But I hadn't anticipated him coming on to me, especially in my costume. He told me that he thought my fangs were sexy. So I leaned over and playfully bit his salty neck. He loved it, and he shook as if he got the chills.

We were just getting to know each other better and have a good time when this strange, not-so attractive girl kneeled down in front of our table and started telling me that she thought that she looked just like me. She insisted upon this, and repeated it to us, with no exaggeration, at least ten times! Jeff was highly annoyed by this skank and asked her to leave. After that incident, we all decided to take leave. Jeff took the initiative.

When we stood up he grabbed my arm, looked me up and down and said, "You're a tall one." We walked out of the restaurant arm in arm. I was happy that the waitress, who was rude to me before, saw me leave with him. Out in the parking lot, we waited for the valet to bring his car around. Jeff stood on the curb while I stood in the street. He wanted to be taller than me. We embraced.

Then he said, "Now this is how it's supposed to be." I was wearing high heeled boots which made me well over six foot tall. I'd guess that he was around five foot nine or so. I usually feel funny being with men that are shorter than me, but for some reason it didn't seem that odd with him.

His friends pulled up in the car, waiting with the engine running as Jeff asked me to go back to his hotel with him. Over his shoulder I could see Kathreen watching and wondering what I was going to do. I think I would have said yes but my parents were visiting me at my apartment back in Thousand Oaks, so I had to decline. I gave him my phone number and told him that I could hang out with him the next night when I had my own car with me. He told me that he would call me. We kissed a small kiss goodnight and that was it. Boy, how I was wishing that I lived in Hollywood... or London for that fact! Oh well, Kat and I returned to our boring hometown of Thousand Oaks.

All night long, I was so excited lying in my bed. I could not sleep thinking that Jeff Beck might be calling me at my house. It was just too much to comprehend. I felt like a schoolgirl who was just about to go on her first date! Of course, I barely knew him. All I knew about his guitar playing was that he was the cute guy playing guitar on Rod Stewart's video, *People Get Ready*. It was on MTV every second of the day when I was in High School. But there was something about him. That special feeling you get when you know that you are standing in the presence of someone who is very powerful and gifted. That was what Jeff Beck was like for me.

The next morning the phone rang. I picked up the phone and heard a British man say to me, "Hi, it's Jeff," as if he was a long time pal of mine. I was so nervous. It did take me a couple of seconds for it to register in my mind and to realize who it was before I finally responded. He asked me if I wanted to go out with him that night. Of course I said yes, without trying to sound too excited. The rest of the day was spent with Kathreen at a Thousand Oaks used record shop looking through the Jeff Beck LP section. We bought all of his albums and took them home to listen to, and drool over the pictures. That's why we bought albums opposed to CDs. So much of the artwork and photos are lost on CDs.

As the night grew closer, I started getting ready for my date. I was excited for Jeff to see me out of my Halloween costume. He told me to meet him at the The Whiskey Bar in the lobby of the Sunset Marquis Hotel, where he was staying. I wore a leotard that had long lace sleeves. The front showed some cleavage with a neckline that laced up. Over that, I wore a long black skirt and my shortest heeled boots I could find. I was off to Hollywood.

I parked in a lot up the street from the hotel and walked down. As I walked in I immediately spotted Jeff sitting on a couch... with the same friends from the prior night. When I saw his friends I knew this wasn't going to be an intimate date with just the two of us. The plans for the evening were to go to dinner at a restaurant on Santa Monica Boulevard called Dan Tana's, owned by Bruce Springsteen. I excused myself to the bathroom. I ran to a phone in the lobby, called Kathreen and told her to meet us at the restaurant. After the guys finished their drinks at the bar, we headed downstairs to the parking lot, underneath the hotel. As Jeff and I passed a floor length mirror in the lobby, he grabbed my hand and yanked me gently backwards so the two of us could see ourselves in the mirror.

He asked, "Don't we look good together?" I was flattered.

The group took two cars. Jeff and I ended up in the back seat of his best friend's small black convertible. I couldn't really tell you what kind of car he had but it was fun being in a convertible. That was something that I just didn't do that often being a native Californian. I had my camera with me. I gave it to his friend. He took a picture of Jeff and I in the back seat with the wind in our hair. That would be the only picture I would get of Jeff and I together. At the restaurant he acted embarrassed and refused my request for the waitress to take a group shot. He made me feel stupid, like a silly child or an obvious groupie.

Everybody at the table had a date with them, except for Jeff's friend, Jed. Jed had handed me his business card for his studio the night before. So I was happy when Kathreen finally arrived and sat next to Jed. There was an obvious instant attraction between the two. Someone at the table made a comment about it, which made them both blush. It was a little awkward sitting at a table, eating spaghetti, with a bunch of strangers but it was entertaining listening to all of them talking and joking around. They got a little tipsy on their imported beer. I was just fine with my good ol' Coca-Cola and garlic bread. I found out that one of the guys that I was sitting next to was a studio musician for my all-time favorite singer, Stevie Nicks. That was really interesting for me. Jeff and I didn't have much to talk about, except for a few short questions here and there.

One of those questions from Jeff was, "So, where is YOUR man this evening?" with a slight "cockiness" to his voice.

I replied with, "If I had a man, I wouldn't be sitting here with you right now!"

Looking back, you always think that you could have come up with something better to say.

If I was more quick witted with my answer, I should've said, "Right here!" But I did ask him if he had a girlfriend. He confessed that he did have one back in London but infidelity caused things to never be the same between the two of them. I wondered to myself, "Who's infidelity?" I didn't ask.

We finished dinner and went outside to wait for the valet to bring the car around. Jeff was still inside waiting to pay the bill. All of a sudden, I heard Kathreen say under her breath, but loud enough for me to hear, "Oh my God, it's Lindsey Buckingham!" Once again, "Miss Eagle-Eye" spotted another celebrity. But this was not just another celebrity. This was a close encounter with a band-member of my all-time favorite artist. He was standing on the sidewalk, with a young blond woman, waiting for his car as well. I watched dumfounded as Kathreen whizzed past me. With a pavlovian instinct, I followed. By this time I had completely forgotten that I was out on a date with Jeff Beck. I lost my composure and went into complete "groupie-mode!" Kathreen was the first to speak.

She said, "I love your guitar playing. I can play all of your songs!"

He rudely replied, "Oh, so they're that easy?"

Kat didn't know how to respond. She just stood there, shook her head and hesitated with uncertainty in her voice as she said, "No..."

I interrupted and blurted out, "I love *Fleetwood Mac*!" And then I looked down at my long skirt and pulled it out on both sides and continued to say, "See, I love Stevie Nicks so much, that I dress like her."

Lindsey then very rudely looked me up and down in an obvious way and suggested that I needed to "get over it!" as he put it. Despite his rudeness, and even though I was highly disappointed in his behavior, I still wanted to have my picture taken with this asshole. I rushed over to Jed, shoved my camera into his fist and asked him to take our picture. He reluctantly obliged. When I hurried back over to Lindsey and Kathreen to pose for the picture, Lindsey's girlfriend rolled her eyes as if to say, "Oh God, not this again" and moved out of the way. I told her, out of respect, that she didn't have to leave but she didn't respond and walked over to the curb. You can see in the photo that Lindsey looked over at his girlfriend with a smirk on his face as if he was helpless and the situation amused him.

Kathreen, Lindsey Buckingham and Wendy Moore

The "get over it" remark really hurt me. The saying of how you should never meet your heroes really applied here. Thank God Stevie Nicks has never disappointed me.

Jeff finally came out of the restaurant and apparently didn't see anything that had just occurred. Lindsey had already taken off with his girlfriend. Everyone else was just hanging out, "enjoying" the fresh air and being hypocrites by smoking cigarettes to cancel out the fresh air. In London you can still smoke indoors (something that was banned in L.A. a few years ago, which is fine with me since I hate singing in small, smokey bars.)

We all decided to go back to the Whiskey Bar for our nightcap. On the way there, it got chilly in the back of the convertible and Jeff asked me to cuddle with him. I thought out loud and exclaimed to him, "Wow, a man that actually likes to cuddle!"

After we pulled into the underground parking garage, Jed wanted to show Kathreen and I his recording studio underneath the hotel. As we entered this plain looking door (that looked like it might lead you into a janitor's closet) I thought, "this is like the best kept secret in L.A." We ended up entering this beautiful, posh studio that easily looked like it cost thousands of dollars a day to use. Jeff uses it a lot and so does *Aerosmith*. Jed handed me a CD case that he called his studio's "calling card." It had all his information written on the inner and outer sleeve with a milk chocolate disc inside. It was very cool. Behind the soundboard, up on top of a drum riser-type carpeted step, was this long, beautiful, dark purple velvet chaise lounge. It resembled a sofa that you might see in a stereotypical, movie version of a psychiatrist's office. I envisioned Elvira stretched out on it for some reason. I laid out on it in delight, trying to emulate my thoughts.

After the tour of Jed's studio, we went upstairs to the lobby and into the bar. As we were walking by, I noticed a guy leaning on a wall, holding a guitar. It was obvious that he was waiting for Jeff. The whole entourage walked by and ignored him. In the bar lounge, we sat down on the same couch that we were on before we left for dinner. I entertained everyone by telling jokes. During the course of the evening, with all the beer that Jeff was consuming, he finally had to make a trip to the little boy's room. That's when the guy that was holding the guitar approached me and asked if I was with Jeff. It was a rhetorical question as it was obvious I was with him. I was surprised he was still hanging around. He shyly asked if I could possibly get him to autograph his guitar for him. He was so humble about it. I told him to wait and that I would try my best. At the same time that Jeff was gone, his best friend took the opportunity to scold me for the way I had acted outside Dan

Tana's with Lindsey Buckingham. He was so disgusted with my behavior.

He asked, "What if Jeff saw the way you acted?" He told me that when you are out with celebrities that you are not supposed to make a big deal out of it. He continued to tell me how "uncool" I acted and how improper it was for me to treat Lindsey Buckingham that way. Especially when I was out with Jeff Beck "for God's sake!" As he redundantly made his point, I again, felt like a child that was being scolded. Thank God Jeff finally returned to his spot on the couch next to me as the reprimanding stopped when Jeff reappeared. In the doorway of the bar I could see the guy with the guitar motioning at me for an answer. He was putting me on the spot, especially after the scolding I had just received. The humble guy was now being a pain in the ass. I shouldn't have made any commitment.

I finally asked Jeff, "Didn't you see the guy with the guitar..." as I pointed over to the poor guy who was still patiently waiting. Jeff said, "Of course I saw him. I passed him when I went to the restroom."

So I asked, "Well, aren't you going to sign the guy's guitar for him?"

Jeff replied, "Why? So he can bloody sell it!?"

I finally guilted him to sign it by telling him how fortunate he was to be famous and to have fans ask him for his autograph. Instead of motioning the guy over to the table, Jeff got up, walked over and signed the guy's guitar. The guy gave me a thumbs-up with a shit-eating grin on his face. I was happy I made this

stranger's night but now I was worried that I guilted Jeff into doing something that he did not want to do.

As Jeff was busy auto-graphing the guitar, Kathreen decided that she had to go home because it was getting late. She got Jed's phone number and quickly left. I wasn't quite sure what was to become of me as everyone was calling it a night after Kathreen's cue.

Jeff returned to the sofa. Jed leaned over my back to say to Jeff, "Looks like you

The only picture of Jeff Beck and I together.

are going to get lucky tonight, eh, mate?" I pretended not to overhear the comment as I listened to Jeff's response.

To my shock, I heard him reply with, "Yeah!"

So I caught them both off guard by saying out loud, "I heard that!"

They both laughed. Jeff seemed to have been embarrassed. But deep inside, I WAS wondering what we were going to do, because I really did like him.

Soon it was just the two of us in the bar as all of Jeff's friends filtered out for the evening. I was a little embarrassed that they might've thought that Jeff was going to get "lucky" with me as they left the two of us alone.

But I thought to myself, "I'm not a virgin. I can handle this. But why am I so scared?" Perhaps, because I had never had a one-night stand before that time, let alone with a rock star!

Jeff led me to his hotel room. It was on the same level, poolside. As I entered the surprisingly neatly kept room, I noticed my name and phone number written on a piece of paper by his bedside. He wanted to order room service right away, so we did. We got coffee and french fries. When room service arrived, I set everything up on a small round table.

Jeff said, "Let's be crazy and eat on the bed!" He turned on the small TV set. How ironic it was for the movie *Blow-Up* to be on! Such an obscure movie to be on at that very moment. I thought that he was playing a trick on me. I was the one to say something first on how twilight zone it was that it was on. Jeff was impressed that a girl of my youth would even know that movie, let alone know that he was in it! Little did he know that I am totally into sixties and seventies nostalgia and music. But for that movie to be playing at that moment was very strange. As we sat in bed watching it, Jeff told me how all of his friends did drugs and most of them died at an early age. He told me that he never did drugs. And I believed him because, for a man in his early fifties, he sure looked good! I loved his profile, especially his hair. And I could've listened to that British accent forever. We cleared the bed after we finished our fries and coffee. Jeff decided that he wanted to take a shower. He disappeared into the bathroom, closed the door and turned the shower on. I sat in bed and thought how trusting he must be. I could've taken off with his guitar or his wallet that laid visible on the night stand.

After the shower shut off, he finally opened the bathroom door in a white, terry cloth robe. He looked so cute with wet hair. He walked around to his side of the bed and slipped under the covers while still wearing his robe. I found that to be a little odd, especially when he slipped the robe off while he was still under the covers. Then he slid the robe out onto the floor next to him. Maybe he was self-conscious of his cock? I wouldn't know as I didn't get a chance to see it at that moment. It just made me more curious. Maybe that was the desired effect. Maybe he was hung like a horse and thought I would be scared away.

Now I had a shy, naked Jeff Beck under the covers next to me. I was still above the covers on my side. He then grabbed me and pulled me on top of his bare chest. It was a nice chest, with just the perfect amount of hair. We began to kiss. It was cute the way he got so easily aroused with me. Not shy at all about showing any feelings. I had only just begun to stroke his chest and kiss it and he immediately moaned aloud. When I kissed his nipples and gently sucked on them, it was all over! I couldn't believe how receptive he was to my every touch. His hands went up my skirt. I got up and took my skirt off, leaving just my leotard on, which had a thong bottom. I got back onto the bed teasing him. I remember noticing how gray his roots were as I stroked his hair backward from the scalp. He did have a good head of hair.

I thought, "He won't be balding anytime soon." He finally had his hands on my butt cheeks, grabbing them. We continued with this innocent make-out session for a little while, and then his hands disappeared under the covers in front of him. It wasn't hard (no pun intended) to figure out what he was doing. I guess he figured that I wasn't going to take off any more of my clothes and he didn't want to insist or impose anything on me... what a gentleman. I decided to "help" him with his quest for ecstasy by licking in his ear and whispering pleasurable sounds. I couldn't really see what he was doing, but I glanced down and caught a glimpse of the head of his cock with his hand wrapped around it. I couldn't see much else. I was disappointed. I guess he was shy about the size of his cock, after all.

After he came, I got up and got a small washcloth from the bathroom, rinsed part of it in warm water and brought it over to him. I made a point not to watch so he didn't feel self-conscious. By this time, it was almost five in the morning. I got under the covers with him and snuggled up behind him with his buttocks fitting nicely into my crotch area. We laid there spooning for about an hour, but Jeff had fallen asleep soon after I had gotten under the covers with him. It felt so nice being there with him. As I was listening to him breathe as he slept, I heard and felt another noise come from another part of his body. Yes, you guessed it. He broke wind. It was a long whistle sound with no scent, thank God. I smiled and giggled with amusement. I thought to myself that this whole night had just been too funny, and that this was a perfect ending (once again, no pun intended). I actually thought it was cute that he farted (a lot of people think that I'm a weird girl).

I looked at the clock and it said six a.m. I realized that my parents were still staying at my house back in Thousand Oaks, so I got up and started to get dressed. Jeff woke up and asked me where I was going. I told him that I had to go home because my folks were in town.

He then said to me, "Well, that's okay. I'll call you tomorrow during the day and we'll go out on a real date."

I said, "Okay," as I reached for the door. I looked at the nightstand and made sure the note with my name and number was still on it. He remained in bed as I shut the door behind me. I got home around a quarter to seven. I couldn't really go back to sleep. I was actually having the insane feeling that I was in love with him. I remember daydreaming that I would move to London if he asked me to. I was excited that he would be calling me again.

It was now Sunday, and after I got up I made sure that I was ready when he called so that I could just get in my car and drive out there. I waited for his phone call all day, but it never came. I knew that he was under an assumed name at the hotel. I didn't want to be the one to call anyway, especially when he said that he was going to call me. I was the type of girl who didn't believe in calling guys.

As the day turned into night, I sat by the phone in a green recliner in my living room eventually conceding that he wasn't calling. I bawled my eyes out. My parents had already left early that morning and my brother thought I was crazy for crying over it. I knew that it was his last day in L.A. and that I would probably never see or hear from him again. And I was right. For the next two weeks, I couldn't stop looking at all the albums Kathreen and I bought. When I had enough mourning, I took all the albums and threw them out.

I tried keeping in contact with Jed. I would stop by the Sunset Marguis Hotel every time that I heard Jeff was in town. One time, when I sat in the lobby for about an hour, I heard that I had just missed him by only five minutes. What can I say, the guitarist of my favorite group, *Fleetwood Mac* had let me down, and Jeff Beck had broken my heart.

To this day, I wonder if it would have made a difference if I would've had "real" sex with him or not.

CHAPTER 18
LOVE AT FIRST BITE?
BY WENDY MOORE

The next two chapters are geared towards our female readers (if there are any left still reading).

It was 1996 and I was still living in Thousand Oaks, California ("T.O." is about a half an hour or more from Hollywood.) My friend Carla and I went to a club in Hollywood on Highland Avenue called Stigmata. Carla's a bit of a wild one, covered with tattoos and body piercing. I'm a bit of a wild one myself, but I only have one tattoo and just my ears are pierced. I like to go out to all kinds of clubs. Carla's really into the gothic scene and that's what Stigmata was like. They played a lot of good, old songs from the 80's that reminded us of high school, so I liked it. Wearing a dark velvet dress with a plunging neckline and a black "Stevie Nicks-ish" type scarf over my shoulders, I let Carla lead me around by a leash attached to a leather dog collar. Once inside, we had a few drinks and danced together. I guess we were getting a little too wild because we had the whole place watching us. One of my breasts came out of my dress and Carla was fondling and sucking on it on the dance floor. This wasn't anything unusual for us when we would drink and hang out together. It didn't really mean anything, we were just having fun.

Soon we got separated and I was hanging out at the bar by myself trying to get another drink. It didn't take me long to get drunk because I rarely ever drank, but when I did... look out! After that, nothing too exciting was really going on until Carla ran up to me and said, "Oh my God, do you know who Marilyn Manson is? He's here! Marilyn fuckin' Manson is here!"

I knew who he was from an MTV video of his band doing a *Eurythmics* cover song, *Sweet Dreams*. He was sitting with two girls and another guy who was bald. I couldn't tell how tall he was because he was sitting down but he was skinny with black hair, so he looked pretty good to me so far. I don't remember

Wendy Moore

what he was wearing because it was so dark in the club, but it looked like it was all black. But I do remember these eye balls and squiggles that he had tattooed all over his arms.

It took me a while to figure out why his face looked kind of strange to me. Besides the fact that he was wearing a colored contact in one of his eyes, he also didn't have any eyebrows! I guess he shaved them off. Carla introduced herself and asked him for an autograph. He grabbed the pen and she pulled her top down. She wanted him to autograph her tits. And he actually did!

Then I introduced myself. He just looked at me and asked me if I had a penis! So I replied, "I do if you want me to."

Then I plopped myself down onto his lap and asked him, "Aren't you going to ask us what we would like to drink?"

He bought us both a cocktail. I had a Long Island Ice-Tea. Then he introduced us to his friends, two rude girls in leopard print clothing and one of his band members, Twiggy. We got on the subject of Courtney Love for some reason, and Marilyn told me that she had sex with one of his bandmates when they were on tour together. Carla was in complete shock and just stood silent freaking out over Marilyn. For some reason they couldn't stay long, and the two girls he was with were acting as though they were jealous and fawned over him. They pulled on Marilyn to leave. He told me that they were going to hit another club, but they didn't invite us. I was kind of surprised when he asked me what I was doing the next night and if I wanted to go out with him. He then asked me for my phone number. So I wrote it down for him on a napkin and watched him slip it into his pocket. I didn't really think that much about it, I mean you can't get too excited when a man asks you for your phone number because nine times out of ten, they don't call you anyway. After they left the club Carla went wild. She couldn't believe that Marilyn asked me for my number and asked me out. It definitely should have been her instead of me, because she was really into him and I barely knew who he was.

Carla looked a little more stylish than I did as far as piercing and tattoos went. She even had her nipples pierced with two little silver barbells. I saw them for the first time that night in the ladies room. I thought they looked really sexy on her. She has really nice breasts to begin with anyway. She kept hanging on my arm all-night singing, "Marilyn Manson wants to fuck you!" We stayed until the club closed around two a.m. and then went home.

The next morning my phone rang. I jumped out of bed and ran downstairs to pick it up. To my surprise it was Marilyn on the other end. I didn't expect someone like him to be conscious that early in the morning! It was ten a.m., which was way too early for me, let alone a rock star that partied all night long. My only conclusion was that he probably hadn't gone to sleep yet.

After I said hello, he said, "Hi, it's Manson."

He invited me to go to The Dragonfly (a popular club in Hollywood where live bands play). He wanted to meet me at the club, which I thought was strange. I asked him why I couldn't just meet him at his hotel so we could go down to the club together? He told me that he has very protective friends that are driving him to the club. So I agreed to his conditions. I couldn't wait to tell Carla all about it. I called her after I got off the phone with him. I would have invited her if I had known that it wasn't going to be a "date" with just Marilyn and me, but I didn't find that out until I got down there. I wore a black unitard that was low-cut in front and laced up the back with a see-through, burgundy mesh top and long matching lace skirt over it. Then I had on a pair of black suede, lace-up boots. I was probably dressed up too nice for a night out with Marilyn!

I showed up at the club and gave it a "once around" inside to see if he was already there, but I didn't see him. I then asked the girl working at the front if she had seen him. She looked puzzled at me and just said that she hadn't seen him. So I stood in the center of a crowd of people, watching the band and keeping one eye on the door. I saw him walk in with his entourage of friends, the same people he was with the night before. I turned my head away but made sure that I was in full view for him to see me. A few seconds went by, I looked back to see if he had noticed me yet, but he just walked straight through the club without even turning his head to look for me at all! I was highly insulted and reluctantly followed him out to the outdoor patio. By the time I got out there, he was leaning on the bar surrounded by his friends with a beer already in hand.

I walked up to him and said, "Hello?" with a tone of voice which suggested, "Aren't you even curious to see if I'm here?"

He just looked at me and swigged his beer. (We're talking major "rock star" attitude here!) He finally said hello to me and I got him to buy me a drink again. Standing next to him I noticed that he was a lot taller than I. In my boots I was already about six foot three, so I was wondering how tall he really was. I looked down to see what kind of shoes he had on and sure enough, he was wearing these black "Herman Munster-type" boots with a very thick, high sole. His two girlfriends were rudely whispering and laughing to each other with their little leopard-print handbags. I felt really uncomfortable. I didn't understand why he had to have these two girls with him everywhere he went. They were like his bodyguards or something. Some bald guy was also with him. I was wondering why they were hanging out with us when I thought that he had invited me out to spend some time alone with me, like a real date. I wasn't as bold and out-spoken as I am today, otherwise, I would have said something about it to him.

It must have been "18 and over night" because there were a lot of young girls in the club. Marilyn started talking with some of them. I joined in and asked them if they had ever heard of "Marilyn Manson", but they said that they hadn't. I even sang a few lyrics from *Sweet Dreams* for them, but they still didn't know who he was... a crushing blow for this "egomaniac." After a while, Marilyn wanted to go to another club called Sinamatic. On Saturday nights this bar turned into a dark, gothic scene with non-stop trans-techno, industrial-type music playing all night long with go-go dancers decked out in rubber and patent-leather clothing. I was certainly not dressed for the occasion but it didn't stop me from going. I had to follow Marilyn and his friends in their car. I had asked him to ride with me, but he told me that his friends wouldn't leave him alone with a stranger ever.

I thought to myself, "You're a big boy aren't you? This is ridiculous!" Oh well, so I followed them to Sinamatic. The people at the door at least knew who he was, so we didn't have to wait in line and we got to walk in for free. I was annoyed by the way Marilyn walked in front of me inside of the club the entire time; it was as if I was invisible! He didn't want to dance or stay in one place. He just wanted to strut around to see who would recognize him.

During the course of the evening he asked me if I would go back to his hotel room and if he could shave my legs. A very unusual request but I actually thought about the unitard that I was wearing and how, since it was one piece, I would have to get completely naked for him to be able to shave my legs! I was going to ask him if his entourage would be there also. I was intrigued to see how the night was going to turn out so I agreed. I actually felt myself getting annoyed and jealous while he flirted with all the girls in the club. There was this one girl in a cheesey leopard print cat suit with her fake tits bulging out the top. I didn't think that she would be his type at all because she had heavy metal hair and a tan body, but I overheard him asking her to come back to his hotel room too! That's when I decided that this whole thing was just really lame, and even though I still wanted to talk to him about music, I had had enough.

I said to him, "I don't care who you are, but I am not having a very good time with you the way that you are treating me. I don't even know why you wanted to see me, I'm leaving."

As I spun around on my heel ready to walk away, he grabbed me by the arm and said, "Don't leave, I still want to shave your legs!"

I don't know how but he convinced me to stay. Maybe his attitude would improve enough for me to go back to his hotel room… to discuss music with him. But he obviously didn't have much respect for me or any woman. He was hardly a gentleman. I ended up following him around all night until he decided that he wanted to leave. We gathered up the rest of his "posse" and he told me to follow them back to his hotel. I finally did ask if we would be alone once we got to his hotel room, but once again he told me that his friends were very protective of him. That meant that they would be there too. He told me to look him up under the name Warner once I got to the hotel. He was staying across from the Beverly Center on Beverly Boulevard. I got lost trying to follow them, so it took me a while to get there.

I went up to his room and knocked on the door. When he opened the door it was obvious that he wasn't expecting me after all. His room was in "true rock 'n roll form" with plates of food all over the floor and clothing draped everywhere. But that's not why I knew he wasn't expecting me, it was because he had removed the colored contact from his eye.

With a shocked look on his face he said, "We thought that you decided not to come over after all." I told him that I got lost. He invited me in and I sat down on his bed. His friends had left, I was finally alone with him. I was wondering if he still wanted to shave my legs, but the subject never came up again. I had never been shaved by anybody else before and for some freak reason, I was actually up for it. I think he was just saying that for shock value anyway, trying to live up to his so-called, weird creepy, persona. It worked on me.

I asked him why he used the name Warner. He told me that his real name was Brian Warner, but he preferred to be called Manson. I asked him if he was concerned that his only hit song was a cover of someone else's. He did seem a bit annoyed that I pointed that out. We both sat on the edge of the bed watching TV. I brought over a one-song demo tape and an 8x10 promotional picture. He took them and wrote down an address in New Orleans where I could send my full-length demo to once it was completed. He told me that he was living in New Orleans. I got more comfortable by taking off my boots and scooted back further onto the bed. Soon we were both lying down on the bed facing each other and talking. I was surprised when he mentioned to me that one of my breasts was coming out of my top! I was more surprised by the fact that he mentioned it to me, than I was about my breast actually being exposed. That was the only time that he showed any kind of respect or acted like a gentleman.

Out of nowhere we started kissing. In-between making out, I looked down at his crotch area. He was wearing very tight, black pants. I remember thinking to myself that it looked like a Barbie doll's crotch! There was no sign of a hard-on in site. It looked as if he didn't even have a cock. If he did, it was very small. We just continued to kiss. I didn't feel any chills or anything. There just wasn't any chemistry between us at all, at least not any from my end. He didn't even try to "feel me up" or anything. Our lips and tongues were basically the only things that were touching each other. It was weird, like a first time kissing session. Then, just after I was thinking that, he suddenly pulled my skirt up and bit my inner thigh extremely hard. I had to keep myself from shouting out loud! I knew that this was another one of his antics to try and shock me.

I pulled back as if nothing had happened. I sat up pulling my skirt back down and asked him if he had a girlfriend. He told me that he did. I don't remember where he said that she was at the time (maybe in New Orleans). It was getting really late and I knew that I didn't want to stay the night with him, so I put my boots back on and stood up. He led me to the door and gave me a hug. I knew he was skinny but I wanted to find out how much he weighed, so I lifted him up. He was about 120 lbs. at the most and around six feet tall! After I put him back down, he finished off our hug by digging his nails into my sides. I guess he wanted to give me something to be able to tell my girlfriends about since we didn't sleep together.

He did draw blood on that one, down both sides. Once again, I didn't really respond to his antics and sarcastically said to him, "I guess it would be too much to ask of you to walk me down to my car, right?" He didn't respond. He just handed me money for the valet. I shamelessly took it and went on my way.

At home, I examined my rock 'n roll war wounds. It looked like a cat had scratched down both of my sides. I had long lines of bloody scabs that were starting to form from where he dug his nails. And of course, I had the bite mark from where he had bit my leg. It had a bruise around it. Then when I looked in the mirror, I couldn't believe that he neglected to tell me about the black lipstick that was smeared all around the outside of my mouth! (Oh, didn't I mention? He was wearing black lipstick!)

After his second album was released, Carla and I went to one of his concerts. Carla was one of the only blondes in the entire place! I ran into "Manson" about a year later at a popular used clothing store on Melrose Avenue called Wasteland. He was in some sort of disguise but I knew it was him. He had a film crew with him. I was with my friend Jenny who happens to be very short. He was very tall in those big "Herman Munster" boots again.

While Jenny and I were shopping he followed us around and would stand hovering over her looking across at me. He was obviously trying to get a reaction from me, but I just ignored him. He probably didn't remember me. He had on thick, yellow and green glasses and a bright red "Bozo the Clown" wig. He was a lot more famous by this point than he was when I first met him.

So that was my experience with Marilyn Manson. Girls, I don't recommend him for anyone who is not a sadomasochist!

CHAPTER 19
PRINCE VALIUM

Cinderella Guitarist, Jeff LaBar had his share of sex, drugs and rock and roll. This is his story in his own words.

There was always some shit going on! The funniest stuff I've ever seen is with other bands that I've toured with. Being on tour with the *Scorpions* in Germany was fun. In Germany, they're gods, you know? And I hung out with *Scorpion* guitarists, Rudy and Matthias and Rick Criniti. (After playing on the second album, keyboard player/vocalist Rick Criniti toured with *Cinderella* as an unseen "secret weapon". He sang and played offstage.) Rick and I got to be real good friends with them while we were on tour. We'd party and hang out till all hours of the morning. This was around '89 or '91. Who the fuck knows?

I remember staying overnight in a city that we had just got done playing. Usually when you were done playing you just packed up, got a blow job and left town. Since it was a short drive to the next city, management decided to rest that night and travel the next day. Instead of sleeping, Rick, Rudy, Matthias and I stayed up all night partying! We were in their room while the sun was rising. All of a sudden the phone rang. It was their call to leave. Their limo was waiting for them outside the hotel. They were like 'Oh my God,' all wired out and shit. I told them they could travel with us and crash out on the bus... but their manager would not allow them to travel with us. I wonder why? We partied so hard that they absolutely sucked the next night! They're great guitar players. I felt guilty partying with them and fucking them up (laughter).

Another night on that tour, Rick and I were up in Rudy's room and we broke out some guitars. We were all drinking and drugging and we started sharing some riffs. After about an hour of this, I remember thinking, "Damn! I'm writing a song with Rudolf Schenker! How cool is this?" Six o'clock in the morning I realize that we wasted the whole night playing the same fucking gibberish over and over. We just played it to death. It was a bunch of idiocy! It's just all nights of idiocy!

Rudy used to just walk around the hotel in leather pants and his Flying V guitar. He'd go up and down the elevators in these leather pants, bare

Cinderella guitarist, Jeff LaBar

feet and no shirt carrying that fucking Flying V, out of the case! I just used to laugh at him; he's so funny!

Seeing *Judas Priest* during the day is priceless. They'd be in the lobby in their fucking little golf outfits! To me, they were like metal gods on stage! And then, during the day, you'd see K.K. Downing and Glenn Tipton ready to golf... just seeing those guys in the plaid knickers, the knee-highs socks, the golf shoes, the golf shirts and those fucking hats with the dingo balls on top. It shattered all my illusions! {How shattered would your illusions have been if you saw Rob Halford with dingo balls in his mouth? And his dog's name is Dingo!}

In 1988, we were headlining all the major arenas. A friend sent me a bag full of valium, xanax, tuies, etc... I was a mess for a week or two. One night, I actually fell asleep on stage while we were performing *Comin' Home*. Along with the electric guitar, I played an acoustic guitar which was on a stand. In the beginning of the song, maybe in the first verse, I rested my chin on the acoustic guitar. And out I went! I just fell asleep! I fell asleep in front of like 18,000 people! Well, the next thing you know, I got smacked in the back of the head! (laughter) It woke me right up and I turned around; it was our singer, Tom Keifer. I finally realized we were in my solo section of the song... 'Oh, here I go!' He was pissed! They tended, by then, to not be too surprised by my antics. He waited a week to yell at me because that whole week I was 'Prince Valium!' I wouldn't have remembered. Maybe he did and I just didn't remember.

That same week, we were ready to check out of the hotel and everyone was downstairs waiting by the bus. I was locked in my room all passed out. They had to break down the door off the hinges because I had the little bar thing across it. I was hammered! I just remember being carried out yelling obscenities at everyone in the lobby as I went by.

That same tour I went through a phase where I drank heavily. The moment I woke up I would drink a twelve pack! Every night I drank Jack Daniel's.

One particular night, at the aftershow party, I passed out on a table signing autographs in front of about a hundred people. The next thing I knew, my security guy carried me out of there, like a baby, to my bunk on the bus. We hit the road and the movement of the bus started making me sick. I was in the top bunk and Rick was underneath me. Well, I just remember blowing JD chunks all over my bunk! It just sprayed out like a hose! And I was like, damn... with the curtain closed and everything, what am I going to do? What am I going to fucking do? So I got out of my bunk, went to the back lounge, curled up and went to sleep. The next day, Rick was in his bunk reading and something was dripping on him!

"What the hell is this? Smells like Jack Daniels!" So they looked in my bunk and there was just puke everywhere! All over everything! They made the tour manager, Steve Wood, clean it up. They took down my curtain, the mattress, my pillows and just threw it all out the front door of the bus and kept going! I felt really bad. Rick, however, found it funny!

See, Rick and me... we were roommates for the first tour; it was low budget then. So I don't know how many nights I would walk in and he'd have two or three girls in bed with him! Nothing of quality of course (more laughter).

One time I walked in our room and he had three girls in bed with him and I was so fuckin' trashed, so I just joined in.

I started going down on this chick and when I sat up Rick said, "Hey! You got a clown face!"

I said, "What?"

Rick laughed, "Yeah, you got a clown face! She's on her period!"

Yeah, my first clown face. Rick was there when I earned my red wings! Yeah, Rick and I did a lot together. We are like war vet buddies. It was fun!

Website: www.Cinderella.net

CHAPTER 20
DANGER DANGER
BY LYNN RAMAGE

I have the dubious distinction of being the one who booked Ted Poley's famous nose whacking show. That night Ted accidentally whacked his bass player (Pete Ruello) in the nose while spinning around onstage during a *Bone Machine* concert! I recall running back into the kitchen to get fresh bar towels and ice for his nose. That incident got caught on video and actually aired on the television show, *America's Funniest Home Video's*.

I hadn't talked to Ted in years when I ran into a mutual friend, Scott Keagy, who helped Ted when he left *Danger Danger* and started Ted Poley's *Bone Machine* which is now *Melodica*. Scott told me Ted was heavily involved in collecting antiques and toys. Scott knew Jonny Z (Megaforce Records) and I were old toy collectors. He thought it would be a nice conversation starter if I ever ran into Ted again. I decided to give him a call. During our conversation we discussed old cool toys... and it turns out he knows more about Barbie than I do (that's a scary thought huh?) We got to talk about *Rock and Roll War Stories* and I told him *Britny Fox's* story about the chocolate cream pie. I guess it triggered some long forgotten brain cells as he had a couple of stories.

Ted Poley: Okay, I'll give you some quick stories. I'll give you my own bus shitting experience. How about that? Then we'll go from the bus shitting stories to the *KISS* story, because everyone loves a good *KISS* story.

We started our biggest *Danger Danger* tour in New York City, went on up to Montreal, all the way across Canada and ended up in Vancouver, went down through let's see... Seattle, where we had *Alice in Chains* open up for us. Huge, huge tour, and my proudest accomplishment was I managed to make it through the whole tour without having to take a shit on the bus (snickering). Anyone who has been on tour, been on a tour bus, or has any inkling about bands on tour, knows the NUMBER ONE ROAD RULE - ABSOLUTELY NO SHITTING IN THE TOUR BUS TOILET!

I hate to dispel everyone's idea of what a

Ted Poley and friend

glamorous life it is on these beautiful tour buses, but what you have to do is basically squat in the back lounge or in the bathroom with a hefty bag. There are always plenty of hefty bags on board for this purpose. You have to do your thing into the hefty bag, wipe and dispose of it properly. It's an art form I did not want to learn to master. That whole tour I feared nature would call at an inopportune time. It's always on your mind on the road. All those years of practicing, wanting to play in a rock band and I completely overlooked this one concern. I guess astronauts are in a worse predicament.

I made it through so many tours until the inevitable finally did come. We were cruising along on a real long stretch of highway through the desert. It was five in the morning and everyone was sleeping. All of a sudden I felt an 'uh oh' feeling. I sensed 'big trouble coming.' I was trying to talk myself out of it. After a futile attempt to psych myself out of it I went up to the bus driver and asked, "How long to the next stop?"

He answered, "Oh, about two hundred miles or so..."

As if my bowels heard the answer, the urge got worse. I really did not want to crap in a bag! There's just something about it that does not appeal to me. I want to sit on a comfortable throne (home throne is the ideal situation), do my business, and when I'm done, away goes trouble down the drain. You know what I mean.

Two hundred miles of nothing... what am I going to do? Force the bus driver to stop and squat in front of everybody? I looked out the window and I didn't even see a cactus I could hide behind. And who knows what could happen... a friggin' snake could be out there to bite me in the nuts or something! Anyway, it's a big no-no to stop a bus for your personal comfort. It screws up the schedule and everyone just gets pissed off at you and then you are fodder for road pranks.

I was standing there in my underwear; the bus wasn't stopping anytime soon, and nature was calling. I made the big decision... CORRECTION... MY BOWELS MADE THE BIG DECISION. I was about to pop my chocolate cherry. It was time for my "big interview" with Mr. Hefty in the back of the bus.

I grabbed a hefty bag and went into the bathroom. It was in the middle of winter in the desert, so the temperature differences were very drastic. It was extremely cold outside and some parts of the bus were cold during the night. I remember the heat blasting on and off to keep us comfortable. I couldn't maneuver myself in that telephone booth they call a bathroom. Hey, I was a virgin. I needed room! It was my first time. I didn't want any accidents.

I went to the back lounge instead and locked the door. Everybody was sleeping anyway.

I looked at the bag and asked myself, "How the hell do you shit in a bag?"

I squatted and neatly wrapped the opening of the bag and conformed it to my ass to try and hermetically seal it the moment I was done. That way the smell would not seep out. This boy was thinking. As I'm squatted, the bus was swaying. You didn't really feel the sways normally but now I'm trying to perform a delicate procedure. The bus swayed and now thoughts of, "Oh my God! What if I miss? It'll be all over the back lounge. It'll be horrible!"

Miraculously, I did my "thing". I was so proud of myself because I did it really quick, and I sealed it up immediately so you couldn't smell a thing! I completely wiped up and quickly disposed of that without a lingering stink. Perfect!! I got the thing successfully tied up and there was only one more step before I could celebrate mission accomplished. All I had to do was open the emergency hatch of the back room and dispose of the offending package "ala space shuttle" style. I opened the vent and there was an opening of about four to five inches. That's not bad. I'll just stuff this thing out of here. The bag was just about fitting in the vent. There was a lot of 'ahem' gas and air in the bag. I was having a difficult time fitting it in. By the time I fit the whole bag in the vent, it started expanding from the temperature differences. The fucking thing was expanding like a hot air balloon and it was stuck. The only difference with this hot air balloon was the hot air was laced with human shit. I couldn't shove the expanding bag out and I couldn't pull the thing back in. Amongst the panic, I scanned my brain for my extensive physics file. What the hell was I going to do? The bag was filling up by the second.

"Houston, we have a problem!" The only answer was to poke a hole in the bag to release the gas and deflate the bag to get the shit out of my life! But that would only defeat the whole mission and everyone would smell failure. This was my worst nightmare. I was so successful up to this point. I had this whole engineering thing figured out and it was literally blowing up in my face. Failure was not an option. So, it was doo-doo or die.

I gently poked my finger through the bag and quickly shoved it out the vent. I ran back to my bunk before anyone could connect me with the heinous vapors.

Since then, I never had to shit on a bus again. I hope I haven't jinxed myself for any future trips. See... it was so good up until the end... just like my marriage!

Hey, since we're doing Ted Poley shit stories I have another one for you. Maybe you should do a whole book on my bowel movements!

We were on the road heading to Wyoming and, once again, I had to go real bad. I was a trooper though and held out for the next stop. We pulled up to this place and it had a general store, gas station, diner and post office. There was only ONE guy running the whole thing. It reminded me of Green Acres where Mr. Haney put on a different official hat for any need.

I asked the man, "Can I use your bathroom?" and he laughed.

He said, "Be my guest. It's outside. Over there!" He pointed to an outhouse WITH NO DOOR ON IT! At that moment I was wondering if shitting in a hefty bag on the bus was a better situation. I went to the outhouse, squatted and looked at the beautiful view of the Great Plains or whatever the hell it was. And the Great Plains watched me.

I sat there thinking, "Rock stardom is everything I ever hoped it would be." As I sat there communing with my thoughts, huge tumbleweeds as big as a house rolled by. Then a few buffalo or bison strolled by to say hello. It was memorable. No, I don't have a picture! Enough with my bowels. Let me tell you my experience with Gene Simmons.

We were in Scotland having lunch with Gene. I guess he went to lunch with us because he had nobody else to hang with (laughter). And no, I didn't have to go to the bathroom. We had a great lunch conversation and it turned out that Gene owns the same type of dog I own. So we kind of bonded over that. Keep in mind, this is not a rock star attitude story, it's more of a 'how cool is Gene Simmons?' story. This story comes out of great respect. I just think Gene is so cool. He's the king of the world, on and off stage. He's intimidating in a cool way. He knows what he wants and gets it no matter what.

After we ate in this beautiful Scottish restaurant, the waitress came over and asked if we wanted anything else.

Gene answered, "Yes, I would like cookies."

She replied, "Well, I'm sorry sir. We have no cookies but we have beautiful pastries, crumpets, crepe's and other desserts."

Gene replied, "No, I would like some cookies please."

And she answered again, "I'm sorry. Can I get you anything else?"

Gene Simmons and Ace Frehley

Gene requested, "Yes, I would like to see the Chef." She left and got the Chef.

He walked over and asked, "Yes sir, can I help you?"

Gene articulately said, "Yes, I would like some cookies please."

The Chef replied, "Well, we don't have any right now but we do have these lovely pies that I'm sure you will enjoy."

Gene asked, "You call yourself a Chef?"

The Chef answers, "Well, yes."

Gene then said, "I assume you have flour and sugar back there (in the kitchen). Well then, I would like you to go back there and please make me cookies. I would like three cookies."

I remember this exactly. He then added, "And don't bring me any mushy cookies." {Ahhhh - very shrewd of Gene to request that the cookies not be mushy… because being a self-important demanding A-hole you might get added ingredients you do not want to eat.}

He then tapped his finger on the table and said, "See this table? Ice this table and bring me three cookies."

It was the funniest thing. The next day I was in the lobby and the same really timid waitress came running up to me. She handed me a box of shortbread cookies and said, "Could you please see that Mr. Simmons gets these?" I was dying.

We also went bowling with them. Gene bowls like nobody you'd ever seen in your life! Wait! Yes, he does bowl like someone else. Twinkle Toes Flintstone! The ball flies down the alley at two hundred miles-per-hour and just hits the surface just before it hits the pins. It's airborne the whole time! The pins just scatter away as if he yelled at them. It's very powerful.

Gee, Lynn this is great now. Gene is gonna read all this, it's gonna read horrible, and I'll never get to do another *KISS* concert again in my life! I love Gene! He's the coolest! We played laser tag with them in England. It was cool. We had a lot of fun!

I hope my stories were good... I hate to come out with my new album, then people read the book and come up to me, "Shit stories? Is that the best you could come up with?"

I've got a million of them, but those stories I remember fondly.

Website: www.TedPoley.com

CHAPTER 21
NASHVILLE PUSSY
BY LYNN RAMAGE

Gordon always wants to give pussy publicity. So we'll give some *Nashville Pussy* some.

As I climbed the backstage stairs of the TLA (the Theater of Living Arts) in Philly, I wondered, "Oh Boy, what is this bunch gonna be like?" I don't know why, but after reading all their wild stories I was almost scared. Their tour manager must have radioed back to them that I was on my way because they looked like little angels sitting around when I walked in. They definitely seemed to know I was coming in. It seemed like I was the teacher walking into a calm class when you know, just moments before, all hell was breaking loose. I just knew something was up as there was a very sweet chocolatey smell filling the whole room.

Guitarist Ruyter Suys, donned only in a see-through slip and cowboy boots, jumped up and yelled, "Goddamn it Blaine! Ya burnt the M&M's again!" Ruyter climbed on top of the sofa, tipped the pole lamp next to it and poured out all these colored M&M's from around the bulb of the light. There was a melted mess inside the dome. I guessed this was a normal, frequent event. Drummer, Jeremy Thompson, popped right down next to me, peered at my notes to pre-read my questions. He started picking on me about my Philly accent. I turned to Ruyter and asked, "Where'd you get him?"

Ruyter: Jeremy is very likeable. We call him "Jeremy the Likeable" (laughter).

Jeremy: You want to know where they found me?

Lynn: From under a rock?

Jeremy: No. Like to hear it, here it goes. Basically, my old band back home in Austin played a show with these guys. We had a big party afterwards. I told them that I hoped the drummer that they had would get goiters on his neck so I could be their drummer. I just saw something I liked and I decided to be this weasel-like guy and do what ever I had to get in. Two weeks later they called me.

Ruyter: He was totally drunk and he kept saying; "Okay, I'm a nice guy. I'm not a bad guy. I don't wish your drummer get cancer or AIDS... I just want him to get a goiter so ya call me and ask 'Jeremy, will ya be my drummer?' Cause I'm a nice guy, I don't want him to get cancer or AIDS I just want him to get a goiter and you'll call me up and go 'Jeremy... would ya like to be the drummer for *Nashville Pussy*?' etc..., etc...., etc...," He said it like 50 fuckin' times! It was so annoyingly obnoxious.

Jeremy: I was being persistent. But look who they called when the time came. They called me. So there! I couldn't have been that annoying!

Lynn: Are ya married? If not, then what's your best pick-up line?

Jeremy: No I'm not. But lots of ladies like me though! Pick-up line? Um... Oh... no...

Ruyter: (laughing) Here's his best pick up line; "Hey baby, I got the fastest go cart in the world and I'm gonna drive ya to Disneyland!" (More laughter) Man, if he ever really did pick up a chick with that she'd be r e a l l y cool. Oh God, this is funny. After this one show there was this boy, he was all of eighteen and he was trying to pick up Cory. He was really young and he said to her, "You wouldn't know how to thank me in the morning." She ended up turning him down. We all wondered, what could this boy possibly do? It was so intriguing. That was pretty damn cocky for an 18-year-old, you know!

Lynn: Do you have any other funny road stories?

Ruyter: There was a time when a certain member of the band happened to buy a whole bunch of valium, no they weren't valium... some super downer drug? Xanax? Yeah, that was it! Well anyway, that certain member gave a shitload of them to Marilyn Manson when we were on tour with them. Marilyn and his whole band were like fuckin' comatose! The day of the very last show of the tour, they were just totally wiped out! Half of our crew was zonked out as well. Our cure for everything is this Habanero pepper. Just gnaw at a Habanero pepper raw and your as good as new. They're the hottest peppers in the world. You can get them in any good grocery store. If ya got the flu, if you're hung-over, whatever... you chew it and it just burns your brains out and you freak out! But then you're over the hump of whatever the problem was and you're back on the side of reality.

Everybody from our team did it and they were, like I said, good as new. Then we went over to Marilyn Manson's dressing room, "You guys got to take one of these man. It'll make you feel better!" And they're like; "No, no, no, we already did like seven lines of coke. We'll be fine." They all went up onstage like cocaine fueled bulls and within a

Nashville Pussy

132

few minutes, they crashed. That was the very last show of the tour and Marilyn ended up having this big hissy fit on stage and walked off early. It caused a lot of shit. There were all sorts of threats, the promoter wasn't going to pay 'cause Marilyn shut the show down early. Fans rioted outside. We didn't see any of it. We were on the inside but we heard that people were jumping on people's cars and shit. Marilyn could've avoided all this (tsk tsk) before the show just by taking one Habanero pepper!

Lynn: Tell us about this Grammy thing.

Ruyter: Yeah, we got nominated for a Grammy. We went and felt real outta place. We were the only band there that looked like we were in a band. I don't know, Blaine what did you think? (As she looked over to her singer/husband Blaine Cartwright)

Blaine: It was like High School all over again, it really was! Here was my group of smart-asses making fun of everything and there's like a bunch of cheer-leaders there... with Madonna being the head Cheerleader and Rosie O'Donnell being head of student Council or something (laughter). We were in assigned celebrity seats. We got to go to some okay after-parties though.

Ruyter: Jeremy actually turned a moderately lame party into a real cool party by stripping naked and jumping into the pool!

Jeremy: Well, I don't think anybody else there thought it was that funny.

Ruyter: I thought it was fucking hilarious! Yo, it was this lame ass party man and Jeremy was raised on movies, where one person jumps in the pool, everyone jumps in the pool right? Jeremy jumped in the pool and that was it. He started splashing all these rich people. Ya know, everyone's wearing their Gucci this and their Gucci that... and finally security came and ordered, "Get out of the pool!" He got out and we draped him in a tablecloth (laughter). Let me see, who was at that party?

Blaine: *Beck*, everyone from *Hole* except Courtney, Scott Weiland from *Stone Temple Pilots*, Twiggy from *Manson*. Besides that, it was just a bunch of fat guys in tuxedos.

Website found: www.nashvillepussy.com

CHAPTER 22
MEGAFORCE RECORDS
BY LYNN RAMAGE

Ministry Stalker and *Anthrax* Pirate Attacks

Everyone in the music business knows of Jonny Z. I remember the buzz around this area when he moved his office from New Jersey to New Hope, Pennsylvania. New Hope is a tourist area. Lots of quaint stores, antiques, flea markets, etc... I have always thought of it as a pricey town.

It is like our own little "Cape Cod." Tubing down the river in the summer is a blast. Of course, there is also boating down the Delaware River from the points in New Hope.

I booked this wretched club called Boomerangs, which was right on the Delaware River between New Hope and Philly. The club held three thousand when their deck was open. I brought in *Love In Reverse*, which was one of Jonny's bands. We were all backstage bullshitting when Jonny's eyes popped out as he grabbed my skinny little wrist.

He asked excitedly, "Where did you get that watch?" It was a *Nightmare Before Christmas* watch that I had just picked up at my local Pathmark supermarket for only five dollars. It had Jacko and a bat on the face. Jonny was all excited especially when I told him how much I paid for it. He collects Disney stuff and he pointed out a Jacko pin he had on his jean jacket. He asked me if I could go back to Pathmark and pick him up as many of those watches as I could and send them to him. I always liked him... anyone into *Nightmare Before Christmas* has got to be beaucoup cool.

As I was approaching the end of this book I thought, "Hey, wait a minute. I bet Jonny Z has a few good tales." So I gave him a jingle and this is what he shared...

Lynn: You have done so much Jonny, surely there are one or two stories that stick out in your mind?

Jonny Z: There's about a thousand of them. You pick the band and I'll tell you the story. You want an *Anthrax* or a *Ministry*?

Jonny Z and family

Lynn: Oh! A *Ministry* would be good!

Jonny Z: *Ministry*? Oh okay... It was *Ministry's* last tour in '97. I believe this was the *Filth Pig* tour on Warner Brothers... the album after *Psalm 69*. The band was on it's southern run heading into New Orleans when some suspicious character came up to guitarist Al Jourgensen and basically said that he was going to kill him.

At first everyone said, "Okay, let's be cool, be cool. It's no big deal. Just idle threats." We didn't think much of it until we noticed this guy started stalking Al. We banned him from our shows but this guy was showing up and getting backstage. We had his name on a shit-list but he kept using different identities to get close to Al. We then started getting concerned that this actually may be a fanatic that may want to "do it."

We ended up calling a former FBI Agent/Secret Service guy to hire as a bodyguard. Al and I flew down to meet him and we hired him to work at a New Orleans show. Al was fitted with a bulletproof vest and he actually performed on stage with it on. If you saw the movie, *The Body Guard*, I was wired up like Kevin Costner. They had me sit in front of the P.A. for the next five shows completely wired to the Secret Service guy who was wired to the police and security. We were watching for those little red dots. Which you know today is very common.

Lynn: Uh Jonny? What little red dots?

Jonny Z: Those little red dots the laser pens emit. Well, when someone wants to shoot you... basically at night, they will use laser light aiming. You point the light on the target, then you fire and basically you will hit your target without error. That's how night-time assassinations are done. We had all those laser pens to deal with. Here we were trying to locate the source of dozens of laser pointers and hoping there wasn't a gun attached to any of them.

It was really crazy because I spent five days working with this Secret Service guy watching everyone in the audience coming and going. We placed special gun checks at the front and hired extra security. At the end of every show, while the band had their finale, I had an inconspicuous car waiting and Al would go directly to the car after the show. We would leave and go to the local airport, get on a private plane and fly into New Orleans. We stayed in New Orleans throughout the entire Texas tour as well, just so he couldn't be tracked in Texas. You have to imagine the stress of a two hour set, sitting there and watching this go on.

Now Al, of course, got sick of the whole thing. He was tired of performing in the bulletproof vest. Right in the heat of one of his shows, with all the little laser lights hitting him, he cracked, "The hell with this shit! If they're going to kill me, let 'em kill me!" and he threw off his bulletproof vest. It was all very intense. And getting out of the place, you just really felt like you were escaping for your life. It was basically a week and a half of complete insanity. I remember when we were in New Orleans, we went shopping in this Voodoo shop and this Voodoo lady set him up with all these protective charms. It was really crazy (laughter). Al went on stage with all these charms, trinkets and oils, as well as the bulletproof vest!

The ordeal lasted three months. Mysteriously everything quieted down when the tour was over. It was an incredible experience!

Now *Anthrax*, on the road, used to do "Pirate Attacks!" You never knew when it was your turn to be attacked!

What they would do is dress up as pirates and get into your room when you weren't there. When you walked in they would attack with water balloons, toilet paper, god only knows! If you weren't in your room they would leave it in such a horrible condition that it was not fit for any human being to inhabit. Their preferred method was the "spy method." This was, if you had a roommate on the road, they would basically have your roommate leave your door open and disappear from the room. If that wasn't the case, other methods included climbing outside their own window, outside the hotel, just to get inside your window. Shimmying across tenth floor balconies was not out of the question. Whatever it took to get in your room, they would do it!

One of the most vicious attacks of all time fell victim to Eddie Trunk. Ed worked for my record company then and is now a DJ on 104.3 radio in New York City. We were at the Monsters of Rock Festival in Europe with *Metallica*.

Eddie got it real bad. I really can't describe his room... there was feces on his pillow and stuff... This is how sick and utterly disgusting this got. That afternoon, we checked out of the hotel and we started to head towards Germany. Ed got on the bus as cool as a cucumber. He didn't even act as if anything happened! You heard the *Anthrax* guys rumbling in the back of the bus and they started to freak out. They started to believe they might have hit the wrong room! And who's room did they do this to? Ed kept it cool all the way to the festival.

Finally the band went to their tour manager and said, "Look! Can we find out who's room we did this to?" They were worried. Were the police after them? Did they piss off some other group? Was it a civilian? They just wanted to know what they did. They kept getting confirmation that it was Ed Trunks' room. Days later, Ed just hung out with the guys like nothing ever happened. So basically, it was a "Pirate Attack" that backfired on them.

When we went to Hamburg, there was a convention going on. You couldn't get a room anywhere. We ended up in this beat hotel that had no locks and I said to myself; "If anybody's gonna get attacked tonight, it could be me!" So I took this giant triple dresser and put it in front of my door. I locked all the windows. Yeah, I had to live like that! It's beyond what anyone can imagine! Just imagine the worst thing possible happening to you except dying. There would be nothing and I mean nothing left to your room or your clothes.

People used to say, "Oh *Anthrax* is so good. Not what you would expect from a rock band. They don't smoke. They don't drink. They're so boring. They don't stay up all night, they go to bed at twelve o'clock." But while you were downstairs drinking, man, your room was finished! And if you happened to be in your bed during an attack, God knows if you'd wake up!

Website: www.MegaforceRecords.com

{At the height of *Anthrax's* career there was rumor that they were getting a commercial deal with McDonald's. McDonald's wanted to show the young generation that they could be hip. The band was going to attract the young rock and roll crowd. The supposed negotiations went all the way to the top of the McDonald's corporate brass. It was a done deal until one McDonald employee pointed out that the band was named after a cow disease! The deal was nixed.}

CHAPTER 23
WHAT CUMS AROUND, CUMS AROUND!

Quiet Riot's Kevin Dubrow can be quite charming. But when asked to contribute to this book, he checked his charm at the door and came up with these gems...

Kevin: Recently, some girl came backstage and did some amazing things with a banana! I didn't participate in that. The funny thing is, our guitarist Carlos participated in this whole thing with the banana, and he's so anti-germ. He's like Howard Hughes! He'll go into a bathroom in a hotel room and he'll sniff the towels first. Then he'll check the sheets for hairs and stuff.

It's really hard, in twenty-five years of doing this, to pick any one thing out. In 1992 we had this drummer, Bobby Rondinelli. Bobby was in *Rainbow* and later *Black Sabbath*. He's an amazing drummer but he used to love to wind me up! One day, he was sleeping in the front of the tour bus in one of the captain's chairs. I went up and pulled my pants down and plopped my cock right on his shoulder and took a picture! Now that really angered him (laughter) and he was determined to get back at me. Bobby is from Long Island... so he's got that New York thing going on!

One of his typical sayings was, "I got a moist ass and I gotta go do a standing wipe." This was his way of saying "I gotta wipe my ass standing up."

While we were traveling in the tour bus, he rattled off his usual, "Ewwweee, I got a moist ass and I gotta go do a standing wipe." I wasn't paying much attention to this as I've heard it countless times before and I didn't realize he was just eating a fudgecicle. So he came out of the tour bus bathroom and had this Kleenex with shit all over it! He started chasing me all around the front lounge with it.

He's going, "Kevin, come over here," and I'm like, "Aggghhh! God, he's got shit on it!" I'm freaking!

I grabbed some potato salad and poured Coca-Cola all over it and yelled, "I'm gonna throw this all over you!"

And Bobby goes, "Ha, that's just potato salad, but this is SHIT!" He's chasing me, and all I'm armed with is potato salad! I'm like, "Oh God," and I'm trying to get the bus driver to pull over but he's laughing too hard. Bobby took the Kleenex, which I thought had shit all over it, and shoved it in his mouth! I thought I was going to lose it! I fucking gagged! So he does that and goes, "It was a fudgecicle you dumb ass!"

That Ex-Lax thing *Britny Fox* pulled is an old thing every band has done at least once. Frankie Banali (*Quiet Riot* drummer) did that to a tour manager once.

Did you know Frankie played with *Steppenwolf*?

At this one particular hotel, Frankie and his tour manager had adjoining rooms, and evidently the tour manager had come in earlier in the day and unlocked Frankie's connecting door. Later that night, Frankie was having sex with this girl and the next thing you know, this tour manager quietly opened the connecting door and tossed a cherry bomb under their bed! Frankie nearly had a heart attack. The girl freaked out. The bed actually caught on fire and the whole band got tossed out, in the middle of the night, into the streets. They ended up having to spend the rest of the night sitting in an airport. Bearing all this aggravation, Frankie had a few ideas for revenge.

Well, this tour manager loved chocolate pudding, Jack Daniel's and Quaaludes, not in that order. So to get back at him, Frankie set him up. He ordered a tub of chocolate pudding from room service and spent an afternoon, on his day off, shaving very fine pieces of Ex-Lax into this pudding. Frankie told me, "Enough for an elephant to shit for a month!" You see, if you are going to do the Ex-Lax gag, the trick is to take the time to shave it into very fine pieces.

So he called the tour manager up and asked if he wanted to come down and watch a game on TV that night. He came down and they started drinking Jack Daniel's. This guy was also popping 'ludes.

Frankie had the pudding sitting over on a table baiting this guy. The manager was eye-balling the motherfucker all night and finally asked Frankie, "Mind if I help myself to this pudding?"

Frankie said, "Sure! Take as much as you want!" So now this guy was chowing down Ex-Lax, pudding, Jack Daniel's and Quaaludes. After a few hours of this, Frankie could tell this guy was getting tired, so he walked him back to his room and helped him into bed. Once his victim was passed out, he handcuffed him to the headboard and moved the telephone so he wasn't able to call anyone when he woke up!

Frankie heard from the housekeeper, who found this guy handcuffed to the bed, that there was shit everywhere! He was just covered in it! It was all over the walls, the lamps, everywhere!

We were never really big on abusing groupies. This one incident happened about a year ago. No one ever believes me when I tell this story. It's so embarrassing.

I was in Vancouver, Canada in a restaurant called Coyote's and all the waitresses were great looking. I chatted with this one beautiful waitress and she ended up showing me the town. We partied hard and she got pretty hammered. We got back to the hotel and she started giving me a blowjob. Now I was lying with my head up on the headboard a little bit and her head was down. She couldn't see me. I laid there doing the normal guy "thing," grunting and groaning like a real pig. I was breathing heavy. She's going and going and going and I guess she could tell I was about ready to cum because just as I'm about to, she pulled her head away. She couldn't see this happen, but just like a smart missile, gloop, right into my own mouth, right into the back of my throat! My mouth was hardly opened wide enough for this to happen. It hit my gag reflex and I fucking swallowed it! It was a one in a million shot!

The next day... I go to the guys, "I have something to tell you. I have a story and this is really truly disturbing!"

So I tell them the story and they go, "You swallowed cum? You're fucking GAY!"

I replied, "I swallowed my OWN cum, that doesn't mean I'm fucking gay?" The debate continues to this day.

And every girl that hears the story says; "It serves you right! That's the big fucking payback for all the gratuitous blow jobs you've had!" Yes, I needed counseling after that one! Website: www.QuietRiotForce.com

CHAPTER 24
GAY CONFESSIONS
BY LYNN RAMAGE

During a video shoot for the video *Just Got Lucky* guitarist George Lynch's guitar solo was shot on an active volcano. The volcano started to erupt causing the rock beneath Lynch's feet to get so hot it melted his shoes. A helicopter had to be called in to get Lynch and the crew off the volcano. Maybe Don Dokken sent George there for a reason as Don Dokken and George Lynch are notorius for having one of the most heated relationships in rock and roll. They despised each other. If Don had it his way he would've probably thrown George INTO the volcano.

One of the most unlikely reunions happened in 1993 when Dokken reformed. After signing a new record deal with Sony the band was to perform live and do an interview via satellite to over 200 stations across the country. Lynch was playing with his guitar and the engineers were worried that George would "mess up the mix" by adjusting his sound. Don asked George to not adjust his guitar when an irate George shouted back "Don't tell me what to do" and threw his guitar down, stormed out, and left the station. The band ended up having to play their recorded sound check and passing it off as being a live performance. During the band interview segment bassist Jeff Pilson disguised his voice and answered questions intended for George. Lynch left the band for a second time a few months later.

Back when George was in the band, I went to the rock club the Birch Hill in North Jersey to cover *Dokken*. I met up with everyone after the show on their tour bus. Don and I sat at the table in the back lounge and our conversation got sidetracked. George came on the bus last and you could

JEFF PILSON   MICK BROWN   DON DOKKEN   GEORGE LYNCH

easily see how hot and sweaty he was. All he had on was these patent leather pants and no shirt. I talked to Don and out of the very corner of my eye, I saw George peel off these hot pants! Whoa! So there he was in his skivvies. It was really hard not to turn around and gawk! Don amusingly watched my reaction the whole time.

In my head, thoughts were racing, "Okay, you've got to be professional here. You know you just want to pounce on him but you can't and you won't!" If that wasn't enough, he came over and leaned across me to reach for a travel bag under the table. Now, I was dying! Aye yi yi! I had thee George Lynch half-naked across my lap! He didn't do anything wrong or out of line (and he couldn't in my eyes), but I was having a heart attack. Don busted out laughing. Ahhh, the little magic moments in journalism.

George is back in *Lynch Mob*, which is a killer band. I got to interview George to promote the *Lynch Mob* album called *Smoke This*. I actually told George the story how he got me all excited, like a teen-ager, back on the bus when he was in *Dokken*. George is such a humble person. He was actually embarrassed and explained the bus is their home, their dressing room. He tried to apologize. Apologize?! Hell! That was one of the highlights of my life!

I asked him, "When you were in *Dokken*, did the guys play pranks on each other?"

"Well, I don't know exactly what you're looking for, but yeah...we sent Don in to get a blowjob for his birthday one year. We sent him into this dark room when we were on tour with *Judas Priest*. It was like around 1986, but the thing was ... the person waiting in the dark room was one of Rob Halford's boy-toys. I thought that was rather funny! All the stories I can think of are sex related. I'm a married man now with kids that can read! We're just not going to go there. Let's just say most bands' buses are well equipped and have an array of video cameras strategically positioned."

"But I will tell you this one gag we played on drummer, Wild Mick Brown. We were at Amigo Studios doing *Under Lock and Key*. We spent hours and hours, that went into days and days, that became weeks and weeks, just in the stu-

Lynn Ramagé and Don Dokken

dio. When you are not involved with the day's recording, you have to think of things to pass the time."

"We accidently discovered a gay, bondage magazine actually called 'Drummer.' Why would a gay magazine call itself Drummer? That was neither here, nor there, but we were going to use this to our best advantage."

"So we thought, 'you know what? Mick Brown is going to be on the cover of the gay Drummer magazine.' We got photos of Mick and we used the studio's copy machine to enlarge and reduce the images to make sure his head fit on all these faces on the cover of the magazine. Then we Xeroxed the "new" magazine cover and inside! We sent copies to everyone! We went to a print shop and had them make reams of these. We sent one to his folks! The cover was a picture of this guy, with rope around his hands and ankles, tied up with a ball in his mouth and something up his ass. And it was Mick's face! Then every single picture in the magazine was Mick. Mick giving himself head, Mick getting fucked in the ass, a bunch of Micks in a gang bang. It was awesome! He never forgave me for that one. He did see the humor in it though."

"He always said, 'Why couldn't it have been a gay magazine named Guitar?'"

"Another time, we had this one producer that we weren't too keen on and we were all wondering if he should really be producing us. We decided we would work with him but we would have our fun at his expense. So we had the engineer plant a tape recorder under the console and this guy would come in late at night and tell all these funny stories. After the producer left, the engineer would take the recorded conversation and put it in the 'Fairlight' (a digital recording sampler computer that can manipulate sounds). We took everything out of context and we diced, mixed and scrambled his whole dialog where he admitted 'being gay, blowing this guy, etc...' We just diced everything up to sound like a gay confession! And then we sent it out to every record label. I heard he did an interview with the L.A. Times where they asked him about it!"

Website: www.GeorgeLynch.com

146

CHAPTER 25
MORE DIRT!

Lizzy West was friends with *Motley Crue* bassist, Nikki Sixx in the late 80's. Here is an account of one of the first parties she went to at Nikki's house.

Nikki was having a huge party... it must've been around '87. They'd just come back from Eurohell...and everyone was invited to his Laurel Canyon house. The whole band was there and after the consumption of many bottles of Jack Daniel's...the party was getting HOT!!!

Nikki has the most exquisite taste in furnishings. His house was immaculate and earthy...he has a fish tank the entire length of one wall...like 12 ft. or something, a gorgeous stained glass piece separated his kitchen and dining room...he has a pit that was doe colored and soft mauve rugs... His personal bathroom was RED! And he had a framed picture of this blood shoot that he did...like a framed composite sheet...right over the toilet...and guess what...he used Suave shampoo! He must have a bad tummy... Rolaids and Mylanta everywhere.

His kitchen was well stocked... I remember that...lots of spices and food...lots of gourmet food...cheeses and caviar...not for the party...just in the shelves and he likes to buy champagne by the case.

I was getting pretty loaded...and I decided to go see the rest of the house...Timmy Luzzi, who was Nikki's right hand man offered to show me around.

Nikki wasn't married at the time. The house was moderate...but beautiful... tucked in gorgeous hills... He had just gotten a black jeep wrangler...and a Harley. They were parked in the driveway.

I went with my girlfriend Pam who went out with Cliff Burton (the bass player from Metallica) before he died. Cliff died the year before when *Metallica*'s bus skidded on ice while the band was on tour in Scandinavia. Cliff was thrown out the window and crushed.

Timmy showed me around the house and right before we got to Nikki's bedroom...he told me to close my eyes.

I said "What?"

Timmy said, "Close your eyes and check this out...you're gonna think this is bizarre."

I asked myself, "What are you nuts trusting a

Lizzy West and Nikki Sixx

guy that hangs with *Motley Crue*."

I did what he asked and he led me into Nikki's room, and then he tried to get me on the bed... I was like "what the fuck?"

While he was trying to get me on the bed, he said, "no really ...trust me. Keep your eyes closed and lay on the bed" So I sat, then laid down... I heard him walk away and he said keep your eyes closed. I heard all these switches clicking.

Finally he said, "Open your eyes"...and I did...and I looked around and all these glowing eyes were looking at me...like a 100 pair! I was in the middle of Nikki's bed and there were dolls everywhere positioned to look straight into the center of the bed...some had their own lights! It was fucking bizarre... Some were marionettes and most were pieroet dolls...you know those porcelain ones? With the hand painted faces and red cheeks...sexy eyes. Apparently...he got a lot of them in Europe, some were really old and valuable. Others were gifts, I suppose...obviously a collector.. he has a lot of art...beautiful stuff on the walls...let me tell you ...elegant taste... whew... except those dolls! The dolls were creepy.

I saw some clothes lying on a chair and I picked them up...they smelled like him...yummy! And I decided it would be funny to put them on... They were like Indiana Jones clothes...I felt like Mel Gibson. And there was a hat... I ran downstairs and announced that I was gonna be the "real Nikki"... just call me Frank... for Halloween... *Motley Crue's* FAVORITE holiday...everyone laughed their asses off...

So I went back upstairs to look for more clothes... mind you... everyone was trashed. I looked in his drawers... I stood there dumfounded at what I saw. His clothes were folded military style...I mean to exact dimensions...even his underwear and socks...I felt like I was looking at the Colonel Major's locker!!! I looked in his closets...his hangers were just "so" apart and straight... made me feel like I had bad posture! He's totally disciplined or ANAL as hell!!! Shoes and boots to the ceiling... stacked, marked and alphabetized...I shit you not.

Anyway...I found some rock and roll stuff to put on...black leather pants and the hottest pink jacket you ever saw. I went back downstairs and Nikki was laughing his ass off... you know what he did? He gave me the jacket as a gift. I still have it. He's extremely well read...has books with leather coverings, first printings and all.

Basically...we partied till the wee hours...

Lizzy West today

148

and no I didn't get laid... although Vince kept saying...come on...just once??

NURSE!

I received this letter and I asked the writer if I could share this with my readers. Here ya go!

Dear Gordon (May I call you Gordon?),

I read your book *KISS and Tell* and your chapter about your experience playing with *Motley Crue* reminded me of my experience playing with *Motley Crue*. I think my experience was a little, ahem, different from yours.

This is going to be very strange; I'm going to give you a brief history about how I ended up with the story I'm about to tell.... I'll try and make it interesting for ya.

For as long as I can remember, I have had infatuations with musicians, so going into the groupie world was a natural progression for me. I've only seriously been in "love" about three or four times in my thirty-two years. Three of the four times have been guys in bands. I was exposed at a very early age to the rock and roll lifestyle and all that accompanies it, good and bad. I blame it on the public school system. I was a "gifted" (their word, not mine) child. I got moved up and graduated early. Big mistake.... when you factor in my penchant for rockers, my raging hormones, and the fact that I was OUT OF SCHOOL at age SIXTEEN.... did I mention that I am also incredibly resourceful too? Well, you get the picture... I had way too much free time on my hands and *Motley Crue* was at the top of my "to do" list.

Fast forward about a year after my Graduation. *Motley* is hitting the road with their new tour. My dilemma... I have no car. I must find a friend with not only the same goal but with some wheels.

Enter, Connie, an older woman (twenty-six) that spent her nights looking at the boys in my boyfriend's band. I knew she was ripe for the job.

I spent some time cultivating a friendship with her. I had some ulterior motives, as did she. I think she was hoping that I could hook her up with one of the guys in my boyfriend's band. Anyway, it was a mutually satisfying situation for both of us. She was also very interested in *Motley Crue* especially Vince Neil... God only knows why. We decided that we had to meet them by whatever means necessary. As I said earlier, I am very resourceful... comes from being "gifted"... I thought we should find the smallest, po-dunk town that they were playing and hit the road.

Evansville, Indiana turned out to be the charm. Not being as big as our home city of Atlanta, I figured that in a smaller town it would be easier to meet them... less girls, less competition. A few phone calls later. Bingo! An in-store record (yes, I said record) signing. We had hit the motherlode, so-to-speak. I had to explain to Connie that the ten hour drive would be well worth it. We would be able to waltz into a record shop in Bumfuck, USA and meet *Motley Crue*. We could not have asked for a better set-up, perfect. Now, this is where it gets interesting....

I picked my brain for days trying to figure out what I could do to make a lasting impression on the guys. It had to be something very special... it would need to involve some mode of dress, a costume of sorts. But what??? The traditional metal girl garb would simply not suffice. Too ordinary. I... WE had to stand out. Aha! NURSES!!! All I had to do was convince my partner that we HAD to do this. It was glaringly obvious. She loved the idea. I remember getting so turned on when I went to the uniform store to get my cap. I felt so naughty. I can remember it like it was last week. Then it was on to Frederick's of Hollywood to get the most amazing white bustier, complete with garters and stockings (lines up the back and all!!). Oh yeah, I forgot the trip to the toy store for the nurse's bag (later to hold various scarves, airplane bottles of booze, condoms, and my handcuffs).

In the weeks leading up to our trip, I was obsessed with thoughts of how it would turn out. My boyfriend at the time was even supportive. I think in a way the whole scenario turned him on, too.

Finally, after painstakingly putting together our nurse outfits it was time to hit the road. You can't begin to imagine how long the drive was. It seemed like we would never get there. We were like two children on a long family vacation, each hour more torturous than the last.... Then it appeared like an oasis in the desert, Evansville - Fifteen miles. Holy Shit, there were only fifteen miles separating me from *Motley Crue*. My hands were sweating. I could feel something deep in my loins starting to wake up. It was nauseating and amazing all at once. It was lust in its highest form.

So, we finally reached our destination. We went over to our hotel. It was some sort of Holiday Inn. Prior research told me this was also where *Motley* was staying! Never underestimate the resourcefulness of a horny woman!! I didn't even have a computer with Internet capabilities back then.

We had only about an hour before it would be time to go to the record store. Not much time to prepare for a meeting of this magnitude. We got dressed up in our gear. I had to admit I was getting really worked up. If things went as planned this would be something they would remember for years to come. We admired each other's outfits (mine was better) and patted ourselves on the back for coming up with such an elaborate scheme. It was also around this time that we started getting into the airplane bottles. We had to drink ourselves a little courage. Off we went, Showtime...

We arrived at the store to find hundreds of fans wrapped around the block. I started to panic, all these preparations. How were we going to get in? We didn't even have tickets for that evening's show.

Motley's manager was walking around outside and spotted us. He grabbed us and shuffled us past the crowd right to the front of the line. I felt like a SUPER-STAR. You should have seen the other girl's lips curling up as we were ushered along. It was at this point I started to think, "oh shit, what am I gonna say when I get face to face with them?" I had nothing planned. I was drawing a complete blank. I was completely dumbstruck with the men of my dreams within spitting distance. Connie, despite my disapproval, started to snap pictures. I'm not a picture taker. I didn't want to look like a mere fan. I was a nurse, for crying out loud. I wanted a patient to examine and I wanted it to be Tommy Lee or Nikki Sixx!!!

At this point we were in clear sight of the band's signing table. They were all staring and pointing at us as we approached them. I was about to cream in my panties. I loved the attention. Not only did I not have anything for them to sign; I didn't have one clever thing to say. Pitiful, huh?

I first passed Vince. He made some stupid comment like, "Are you guys really nurses?" I just smiled and kept going. Next was Tommy, my dream fuck.

He had his pen out and wrote down the hotel name and room number on my hand. AHHHH, an invitation. I could have died right then and been a happy woman. He asked if he could see inside my doctor's bag. I, of course, obliged him. He pulled out the handcuffs and held them up grinning.

I went past him to Nikki. He just sort of gazed up at me, like he didn't know what to say either. He asked if we were going to the show. I told him we didn't have any tickets and he said not to worry... we were going. I towered over him. He seemed so small to me. I'm about five foot, seven inches and I had five inch pumps on. I think he was a little intimidated... It all happened so fast. Next thing you know we gave our names to their manager so that we can get into the show that night. We were also invited back to the hotel right after the record signing. We didn't mention that we were staying in the same hotel.

We waited until they left and caravanned back to the Holiday Inn. Connie had a convertible Camaro, so what would you do in this situation? Of course, we flashed them. They were hanging out the windows of the van and encouraging us. I had to do it. I'm a little bit of an exhibitionist at heart.

We all went into the hotel together as an entourage. I tried to seem as nonchalant as I could be on the outside but inside I was freaking out. I mean we were drawing some serious attention from other hotel guests, employees, etc... After all, it was the middle of the afternoon. We went up in the elevator with everyone. At this point, I had Tommy Lee on my mind, no one else. He just kept leering at me, putting his hands on my ass. I was about to explode. I would have fucked him right there in front of everybody. We got off the elevator and went into Vince's room. He is the one that brought up the photo session. He asked us if we would like to be in *Motley* Magazine.

Of course we said, "YES!" He then went on to explain how we should feel honored to be asked because *Motley* Magazine is for the creme-de-la-creme of the groupie corp. I truly felt like a superstar now. He had a Polaroid and asked us to take our clothes off and if we would eat each other. I declined. I was not, in any way, interested in Connie, even if it was for such an upscale publication!! She just wasn't my type. Mick Mars was not around, thankfully. He gave me the creeps. Also, Tommy and Nikki were giving us suggestions, like "show us your tits".... "let's see some skin." You know, the typical male banter. I took off my top to reveal my beautiful bustier. That went over very well. They displayed my tits very nicely. Connie had already gotten down to her panties. She was topless and going for bottomless any second. We posed with each other to please the guys porno-lesbian fantasies. I held her tits. We had our nurse caps on the whole time. After much prompting, I lost the bustier and went down to the garters and white panties and stockings. I put my stethoscope on my bare chest. That was well received. That was as far as I would go for the camera. Connie did some full frontal stuff while I got cozy with Tommy. Nothing too heated. He helped me fasten up my bustier and we had a little touchy-feely kind of vibe going. Nikki and Vince were all over Connie, telling her to masturbate and God only knows what else.

By this time it was getting late and they had to get ready for the show. We excused ourselves and said we would see them at the arena. I remember feeling so totally in touch with my body when we left that room. I wanted to go somewhere and be alone to see where it would take me. I was dripping wet. The anticipation of the night ahead was killing me. I was also a little embarrassed to look Connie in the eye. To this day, we have never discussed her masturbating in front of *Motley Crue*. I was just glad it hadn't been me.

We were on our way to the concert. I can't even recall who was playing other than *Motley*. I want to say *Guns 'n Roses* opened the show but it was really unimportant. All I know is that we were invited guests of *MOTLEY CRUE*. We picked up our tickets and passes at the will-call window. I breathed a sigh of relief when the tickets were actually there. We proceeded into the show feeling very happy with ourselves. It was like we had a big secret, or that we were the only ones in on a joke. It felt naughty and I enjoyed every second of it. We proudly displayed our passes for all to see, particularly the other girls. We saw Nikki walking around before the show. He was carrying around some Polaroids and when he saw us he put them in his pocket.... Hmmm.... He told us how much he dug our outfits and asked us if we would be coming back to the hotel for the after-show party. We just coyly smiled. Inside I said, "You bet your sweet ass we would be there." He had to go and politely excused himself. He would not let us see the pictures he had in his pocket and stated firmly that they were *Motley* property now!

The show kicked ass but I secretly couldn't wait for it to end. I had business to take care of. I kept playing out different scenes in my head about how the evening would turn out. Me, alone in a room, with Tommy Lee. What I would do to him? How could I please him, taunt him, mesmerize him, and make him want to please me? The scenarios were limitless. I honestly don't remember much about the concert. I was knee deep in thoughts of sexual rapture. Of course, so were the other groupies in Evansville, Indiana. I never thought about that scenario. I should have, because, lo and behold, when we got back to the hotel, there they were. There must have been at least twenty other girls. Suddenly, I felt threatened, like somehow they had invaded our private

party. I started to feel like my night of passion was not going to happen. I would lose my Tommy to the grips of some blond with big fake tits. I was getting jealous. Connie had laid the groundwork for her evening with Doug, the manager, also securing us free passes to any future shows... smart girl. I was left in my own little pitiful world of envy. What to do, what to do? I had to do something. There were a lot of people crammed into a two-room suite. A lot of drugs were being consumed, music blaring, strippers, you name it. I felt like I had to make a move. I approached Tommy and told him I wanted to "talk" to him privately. I had every intention of sucking his cock in the bathroom.

Nikki walked up to me and said, "Just where do you think you're going?"

I could see my window of opportunity fading. I was pulling Tommy by the hand and Nikki was pulling me by the other. It was a tug-of-war. At this point I could tell that Nikki was genuinely interested in me. Tommy would love to have had a good blowjob but he had his sights on some strippers. So, I reluctantly let go of Tommy's hand. He reached down and unzipped my skirt and put his hands all over my ass. He made sure to lightly stroke my crotch and he told me he'll be back to finish the job later. LATER? I'm friggin' dying here and he says he'll be back later? Forget that!

Nikki, who had been very patient, was still holding my hand. He asked me if I wanted to stay with him. While not my dream fuck he was second on my list. I said, "Yes." Nikki was still a cutie. We had a few drinks. As I left to go to Nikki's room I told Connie that I was staying with Nikki and I would see her in the morning.

As we walked down the hall of the Holiday Inn, I suddenly felt like I might be making a huge mistake. I had pretty much committed myself to sex. I had second thoughts of not having sex with Nikki. It might ruin my chances of ever being with Tommy. A whole new can of worms was being opened in my mind. I was definitely attracted to him but I was just so sure that I was going to be with Tommy. I had not thought of how I would make Nikki my "love slave" for the night. It could be done, no doubt about it. But I had my heart set on Tommy.

We had both been drinking and fairly intoxicated when we got to his room. It was non-descript, a basic hotel room. From the doorway I could see clothes were everywhere. It had two beds in it. On one of them was an open guitar case, some new toy he had just gotten. I don't think it was a bass. I'm pretty sure it was a regular guitar. Only a few steps into the room and we started making out like crazy. More clothes went flying through the air. It was pretty intense. It had been building up in me for hours. I was ready to get fucked. There is a huge difference in wanting to "make love" and wanting to simply get-off. I thought I would take matters into my own hands (literally and figuratively) when I went straight for the kill. He seemed taken aback when I reached down between his legs and unzipped his leather pants. Not saying a word I slowly, gently, took him into my mouth and started teasing him with my tongue. Playfully at first, then a little more intense. I went for those certain spots that I know drive men to tears.

At this point his pants were not even past his knees and he fell backwards into the wall with me right on top of him. Just the position I like to be in... a position of control.

I still had on my panties, sopping wet by now. Garters exposed, my skirt hiked up to my waist. My pussy was on fire. I got his pants off after wrestling with the boots... We pretty much just went for it on the floor. I stayed on top for most of the time. I like being able to set the pace, also it's much easier for me to climax that way. I find that I am able to cum about eighty percent of the time being on top, and this was no exception. It didn't last as long as I had hoped, but all in all it wasn't a bad experience. Even in our inebriated state we still managed to have a little dialogue. I like dirty talk and I must say Nikki didn't score big in that department. I also like explicit directions, and again he was very passive. I would have liked him to have just said "Hey, it drives me wild if you stick your finger in my ass" or something like that. I could have really blown his mind!!! He did score big points in the department that matters most. He was very orally inclined. I didn't even have to direct him to my clit. He found it all on his own... Bravo, Nikki!

He was also very cuddly. We slept in the "spoon" position and when we woke up, instead of feeling awkward, we hopped in the shower together. It was a nice end to a fantastic trip. I've seen him several times since our evening together. I heard he is happily married and has conquered his addictions. He is also a proud papa. I also heard he is coming to Atlanta soon. I've long ago hung up my nurses cap... but ya never know... I wonder where they got the idea for the Dr. Feelgood Tour?

Nikki Sixx and Vince Neil

155

CHAPTER 26
STERN S RAT PACK!

It Was Not a Date!

I (Lynn Ramagé) met Kenneth Keith Kallenbach through my friend, Gina. Kenneth brought her to the "Stern Show" and she got momentarily naked. After the show, Kenneth left her stranded on a corner in New York City. She had to find her own way back to Philly. I can't believe she even spoke to him after that.

So Gina called me one night and said, "Like yo man, Kenneth Keith Kallenbach from *The Howard Stern Show* wants yur (she talks with a thick South Philly accent) number so you can go out and review his band."

I'm like, "Yeah, whatever." We got to talking and she's still very vague whether she ever really "did him." When we start talking we're like a pair of old yentas.

All she said was, "... at least he knew what to do."

Well, it's questionable how one could take that if you knew Gina. I am still under the impression that she didn't do him... and try real hard not to even get a visual of that possibility. He's probably the least likely guy in all of America that I'd ever want to fuck! I reluctantly gave her permission to give him my number. I instructed her to tell him to call me ONLY to review his band, nothing else.

Gina is an original, quite the colorful one, and easily spotted at shows like the *Cramps*, for instance, dressed in a leopard cat suit! She kinda reminds you of a cross between Joan Jett and Grace Slick. She's a trip. She sent a video of herself to WYSP radio pretending to have an orgasm on a washing machine while looking at the centerfold of Peter Steele from *Type O Negative*. DJ John Dabella supposedly loved it! I can still hear her moaning all across Philly's airwaves.

So a few days went by before the

Gina and Howard Stern

157

phone rang and it was Kenneth. We ended up yapping for an hour. I really felt sorry for him. He seemed like the lonely type. So, being the sucker that I am, I invited him "to hang" with my friends. We were all going to a club called Shooters. It was Thanksgiving Eve. He came up to my house in a mini-van and met my clan of friends. My girlfriend Sandy and her boyfriend decided to drive all of us to the club.

Once we got to Shooters everyone recognized him from Howard's show. This guy was being treated like a huge celebrity even though his claim to fame is he can supposedly blow smoke out of his eyes. It's a shame. He seemed like a very nice guy, but all I saw was Alfred E. Neuman (from the front cover of a MAD magazine) with long hair! Ughhhh, if Gina "did" that! - I couldn't quite imagine him on top of Gina. While he was busy off signing autographs and being social, I happened to run into my ex-boyfriend. We reminisced about the old days and we got cozy on a shuffleboard table in the back-room bar. Kenneth came back there and got perturbed about the attention I was giving my "ex." While my ex and I were sucking face, Kenneth tried to hold my hand. It was really weird.

All kinds of thoughts ran through my head, "What the hell is he trying to do? Is he trying to make this a threesome or something?" I only asked him to hang with all of my friends because I felt sorry for him. This was NOT a date and I gave him no implication that it was a date.

As the evening came to an end, I bid farewell to my lost love. Kenneth was still trying to hold my hand in the car on the way home. It was creepy how he just didn't get it. Just as Sandy dropped us off and drove away, I noticed the keys in my pocketbook were gone! Christ, it was the middle of winter and I knew my

apartment was locked up solid! There would be no way into my ground floor apartment. Of course, Kenneth generously offered to have me go home with him. I politely refused.

I thought, "I'll stand out here and freeze first." I was determined to get into my apartment even if I had to bust my way in. I stood on a lawn chair and finally was able to move my bedroom window. I had Kenneth give my ass a boost to get through the window. That was a big mistake but there was nothing I

KKK and a stunned Lynn Ramagé

could do about it. After I got back into my apartment I reluctantly let Kenneth in to get warm. If it was summer I would've just dismissed him. He continued to try to hug and kiss me. Ugh, I was getting douche chills. It was like fighting off a dumb animal. His advances were getting so bad I had to come up with something real quick. Something that would work on a dumb animal. I clutched my stomach. I feigned sickness. I thought for a second using the ol' time of the month excuse but I figured this dumb fuck would then bug me to blow him. I faked diarrhea pains so he would go. Nothing like a woman resorting to telling you she has diarrhea to ward off your clumsy advances. Who knows? He might've gotten more excited! I took my chances.

The next day my friend George, the manager at Shooters, called to say they found my keys in the men's room. In the MEN'S room!!!? I was spitting bullets! Now it was Thanksgiving Day... the club was closed. I had no way to get my keys, which also meant I couldn't drive my car, which meant I couldn't go anywhere... (Blondes never have spare keys and if they do, who knows where they are?) so I had a frozen dinner for Thanksgiving that day! Thank you very, very much! I can only assume that when I was hanging all over my "ex" he must have taken them right out of my pocketbook and ditched them in the men's room! Who else would have done this? Right? Well, I certainly wasn't in the men's room! He was the only other person near my pocketbook to have that opportunity! I kept thinking, "what a little jerk-off!" Well, after all, he did leave Gina stranded in New York City! I never spoke to him again after that stunt! Whether he did this or not, I'll never know for sure. But the detective in me, and my gut instinct, sure lead me to that conclusion.

Epilogue: Kenneth e-mailed me a few months later. I e-mailed the little runt back, "eat a box of Wheaties!" So for the record, I did not have a date with Kenneth Keith Kallenbach! May some girl someday take his keys and hide them in a ladies room somewhere in America.

Ever since that incident I hate seeing a MAD magazine.

SAL THE STOCKBROKER

The Smoking Gun Web Site (www.thesmokinggun.com) became famous when they revealed that Rick Rockwell's former fiancée had filed a restraining order against him. What does this have to do with rock music besides the "Rock" in Rockwell? Well... payback is a beautiful thing.

I was getting some heavy flack from some asshole *KISS* fan named Sal because he took offense to my book *KISS & Tell*. The moron sent some really wacky, threatening e-mails defending his beloved *KISS* idols. It turns out Sal is Sal The Stockbroker, one of the wanna-be pseudo-celeb-whatever-the-fuck he is supposed to be, from *The Howard Stern Show*.

Here is an article about Sal's behavior with his favorite rock band:

Stockbroker KISS-es Off Rocker

From: Pagesix.com

Gene Simmons - the bass player for KISS, who has the longest tongue in rock 'n' roll history - seems to be under endowed in his sense of humor. When KISS played the Mohegan Sun in Connecticut on Tuesday night; Simmons lost his temper at a fan in the front row and refused to go on with the concert until the man, Sal Governale, left. Governale is better known as "Sal the Stockbroker," a frequent guest on the Howard Stern radio show who delights in calling Stern's producer, Gary Dell'Abate, a "horse-toothed jackass." Sal confesses that when Simmons stuck out his anaconda-like tongue, he stuck out his tongue as well, while putting his thumbs in his ears and wiggling his fingers.

"I did it to make Gene laugh," said Governale, who works at Millennium Securities. But Simmons wasn't amused. "Gene pointed at me and said, 'You're out of here.'" Sal, confronted by security men and a burly roadie, soon left the arena voluntarily. "I didn't want a riot, which was the next step," said Governale. "It was ugly."

But KISS' manager, Doc McGhee, denies Sal was threatened. "They went over and asked him to cut it out," and he said, "'I feel uncomfortable,' and asked to be escorted out," said McGhee. "He did a good job of annoying Gene. He's got to learn how to act in public."

One of Sal's biggest sleazeball moves was negotiating a secret agreement with an Internet firm to plug the company on Howard's show--unbeknownst to Stern & Co.--in return for at least $45,000 in cash. Bonus payments were also negotiated if the plugs were aired on Stern's television show. The agreement was made and then the company stiffed Sal on the illegal deal. In other words, they got plugs from Sal and then fucked him on the payoff. How this came to surface just shows the brilliance of Sal. He took the company to court to sue them for the illegal payoff. Howard, this is the price you have to pay working with idiots!

Check out www.TheSmokingGun.com for the hilarious details on this knucklehead. Just go to their home page, click on "Search TSG" and type in Sal and have fun.

Last report of Sal was he was suing Gene and *KISS* for some ungodly reason. Have fun Gene and Paul. You must love those exuberant fans.

CHAPTER 27
METAL SLUDGE

"I ignore that site and the lies they persist in spreading. Anyone who wants to visit it, it's their business but I would appreciate it if you don't come here and reprint this crap." - Gerri Miller, June 28th, 1999, on the Metal Edge Bulletin Board.

Gerri Miller

I don't have enough metaphors for Metal Sludge. Metal Sludge is the Mad Magazine of Metal. It is the Friar's Club of the rock world based on a parody of Metal Edge Magazine. It is a web site that rips on everyone and anyone worth a mention in rock and roll. Unfortunately, past editor, Gerri Miller received the brunt of all the abuse on the Metal Sludge web site. Gerri Miller, felt the pressure and left her job. I do have to say Metal Sludge went beyond the Friar's club theme of making fun of people out of affection. Metal Sludge at times can be just plain vicious! But that's the entertainment business, you have to take the good with the bad. There are quite a few rockers on their "bust balls" list. Some take it with a grain of salt, others can not handle it. Ask Stefen Adika from *L.A. Guns.*

Metal Sludge sometimes hooks up a great Q&A with a rocker or better yet; a model/actress/groupie/rocker girlfriend. They have a section called 20 Questions (Sometimes they don't know how to count and they ask more, which is fine by me. Love those bonus questions!).

Another section of Metal Sludge is their Metal Sludge Advisor. You won't be getting sound Playboy advice in that section!

The most visited and talked about section is Donna's Domain. This section is full of brutal gossip and graphic details on practically every rock musician worth mentioning. This is where some musicians wish they did not go into the entertainment business. The age of the internet means networking of information and groupies take full advantage of this technology.

Web mistress Donna Anderson's moniker is obviously a fake name combining Donna D'Errico's and Pam Anderson's names. Donna's sections include "The Long & Short Of It" which includes a Penis Chart along with groupies detailed "reports" of their sexual activities with rock stars. Donna's "Ho-Bag" is where she answers her mail. She also has a "Groupie Chart" that lists various groupies and info about them. If you have any gossip or something you'd like to say to her, then just e-mail her at DonnaAnderson@metal-sludge.com. Other sources of rock gossip on the 'net is Groupie Central and Nico's Intimate Notebook.

Lynn Ramagé caught up with Gerri Miller and asked her for her most memorable rock story in her illustrious rock journalistic career. Here is her story and then we'll continue on to other Metal Sludge.

One writer I admire here in America is Gerri Miller formally of Metal Edge Magazine. Who hasn't picked up a Metal Edge at least once in their lives? If you're reading this book, you have to have read at least one of Gerri's stories over the years she was with that publication. She, I'm sure has been an inspiration to many a journalist. Upon the undertaking of this book... it was sometimes difficult to think; hey who has a good story? So I approached Gerri who is still contributing her freelance writing to numerous magazines and websites and she said, "Boy, let me think on this one." So I called her back a few days later and this is her war story.

120 Degrees in The Desert by Gerri Miller

"Last summer, in July sometime, there was this tour that really never became a tour. It collapsed but the very beginning of it was this date in Las Vegas. It was *Bang Tango, Enuff Znuff, Bullet Boys*, and *Pretty Boy Floyd. Enuff Znuff* were traveling on their own tour bus. *Pretty Boyd Floyd* and *Bang Tango* were traveling from Los Angeles by another bus. My photographer and I were going to fly there but they said, "No come with us." We figured okay, what the hell. Okay, we'll take a ride with them, hang out, have fun and just fly back. They even picked us up."

"So we were on the road with *Bang Tango* and *Pretty Boyd Floyd*. Well, the bus was rather ancient, probably dating back to the early 70's and it started having problems in the middle of the desert! It was fine for about the first hour, but then we started having problems. The air-conditioning seemed to be struggling and the heat was beginning to win over the air conditioner. The driver informed us that he had to go slowly to conserve it. Well, by the time we got to about Barstow in the middle of god-knows-where... it was an inferno in there! The only thing we could open for air was a little hatch in the roof (meaning the windows on this rig didn't open) which really didn't do much at all. I just can't tell you how hot it was! We passed that big thermometer in the desert, it was a one-hundred-twenty-some odd degrees! We were all dying! We were just trying to conserve energy. I felt really, really ill. Like really ill."

"We had to go slowly otherwise the bus was going to blow up. We had to stop on the road a couple of times too as the engine was just overheating. It turned into a seven-hour ride! It turned into one of the most awful experiences I ever had!"

"At one point we had stopped at a convenience store in the middle of nowhere. It wasn't a name brand place, just a truck stop and I bought a five-pound bag of ice. I held it and I cradled it like a baby, just letting it melt all over me. I didn't care! I put some of the cubes on the back of my neck and I just sat there and held it like a pillow and tried to cool myself down. I was really dizzy. This was just like being in a sauna. It was really horrible. By the time we got there we were all ready to collapse. We were a wreck! Everyone was just totally soaked in sweat, and to top it all off, there were problems at the hotel. They weren't reserved properly and we had to wait to get a room. I just about cried, I really did. I was very exasperated by the whole thing."

"It was just a horrifying experience. The show was great though! Whenever I see those guys we say to each other, 'Ha, ha, remember Vegas?'"
Website: www.mtledge.com

I'm sorry Lynn but I beg to differ on your praise of Gerri Miller. Out of all the years involved with rock and roll bands that is the best war story Gerri Miller could muster up? And she had a few days to "think it over." No wonder Metal Sludge rips her so much. She was never very kind to me either. She was too busy licking Ace Frehley's asshole.

On to hilarious outtakes of a very funny web site - www.Metal-Sludge.com
Fans of the site watch Gerri's every move. Here's one "report" that I know for a fact was true;

Hey kidz.... It's me again... Well, well, well, do I have a FUCKING GEM for ya!!
In Sept-October KISS was rehearsing for the BORING CIRCUS tour in L.A. next door to where some friends were in pre-production for their major label debut. Booze Hag Gerri Miller was interviewing KISS. KISS did something to piss off Gerri (don't know what it was...maybe they told her she was an unattractive sideshow and she needs to die). After getting pissed and throwing a fit, Gerri storms out of the building and gets in her little ass piece of shit car, slams it in reverse and RIGHT INTO ACE FREHLEY'S RENTED MUSTANG!!! Then-get this-SHE FUCKING DRIVES OFF!!! So, her license number was written down and reported to the LAPD.
Thanx guyz-keep up the GR8 WORK.

Metal Sludge nails some great interviews despite a lot of stars refusing (mostly in fear of being ridiculed). Here is a slice of an actual Donna D'Errico interview for you to savor.

BEST OF...

Metal Sludge presents you with 23 QUESTIONS WITH... Donna D'Errico (Actress, Supermodel, Mom, and Nikki Sixx's Wife!)

In our opinion, this is one of the best interviews we've done! As most of you know, Donna is married to Motley Crue's Nikki Sixx. She was also Playboy Playmate of the Month for September 1995, Playboy cover girl for November 1996, a star on Baywatch and Baywatch Nights, and other cool shit like that. If you wanna know more about Donna's bio then go to fucking E! Online or some shit like that. Donna was so honest and brutal in this interview, she is the 3rd recipient and 1st female winner of the Metal Sludge Super Balls Award!

Donna D'Errico: SORRY I TOOK SO LONG!!! HERE YA GO——ENJOY!!

2. You recently flew to Japan and had quite an experience. For those Sludgeaholics who aren't aware of the story, could you tell them about it?
DONNA D'ERRICO: *OKAY, WELL I WAS EN ROUTE TO TOKYO FROM LAX AND WANTED TO GET SLEEP ON THE PLANE SO I WOULD BE ABLE TO BE AWAKE WHEN I GOT THERE (THE DAYS AND NIGHTS ARE OPPOSITE FROM HERE).... COULDN'T SLEEP, SO I TOOK A PRESCRIPTION SLEEPING PILL... STILL COULDN'T SLEEP.. A BIT LATER I HAD A GLASS OF WINE... STILL NOTHING... HAD ANOTHER GLASS... FINALLY, ABOUT 50 MINUTES BEFORE ARRIVAL TIME I NODDED OFF.... WELL, I GUESS ALL OF THE ABOVE FINALLY KICKED IN 'CAUSE WHEN THE PLANE LANDED, I COULDN'T BE AWAKENED AT ALL.... I'M TOLD THAT I HAD TO BE CARRIED OFF THE PLANE, AND WHEN I FINALLY CAME TO, I WAS DISORIENTED, WAS SURROUNDED BY JAPANESE PEOPLE SLAPPING MY FACE AND ALL SPEAKING JAPANESE AT ONCE, WAS BEING PUSHED TOWARD CUSTOMS, AND I GUESS I FREAKED.... I GOT IRATE AND WANTED THEM ALL TO LEAVE ME THE FUCK ALONE... SO I SUPPOSE THIS CAME OFF TO THEM AS BEING IN NEED OF RESTRAINT, AND TOOK ME TO THE MEDICAL AREA OF THE AIRPORT, HELD ME DOWN, AND GAVE ME SOME KIND OF SHOT IN THE ARM...THE NEXT THING I REMEMBER WAS COMING TO IN AN EMERGENCY ROOM WITH HAWK (HEAD SECURITY FOR THE BAND) AND MY HUS-BAND BESIDE ME... I LATER FOUND OUT THAT I SOMEHOW GOT TO NIKKI'S HOTEL ROOM, LAID DOWN ON THE BED, AND STOPPED BREATHING... NIKKI WAS GIVING ME CPR UNTIL THE AMBULANCE ARRIVED... THEN IN THE AMBULANCE I FLATLINED FOR A MOMENT... THEY BROUGHT ME RIGHT BACK.... THEN GOT TO THE EMERGENCY ROOM AND THEY DID SOMETHING (???) AND THEN I WAS FINE....*

Also, did you ever figure out what they shot you up with?
DONNA D'ERRICO: *NEVER DID!!*

Are you going to pursue legal action at all?
DONNA D'ERRICO: *NAH...I'M ALIVE, SO WHY COMPLAIN?*

3. How many dates did it take Nikki before he got into your pants?
DONNA D'ERRICO: *HE WOULD CLAIM ONE, BUT I'M STICKING TO TWO WEEKS*

4. What hard rock/heavy metal band should give it up and call it a day?
DONNA D'ERRICO: *KISS.....NEVER REALLY LIKED THEM, AND I'M NOT INTO THE WIG THING*

5. Do you think Pamela Anderson has great acting talent or is she just all tits and ass?

DONNA D'ERRICO: *NORMALLY I WOULD HAVE SAID SHE HAS NO, LET ALONE GREAT, ACTING TALENT. HOWEVER AFTER SEEING HER CRY OVER TOMMY ON JAY LENO A FEW TIMES LAST YEAR, I'D SAY THEY GAVE THE OSCAR TO THE WRONG CHICK.... ON THE OTHER HAND, DIDJA SEE GWYN CRY?*

6. For $10,000: Would you wedge a mature butternut squash in your vagina for an entire day?
DONNA D'ERRICO: *I'D PROBABLY DO THAT FOR FREE, SO 10,000 BUCKS WOULD BE A BONUS!! IS THAT AN OFFER??*

10. Rate the following dudes on a scale of 1 to 10. 1 being a scrub and 10 being a hunk.
Scott Baio.... *1*
Mick Mars..... *I PLEAD THE 5TH*
Mark McGrath.... *WHO'S HE?*
Kid Rock....*6*
Lars Ulrich...*1*
Howard Stern....*2.5*
Bret Michaels....*1*
Vince Neil.... *GONNA TAKE THE 5TH AGAIN*
Gene Simmons...*1*
Dennis Rodman....*0*

11. What rock star deserves a smack in the mouth and why?
DONNA D'ERRICO: *....TOMMY LEE...I THINK THE REASONS OBVIOUS*

12. Pick one of the following:
A. You get a role in the next Adam Sandler movie, which grosses $150,000,000 and immediately puts you on Hollywood's A List. You even get nominated for an Oscar for Best Supporting Actress. However, due to your busy schedule you get a severe yeast infection that makes it so you can't have sex for an entire year. Nothing. Zero. Zip. After that year, the yeast infection goes away and everything is back to normal.
Or;
B. You get a role in the next Pauly Shore movie, your career gets ruined, but your sex life is better than ever.
DONNA D'ERRICO: *THAT'S A TOUGHIE....BUT SEEING AS HOW I ENJOY GIVING AS MUCH AS RECEIVING, AND YEAST INFECTIONS DON'T AFFECT YOU ORALLY, I'D CHOOSE "A"*

13. 2 Part Question:
What is your current opinion of Pamela Anderson?
DONNA D'ERRICO: *JUST THIS: IF SHE HAD AS MANY DICKS STICKING OUT OF HER AS SHE'S HAD STICKING IN HER, SHE'D LOOK LIKE A PORCUPINE*

And, When Pamela is talking, what percent of the time is she full of shit?
A. 25%
B. 50%
C. 75%
D. 100%
DONNA D'ERRICO: *BASED ON MY BELIEF THAT SHE IS COMPLETELY SINCERE IN HER DUMBNESS, I'D ACTUALLY SAY 0%*

14. When can we expect the Donna D'Errico and Nikki Sixx sex tape to be stolen out of your

house and sold through the Internet?
DONNA D'ERRICO: *NEVER—-WE WOULD BE HONEST ABOUT SELLING IT FOR A PROFIT, NOT MAKE UP SOME STUPID STORY ABOUT IT BEING MYSTERIOUSLY "STOLEN"...WHO WOULD DO THAT?*

15. Which do you prefer? Baywatch or VIP?
DONNA D'ERRICO: *BAYWATCH. I'D RATHER LAUGH THAN VOMIT*
Warrant or Slaughter
DONNA D'ERRICO: *SLAUGHTER—SAME REASON*
Metallica or Limp Bizkit
DONNA D'ERRICO: *METALLICA—-BUT THE OLD STUFF, THANKS*
Cinderella or Poison
DONNA D'ERRICO: *I'D HAVE TO TOSS A COIN...*
A Team or Miami Vice
DONNA D'ERRICO: *A TEAM*
Alice from the Brady Bunch or Florence from the Jeffersons
DONNA D'ERRICO: *FLORENCE, OF COURSE*
Pokeman or Pac Man
DONNA D'ERRICO: *PAC MAN!!!!!!*
The Vince Neil sex tape or The Bret Michaels / Pam sex tape
DONNA D'ERRICO: *EEEWWWW!!!!! NEVER SAW EITHER ONE*

16. For $50,000: Tell Mick Mars as part of a science project you want to shave his balls. If you don't persuade him to let you, you don't get paid. You'll get another $250,000 it you grab the shaft and begin jerking it until he jumps away or lets you finish.
DONNA D'ERRICO: *UUMMMMM.....WAS THAT A QUESTION OR A LEGITIMATE OFFER?*

17. Do you give Nikki an all access pass to your 3 inputs?
DONNA D'ERRICO: *YEAH BABY!!!*

19. If Nikki wanted to bring home a chick for a threesome, would you be down for that?
DONNA D'ERRICO: *WHAT'S TO SAY WE HAVEN'T ALREADY?*

21. Do you know if it's true that Pamela had 2 ribs removed and that she has had more plastic surgery then she is admitting?
DONNA D'ERRICO: *THANKFULLY, I DON'T HAVE FIRST HAND KNOWLEDGE OF EITHER ONE. TOO BAD YOU DIDN'T ASK ME ABOUT HER EATING HABITS.*

22. Nikki recently fell off the wagon this summer. How did that affect you and what were your thoughts on that?
DONNA D'ERRICO: *I WAS RIGHT THERE WITH HIM...WE ARE BOTH NOW BACK ON*

23. Time for Metal Sludge's Word Association. We give you a name, and you give us your thoughts.
David Hasseloff / *FENCE WALKER*
Mick Mars / *DRACULA*
Vince Neil / *SAD DAD*
Heidi Mark / *SKINNY, HYPER, SWEET*
Pamela Lee / *CHEESE WHIZ*
Hugh Hefner / *VIAGRA OVERDOSE*

Limp Bizkit / *ON LAST LEGS*
John Henson / *M.I.A.*
Warrant / *FLASH IN THE PAN*
Gene Simmons / *WIG BOY*
Tommy Lee / *A.A.W.B. (AFRICAN-AMERICAN WANNA BE)*
Bret Michaels / *BLUE BOY*
Carmen Electra / *CELEBRITY LEECH*

Metal Sludge is the gossip capital of the internet when it comes to rock stars. Here is another small sampling.
DONNA'S DOMAIN!
DONNA'S WORLD FAMOUS GROUPIE CHART!
Hey everybody, how's it going? I've gotten a lot of e-mail lately on some various wives & girlfriends. So I'm going to start a list of "Groupies" and list all the guys they've fucked. A Groupie Chart. This compliments the Dick and Hair charts. So we are going to start with one of the biggest groupies to date, Mrs. Jani Lane, and work our way down.

ROWANNE LANE has been with:
Jani Lane, Donald Trump, Fred Coury, Michael Monroe, Taime Downe, Jizzy Pearl, Stephen Pearcy, Brent Muscat, Jimmy D'Anda, Eric Brittingham, Vanilla Ice and more!
BOBBI BROWN has been with:
Jani Lane, Tommy Lee, Matthew Nelson, Leonardo DiCaprio, Mark McGrath, Stevie Rachelle, Dave Navarro
PAMELA ANDERSON has been with:
Tommy Lee, Bret Michaels, Scott Baio, Dean Cain, Kelly Slater, Sylvester Stallone, David Charvet, Eric Niles and now Kid Rock.
TAWNY KITAEN has been with:
Tommy Lee, David Coverdale, Robbin Crosby, OJ Simpson
SAVANNAH (Dead Porn Star) was with:
Vince Neil, Axl Rose, Slash, David Lee Roth, Billy Idol, Pauly Shore, Greg Allman, Billy Sheehan, Marky Mark, Jeanna Fine and a lot more!!
ERIN EVERLY has been with:
Axl Rose, Matthew Nelson, Anthony Kiedis, Donovan Leitch Jr, David Arquette
BRANDI BRANDT has been with:
Nikki Sixx, Taime Downe
CARMEN ELECTRA has been with:
B-Real, Dennis Rodman, Tommy Lee

     OLD SCHOOL GROUPIES
PAMELA DES BARRES has been with:
Jimmy Page, Mick Jagger, Keith Moon, Jim Morrison, Chris Hillman (The Byrds, The Flying Burrito Brothers), Brandon deWilde, Tony Sales, Noel Redding, Waylon Jennings, Nick St. Nicholas (Steppenwolf), Don Johnson, Dennis Hopper, Jimmy Thrill, Terence Trent D'Arby.
SWEET CONNIE has been with:
David Lee Roth, Alice Cooper, Peter Criss, Jimmy Page, John Bonham, Rick Springfield, Huey Lewis, Keith Moon, Don Henley, Glenn Frey, Joe Walsh, Eddie Money, Doc Severinsen, Waylon Jennings, Fleetwood Mac, Lindsey Buckingham, and every other band member or roadie who ever came through Little Rock, Arkansas.
If you have any gossip or something you'd like to say to her, then just e-mail her at donnaanderson@metal-sludge.com

It's been public knowledge that Sebastian Bach has had a long-standing problem with me ever since the *KISS & Tell* books were released. He became an asshole when he misunderstood my compliments about his wife. But I think he was more concerned that I wrote about his beloved Ace Frehley. The guy called in a radio interview I was doing in New Jersey and threatened me. He's even gone to the length of harrassing me with threatening phone calls to my home phone. All I can say is "how immature do you want to prove you are?" Well, Metal Sludge cleared up all my misunderstandings on the guy when they took an interview and explained what really goes on inside Sebastian's mind. Read on.

INSIDE SEBITCHIAN BACH'S MIND!

I haven't done one of these in a while, so back up off me if I'm a little rusty. For those of you who don't know what this is, I will tell you what Sebitchian was really thinking during this interview. It is from The Aquarian, which is a magazine in the New York / New Jersey / PA area. The questions Sebitchian were asked are in regular type, his answers are in italic type, and what Sebitchian really means is in bold type! Sebitchian talks a lot of shit about Skid Row here as well, so pay attention. Let's begin.

Question: What is your opinion of Skid Row re-forming with a new lead singer?
Sebitchian: *Who? Oh yeah, Skid Row, yeah, I used to be a Skid Row fan, actually. To me that's a complete joke. They are doing songs from 10 years ago with two guys (who) weren't there in the first place. It's like karaoke night. It's like; "whoever's got black leather pants and long blond hair, okay, c'mon up! Go for it!" I would not be in a band that only does songs from 10 years ago. It's fucking hilarious. What the fuck have you done for me lately? It's unbelievable. It 's, like, funny to me. I have no interest in doing 80's retro metal night. That's not what I'm about.*
What he really means: **I would not be in a band that only does songs from 10 years ago. Well, except for when I play with my band. We do only about 4 or 5 new songs and about 13 Skid Row songs, but that's beside the point. Even though I wear tight black leather pants, a very gay cod-piece, sing songs that were written in the 80's, frequently say 80's rock cliché's, and wear white cowboy boots with tassels, I have no interest in doing 80's retro metal night.**

Question: Your first solo CD, Bring 'Em Bach Alive is a live CD featuring mostly Skid Row material. So what's up with that?
Sebitchian: *There's a bunch of new studio songs on there as well. What happened was Atlantic Records asked me to do a full live record of just Skid Row material. I said, no I'm not interested in doing that. I said, "I'll give you your live album, but I got to add to it some new studio material." They said "okay." If it was up to me, it would be a whole new studio record. But this is what Atlantic wanted. They didn't ask the guys from Skid Row for nothing. I'm not out there like them going, "Here's our new tune Youth Gone Wild." We have two complete different ways of thinking. I'd be pulling a Kurt Cobain if I was on tour right now and my new song was "Youth Gone Wild." It would hit me at 5 o'clock in the morning at the hotel going, "What the fuck am I doing?" They can have a nice time. "Rattlesnake Shake," rock on guys! Have fun and don't hurt yourself on the fucking high notes either.*
What he really means: **There's a bunch of new studio songs on there as well. I wrote a whopping 3 out of the 6 songs on that album, and I had really creative song titles, like "Rock and Roll", and uh...well I forgot what the rest of them were called because they were all poorly written. See, what happened was Atlantic Records found out my solo shit sucks, so in order to sell CDs they had to put Skid Row songs on there.**
But then they didn't want to release it, so they licensed it out to Spitfire, and we all know Spitfire will just about release anything. See, I can hardly write a check, let alone a song. If it was up to me, it would be all Skid Row songs because my solo shit blows goats.

Question: How did you hear the news?

Sebitchian: *I read it on the Internet.*
What he really means: **I read it at Metal Sludge.**

Question: Van Halen and AC/DC successfully changed lead singers, can Skid Row get away with it?
Sebitchian: *I hate to break it to Snake, but he ain't no Eddie Van Halen. Angus Young got Brian Johnson, but Angus Young is ANGUS FUCKING YOUNG. I'm really sorry, Snake. But he owns the name of the band, so whatever. Totally destroy it, wreck it!*
What he really means: **Well they certainly can't do any worse than I'm doing, so why not?**

Question: Could you ever see yourself re-forming with them somewhere down the road?
Sebitchian: *Never. I will never fucking play with those guys again. You will NEVER see that happen. I haven't talk to those guys since 1996.*
What he really means: **I will never play with those guys again! You will NEVER see that happen. Unless they ask me, in which case I'd accept immediately because I'm tired of playing half-empty clubs. Hell, Slaughter's last CD sold more copies than my CD, so after my next solo CD flops, I'll definitely be looking for work. Fuck, I'd sing for Britny Fox or Trixter if they'd let me!**

Question: Why do you think Snake and Rachel have something against you?
Sebitchian: *'cause I'm the only person who tells them they suck! I'll tell anybody they fucking suck, if they fucking suck! They can't handle that in their lives. They think going on tour with no new album and singing songs from 10 years ago is a good career move. Talk to me and talk to Snake; it's like fire and fucking ice. When I did "Youth Gone Wild", it mean something. I was 19 for fuck sake! Those guys are like fucking 40! In your fucking dreams you're the "Youth Gone Wild"! Your fucking 40 is what you are! Jesus Christ! It's ridiculous.*
What he really means: **It's because I'm a self centered, bloated, piece of shit. I'll be honest dude; I'm a dick. I cheat on my wife, I throw bottles at fans, I insult fags...I mean gays, and I haven't washed my hair since Ronald Regan was President. Plus I have lots of zits on my back, and Snake and Rachel kept getting grossed out. Not only that, but I contributed as much to the Skid Row songwriting as Joe C (r.i.p.) would contribute to the L.A. Lakers. Meaning not at all. I was a lazy bastard and they booted me out. What more can I say? Jesus Christ! I'm ridiculous.**

Question: Interestingly enough, the band picked a replacement that even physically resembles you: a tall thin guy with long blond straight hair. What is your opinion about this?
Sebitchian: *I have no opinion. I just don't give a shit. Who cares?*
What he really means: **I have no opinion. I just don't give a shit. Not at all!! That's why in every fucking interview I do I mention Skid Row and rip on them every chance I get. It's because I don't care, you fuck! That makes sense, right? I mean, I don't fucking care. I don't care that Skid fucking Row is opening for *Kiss*, which is something I've never done. I don't care that they play in front of way more fucking people in a few days than I did during my whole solo tour. I don't care that Snake and Rachel haven't burned all their fucking bridges and that people still respect them and return their phone calls. I don't care that Solinger washes his fucking hair once a day and doesn't smell like a trash dumpster!!! NONE OF THAT FUCKING MATTERS TO ME! I'm not bitter! Next fucking question, you prick.**

Question: Would you ever consider going to one of their shows just to check it out?
Sebitchian: *Absolutely not! I'm not going to watch someone sing "I Remember You" who can't hit the high notes. Jesus! At least get a guy who can hit the high notes. All my fans tell me that "I Remember You" is a train wreck. From what I hear he can't even come close to hitting the notes. At least when Judas Priest got Ripper Owens, he could hit the notes.*

<u>What he really means</u>: **Absolutely not! You think I would pay $85 to see Skid Row open for** *Kiss*? **Fuck dude, I can't afford that shit. I blew all my money on pot, beer, comic books, and hookers. If they put me on the guest list I'd probably go though. Can you hook me up?**

<u>Question</u>: Could you ever see joining another band?

<u>Sebitchian</u>: *If the music was good. The only reason I perform under my own name is because I'm not putting 10 years into a band name. I'm not doing that anymore. I got screwed out of the Skid Row name. Slash feels the same way.*

<u>What OZZY STILLBOURNE has to say</u>: **Slash's feels he got screwed out of the Skid Row name? Sebitchian just said that, "I got screwed out of the Skid Row name. Slash feels the same way." What the fuck? When was Slash ever in Skid Row? Yeah, I know he's referring to Slash being screwed out of the Guns N Roses name, but at least explain it better. Like I said before, words just come out of his mouth and he really has no concept of what they mean. I'm sorry I just had to point that out. We'll now continue with the theme of "What Sebitchian Really Means."**

<u>Question</u>: Does Skid Row still have a contract with Atlantic?

<u>Sebitchian</u>: *No. Jason Flom told me that he won't go see them or listen to their tape because he thinks its a fuckin' disaster. He can't believe that they are destroying the name. He told me himself.*

<u>What he really means</u>: **No. Jason Flom told me that he won't go see them or listen to their tape because he thinks its a fuckin' disaster. But you know what, dude? I just realized that if Jason said he didn't listen to them or see them, then how would he fuckin' know if they were a disaster or not? Oh well, fuck it. Jason Flom is a big time music industry weasel so you can't really believe the shit he says. He probably offered them a 10 record deal for all I know.**

<u>Question</u>: Is it difficult having your wife as a manager?

<u>Sebitchian</u>: *Nah, it's great. She's the only person I trust.*

<u>What he really means</u>: **It's great. While she manages my career straight into a downward abyss of shit and piss, I'm in hotels fucking Kendra Jade type chicks. It's great. She's probably jacking me of half my money though, but I'm too stoned and stupid to give a fuck.**

<u>Question</u>: Have you had manager problems in the past?

<u>Sebitchian</u>: *Let's just put it this way, I was asked to join Judas Priest before Ripper, but Doc McGhee, my manager at the time, never told me about it. I didn't find out until it was too late. He wanted to keep me in Skid Row, but then that blew up, so whatever.*

<u>What he really means</u>: **Let's just put it this way, I had managers give me a lot of shit. For some unknown fucking reason they get all stressed when you throw bottles at fans, or insult some cocksuckers, or put your foot in your mouth time and time again. They get all uppity when you walk out on interviews or come off like a total jackass on a late night talk show. Doc was always on my ass about that shit and it gets old after a while. I'm much happier having my wife manage me because if she gets out of line I'll just slap the ho!**

<u>Question</u>: Is it true that you were vying for the lead singer position in Van Halen just before they hired Gary Cherone?

<u>Sebitchian</u>: *No, that was a crazy rumor. There was nothing going on. I think it came from Howard Stern saying I should be their singer. It's totally not true.*

<u>What he really means</u>: **No, that's not true. I didn't try to weasel my way into Van Halen until AFTER Cherone left? Got it? Then I was practically begging for the job during every interview I did and even started the rumor that VH was interested in me. Of course Eddie wouldn't even let me take out his trash, let alone be in his band.**

Question: Eddie Van Halen often speaks about LSD - Lead Singer's Disease. Do you think you suffer from that?

Sebitchian: *The only time I did LSD was back when I used to hang out in arcades.*

What he really means: **The only time I did LSD was back when I used to hang out in arcades...which was at least 2 days ago.**

Question: Let me put it this way...do you have an inflated ego?

Sebitchian: *Dude, what do you think? Yes, I have a big ego. Anybody who gets on stage has a big ego. Every single rock star in the world is conceited, especially Eddie Van Halen. How about GPD - Guitar Player's Disease? If there is such a thing as lead singer's disease, I have an incurable cause and I'm proud of it.*

What he really means: **Dude, my ego is so big when it thunders I take a bow. Gene Simmons ain't got shit on me mother trucker! I'm out of clever things to say down here.**

By OZZY STILLBOURNE (www.Metal-Sludge.com)

Staff at Metal Sludge:
Donna Anderson: donnaanderson@metal-sludge.com
Dana Brittingham: dana@metal-sludge.com
Courtney Ford: courtney@metal-sludge.com
bastard boy floyd: bbf@metal-sludge.com
Lita Love: litalove@metal-sludge.com
Jani Bon Neil: jani@metal-sludge.com
Taime "Sex" Slaughter: taime@metal-sludge.com
Ozzy Stillbourne: ozzy@metal-sludge.com

Thank you Metal Sludge!

CHAPTER 28
CRAZY NIGHTS
BY WENDY MOORE

(Excerpt from Wendy Moore's new book, *INTO THE VOID... WITH ACE FREHLEY*)

Another fun night, Peter Criss came over for the costume fitting for the much anticipated reunion tour. Ace wanted me to greet Peter and the costume designer lady at the door wearing a Catholic schoolgirl uniform. I surprised Ace one time by coming out of my apartment wearing it. I even had my hair in pigtails. I never met Peter before that night. Peter got a kick out of me answering the door that way.

After Peter broke the toilet seat in the guest bathroom he came back out with his black unitard halfway on. I snuck around the kitchen with my camera to take pictures of the fitting. I got one photo of Peter and the costume designer fussing with him. Ace was in the background sitting on the couch grinning because he saw me. Peter looked so funny, like he really wasn't enjoying this one bit. I noticed that he had the number 3 tattooed on his arm. I told him that was "my" number and to take it off. He laughed. I loved his thick, New York accent. It seemed to be the heaviest out of the whole band. When it came time for Ace to be fitted, he was bragging that he was the only one who could still fit into his original costume.

I'll never forget the day that I met the whole band. I had to pick up Ace from Cole Studios where they were rehearsing. I don't know why it didn't dawn on me that I would probably see the entire band, but it didn't. I walked into the studio and asked the men at the front desk what room *KISS* was in. They hesitated to answer but I professionally said, "I'm here to pick up Ace. I'm his personal assistant."

They pointed down the hall to the last room. As I walked down the hall, the singer from *Rage Against The Machine*, Zack de la Rocha, walked out of a studio. At that moment, I was wishing my brother was with me. Rage is one of his favorite bands. When I got to the room Ace was rehearsing in, I opened the door and just stood there staring at everyone staring at me. At that moment I realized that I was in a room with the four original band members of *KISS*.

Ace quickly introduced me as his personal assistant. I could barely see Peter in the back of the room

Ace Frehley on the couch while Peter Criss is measured for the KISS re-union tour

behind a drum set. Paul was sitting on a sofa to the right of me wearing a pink bandanna. I sat down next to him and smiled politely. I noticed Gene in the corner of my eye sitting on a stool wearing black leather pants and a baseball cap. I assumed that both he and Paul were covering up their thinning hair, but I wasn't sure. Gene said hello to me with an annoyed tone of voice, as if he was angry that I didn't really seem to notice him or make a big deal about him. I politely said hello back.

After their break, they began to work on one of the newer songs. Peter seemed to have trouble keeping up. Gene seemed annoyed. They squabbled over new ideas for the song. Without realizing I began to sing along because I heard Ace playing the demo at home.

Gene pointed and yelled at me, "Hey!! You there! Stop singing, please stop singing!" I sank in my seat. Ace looked like he felt sorry for me. I was glad when they were finished and their roadies came in to pack up their gear. Ace and I took off.

Back home, I let Ace listen to the demos that I was working on. He liked a song that my band did called *Mystic Lady*. It was a *T-Rex* cover. Surprisingly, Ace told me he had never heard of *T-Rex* or *Marc Bolan* before and thought it was one of my originals. He offered to come down to the studio with me sometime and play on the song. I was delighted. He told me "it would be a nice change from the pressures of recording with *KISS*." I told my producer about it and he was excited to meet Ace. So we planned on a night.

When the night finally came, Ace asked me who would be at the studio. He

Ace's turn to be fitted for the KISS re-union tour

was worried about me having tons of friends hanging out and stuff like that. I told him that it would be just the band and my brother. (Little did Ace know, my brother was going to secretly videotape the session.) Ace had to get all ready with his "going out" make-up on (base, powder, and black eyeliner.) He got dressed up with all of his rings and necklaces. It was time to leave, but we ran into a problem. Ace could not find his stash of coke (He never left home without it). I nervously sat by the phone, chain smoking and telling my producer how sorry I was that we were running so late. I was hoping that he wouldn't charge me for the time. Ace completely destroyed his bedroom and it was right after I just cleaned it up. He threw everything everywhere. It was like a hurricane hit the place. I stayed clear while he yelled and cussed. He finally found the coke on a shelf in his closet after he had accused me of taking it, of course.

Ace would always accuse me of stealing his drugs. I remember trying a valium for the first time with Ace one night. I told him how much I loved it before I passed out. Unpredictably, he woke up before me the next morning. He grabbed the bottle of valium that he had by his bedside and shook it next to his ear and looked at me with suspicion.

I said, "What?"

He said in an accusing tone, "Some of my pills are missing" as if he could tell just how many pills were in the bottle by the sound.

I said, "You're crazy, not only did I go to sleep before you but I woke up after you. I didn't and wouldn't take your pills!"

He said that he was sure that I took some because of how much I said I liked them the night before. He never did believe me. Even to this day, he probably thinks that I stole some.

There was another time when a bunch of us were hanging out in Ace's condo when Ace, out of nowhere, announced to everyone, "I'm going to leave this room. And when I come back in, I don't care who took them, but they better put my pills back onto the coffee table."

He stormed out of the room for about thirty seconds... during that time we stared at each other incredulously. When he came back in he stared at the empty coffee table like Hitler. It was really funny. He ended up finding his pills right where he had left them. He always accused people of stealing his drugs. And when he found out otherwise there was never an apology. It was just part of the drug-induced paranoia.

One time, I tried to stop him from mailing a bill payment back to himself. He yelled at me and said, "What are you, an idiot?!"

When I was finally able to show him what he was doing wrong, I said, "Do you want to mail this bill back to yourself?"

He didn't say a word... he probably felt stupid. This incident warranted an apology. Again, he would never apologize.

The only time that Ace and I noticed when someone actually did take something was when the one hundred dollar bill that we used to snort cocaine had magically turned into a one-dollar bill by the end of the night. Come to think of it, that happened a couple of times!

Anyway, we finally made it to my recording session almost two hours late. I was a nervous wreck driving there. If you couldn't answer him right away when he asked how much longer it would be before we got to our destination he would throw a fit. He has zero patience.

Once at the studio though, his mood turned around. We made "a trip" to the bathroom together before we got started. Ace played a twelve string acoustic guitar that I had to borrow from the Guitar Center (all of Ace's instruments were locked up in *KISS'* studio). I was surprised at how bold my producer, Alex, was when it came to telling Ace what was good and what wasn't. I sat behind the console with Alex looking in at Ace while he played. My brother was in a dark room-videotaping Ace.

We noticed a problem with the recording. There was a strange sound that was appearing on the tape. We finally figured out what it was and had to stop recording. It was the sound of Ace's breathing (He always sounded like he had a stuffed up nose). We didn't know what to do about it. We tried moving the mic around, but that didn't work. I even took my bra off at one point and put it over the mic to muffle the sound. Finally, a piece of T-shirt material worked. We nicknamed Ace Darth Vader for the entire recording session.

The final result was amazing though. You would never guess that the beautiful acoustic guitar that you hear on my song is Ace Frehley. I love it. Then he laid down some awesome leads on some of my other tracks.

I hadn't eaten anything since the day before, and it was now around five or six a.m. By this time, my stomach was really hurting badly from lack of food. I couldn't wait for them to be done. I fell asleep on the couch for a little bit.

Ace did me another favor that night. He paid the rest of the money that I owed Alex for my demo - one thousand four hundred dollars. Ace probably felt

Ace Frehley in the studio with Wendy Moore

guilty for making us so late. I was so tired and hungry that I just wanted to leave. Finally, about an hour and a half later, we were able to leave.

We drove back over Laurel Canyon when Ace wanted me to stop at a newsstand. It ended up being another forty-five minutes of waiting. He took his time and browsed through the rock and porno magazines. It seemed like forever! I could have just died. I cannot even describe to you the horrible, empty, chemical feeling that I was feeling in the pit of my stomach. I wasn't even sure if I would be able to eat once I got near some food, that's how bad it was. I will never forget that awful feeling as long as I live. It was sick. I was living on a terrible diet of cocaine and one or two meals a day. I was pencil-thin and some of my friends were getting concerned. I know that my brother was the most concerned. It had gotten so bad that I was literally losing my mind with cocaine and my brother threatened to call the police on Ace. I begged him not to. But I can sort of see why, now. I was five foot eleven inches and weighed one-hundred-eighteen pounds! (My normal weight is around one-hundred-forty pounds.) Even my chiropractor commented about my weight. But I really thought that I looked good at the time.

Ace finally bought a couple of magazines and got in the car. I couldn't wait to get through the canyon to the AMPM. I pulled up and scampered out of the car and ran inside the store. I grabbed a cheeseburger and shoved it into my face, then I grabbed another and went over to the condiments and started piling relish and ketchup on it. Ace just stared at me. He had never had their burgers before. He tried one and seemed to really like them. I've always loved them and on this particular night, they tasted especially good. I even took a third one for the road!

It was April 27th, 1998 - Ace's 47th birthday. Eric Singer came over to give Ace a birthday present. He got Ace an electronic drum kit. They spent all day setting it up in the living room and playing around with it. I made hors d'oeuvres in the kitchen. I made a bed of cream cheese with cocktail sauce, topped with fresh baby shrimp on a large glass platter. Then I laid out a plate of triskets to scoop it up with. It was really good. I'm not the best cook in the world and thank God, with Ace, I didn't have to be. The blond girl (Editor's note: mentioned previously in Wendy Moore's book *Into The Void... with Ace Frehley*) was coming over to bring Ace a dinner that she and a girlfriend had made. She didn't know that I was going to be there. She thought that she and her friend were going to have a

Eric Singer and Ace Frehley

double-dinner date with Ace and Eric. The crushing blow for her when she arrived was seeing me lounging in the living room on the couch. She pretended not to be bothered by my presence. It was a good Italian meal and we had tons of leftovers that I ended up taking home. During dinner, Ace and I would slip off to the bathroom, one at a time, to do lines. I don't even think Eric knew what was going on.

At the dining room table, we got on the subject of men and women and Eric got so burned up over the topic it was hilarious! I don't remember exactly what it was that bothered him so much, but he was a little "hot-head!" I think he has some sort of Napoleonic complex. It's so transparent in the way that he acts all of the time. He tries to make up for the fact that he's short by talking about women in a very demeaning manner. He can be extremely offensive. I tried to ignore him most of the time. He always asked me if I had any girlfriends for him, ones with big tits. I wondered why he would want that because a big-breasted woman would only make him look smaller! Eric is your typical "male pig."

Ace wasn't so bad. Sometimes he would say things on purpose to make me jealous about other women. That was about it. He even had the decency to watch his porno DVDs in the other room after I had gone to sleep. He knew how much I hated them. He could have easily taunted me with them. I'm not a prude. I just draw the line at people who get paid to spread their legs and have sex for money. I don't have a problem with tasteful nudity.

One time, while Ace was in bed looking at a magazine called Barely Legal (which features eighteen-year-old girls that look under aged) I was able to get back at him a little. As he showed me a spread of a girl that he thought was "hot," I replied, "Yeah, she's about the same age as your daughter, Monique, huh?" I hope that made him think a little. It didn't seem to phase him.

Ace has a fetish for hermaphrodites. He took me to a porno shop on Hollywood Boulevard one night. He was always trying to find videos with chicks with dicks (Hey guys, wake up. I think you might be in denial if you like that sorta stuff. It's guys with tits… not chicks with dicks!!!). We ended up getting a couple of videos for him and an assortment of sex toys. I got a small white vibrator to replace the one that I already had, which got so over-heated it cracked! Ace also got me this vibrating butterfly that you wear in your underwear, almost like the belts that women used to hold their maxi-pads in place with. It had a long electrical cord that had a remote on the end of it to control its vibrating speed. The butterfly would then vibrate right on top of your clitoris (I call it "the bean"). I tried it but I didn't really like it and never used it again. It sat in a basket full of sex toys by Ace's side of the bed. He also bought this weird contraption, which had different attachments (some of them looked pretty scary!). It also had a remote. I had no idea what it was supposed to do.

Then there was the "vibrating egg". Ace would want me to insert this egg into his ass while he controlled the vibrations. I didn't particularly enjoy doing this, but he sure did! He jerked off while I did this. I don't want to say what I once found on the end of the egg. When I pulled it out, I don't think it was a Baby Ruth. I would sometimes find some of the sex toys (that had the stranger attachments on them) rusted on the floor in the shower. I'm not quite sure what had been going on in there but there sure were some long showers!

Ace always told me that I was like a man because I was the tallest girl that he had ever been with. He said it felt like he was fucking a guy! He also said that I am the weirdest girl that he had ever met because nothing he did would gross me out. And that was truly tested on this one particular day.

I don't know if you are aware of this but if you do a lot of cocaine it gives you diarrhea. Sometimes it is cut with baby laxatives. I came out of the bathroom when I noticed Ace squatting on the floor in the nude. He was crouched in front of the TV, fidgeting around with the VCR. Suddenly he had a really strange look on his face like a little boy who had just done something wrong. He felt around on the floor behind him and then grabbed a napkin and started wiping. I walked over to see what he was doing and found a small light brown spot on the floor. He grabbed a throw rug and attempted to try to cover it up.

As he walked away, I asked him calmly, "Did you just crap on the floor?" He started laughing. I went into the kitchen and found the "Resolve" carpet cleaner and cleaned it up. If I ever go back to house-cleaning, I can tell them, "Believe me, I've seen it all!"

So, back to Ace's birthday - After dinner, Ace and I had plans to meet the rest of the band to celebrate his birthday at The Roxy Theater with *Cheap Trick*. The Roxy is another popular club on Sunset Boulevard that is right next door to The Rainbow Bar and Grill. I wore the most expensive dress that I had. It cost me three hundred and seventy dollars. It was a beautiful black gown that was short in the front and had two long tails in the back, like a tuxedo jacket. Two spaghetti straps held up a low, sexy neckline. I was also wearing my new black velvet platform boots that made me as tall as Gene (around six foot four). I was so upset that there was no film in my camera that night.

We all sat at a small table in The Roxy and watched *Cheap Trick* play. At one point, they shined a spotlight on Ace, who was seated right next to me, and wished him a happy birthday. Ace waved to the crowd. Then before I knew it, all these new best friends of mine, that I didn't know I had, came up to our table and tried to squeeze in and sit with us. There was absolutely no room but they all tried. The place was extremely crowded and very, very hot. I tried to make a joke to Paul by saying, "It's hotter than hell in here!" but I got no reaction out of him. He either didn't get it or heard it a million times. Everyone took off his or her jackets and shirts because it was so hot but Gene kept his leather jacket on the entire time. Ace noticed this and said that he was probably afraid to take his jacket off (even though he had to be boiling in it) because he was so fat. During the show, I had to go to the restroom. It was really hard squeezing out from the table and through the crowd. I found my brother and told him to meet us at The Rainbow afterwards. When I tried to return to my seat, Gene noticed me having trouble climbing over a metal bar, which stood between the table and me. He reached his hand out and pulled me over with such force that my pantihose caught on the rail and got ripped to shreds. Thankfully Gene didn't notice. I was grateful for his "gentleman-like" help. Especially after our first impression of each other from our first meeting... I was very surprised! After the show, we got to go backstage to meet *Cheap Trick*. I got a personalized guitar pick from Rick Nielsen.

I remember when I saw *Cheap Trick* play at The Whisky a Go-Go a long time ago; Rick was in a really bad mood on stage and knocked over all of his guitar amps. They came dangerously close to the audience. Then he destroyed his trademark guitar (the one that looks like him). I will never forget that show. It was awful. I also remember how turned off I was when they had topless girls on the stage wearing panties with the words *"Cheap Trick"* on the back of them. Gene was at that show too. He was wearing black leather pants that had a hole on each side, where his outer thighs shown through. (To this day, I have never seen Gene wear any other kind of pants but black leather!) I tried to chase after him for an autograph for my friend, Marlene but he disappeared backstage.

After everyone was done visiting backstage, we went next door to The Rainbow. The band, Ace's guitar tech, a few other friends and I squeezed into a crescent shaped booth in the middle of the dining room. My brother and a friend sat at another table across from us. Ace asked them to move when they attempted to sit with us. The rest of the band hadn't sat down yet so they were saving the seats. We ordered a pizza and Ace ordered one for my brother and his friend at their table.

When I ordered a coffee, Ace leaned over to me and whispered, "That was very good of you to do that in front of Gene."

Gene didn't want Ace hanging out with a girl that drank because he was under contract with *KISS* that said he could not drink or take narcotics of any kind. I rarely ever drank anyway. I guess Ace didn't really know that about me but I would have gotten that coffee whether Gene was there or not.

During dinner, Gene pointed at my brother and asked out loud, "Who's that blond guy?" He thought he was a musician or something and was probably wondering why Ace ordered a pizza for him. My brother has long red hair. I guess it looked almost strawberry-blond in the dark, but it's pretty orange in color. Ace repeatedly said people who were born with red hair have "The Curse."

Gene spotted a girl in the booth behind ours looking over at us. She was very plain looking and wasn't wearing any makeup. She had a horrible 80's permed hairstyle on a weird small head, but she did have a huge set of "knockers." Gene most likely just saw her huge breasts as the rest of her appearance didn't matter. If Gene did have a preference, he tended to go for over-weight big-breasted women. In fact, every time he would see Ace and I he would tell Ace to "feed that girl!"

The weird headed girl got up out of her seat and walked towards us. Gene had a huge grin on his face as he seductively motioned with his finger to come over to him. Then something happened that was right out of *Spinal Tap*. The girl came up to our table walked right past Gene. She kneeled down in front of Ace and told him how much she loved him. It was hilarious. Gene's ego was embarrassingly smashed for the moment. He felt like such a fool. She talked to Ace for a while and then went back to her seat. No one said a thing.

Ace accidentally dropped his napkin under the table between my feet. As he bent over between my legs to reach for it I pushed down on his head with both of my hands and simulated him giving me a "blowjob." Gene laughed hysterically trying to act as if he was still in a good mood after that pitiful humiliation. Ace got up with his hair in a mess wondering why Gene was laughing so hard.

The night wound down and we all got ready to leave. We stood out in the parking lot and waited for the valet to retrieve our cars. Ace went off by himself to get his own car. I was left standing next to Gene.

Gene broke the awkward silence, "You know, I didn't like you at first but you are like 'one of the guys' with the way that you made me laugh in there." He then apologized for the way that he acted when we first met. I gave him a long hug and told him how nice it felt to hug a big, tall man. I'm not sure what it was but Gene did have something sexy about him. It certainly had nothing to do with his hair, though. That was the one thing that I didn't understand about him. Everyone who sees him says the same thing about his hair, "What the hell is that thing?" I don't understand how someone who has the money like he has, does not get a really good hair transplant or something. I also wondered why his loved ones don't say anything to him about it. Doesn't he know what it looks like? His hair looks like a fuzzy turban of black cotton candy, swirled around on top of his head. It's truly awful.

During our brief conversation, we got on the subject of band names. He told me that he didn't like the name, *Venus Envy*. (This is coming from the man who wanted to call *Van Halen*, "Daddy Long-legs!") He then asked me if I knew of any bands that have made it using a silly name.

I answered, "Yes, *KISS*!" He stood stone-faced. I didn't even get a chuckle. I figured I should quit while I was ahead and said, "It's a joke silly." By this time, Ace had pulled the car up and watched us talk. He honked the horn for me to get into the car! After a brief goodbye with Gene I got into the car and Ace queried me on what Gene and I talked about. I explained our conversation and I told him that Gene apologized to me. Ace couldn't believe it! He said that Gene never apologizes to anyone and that he must like me. It was an offhanded jealous remark. I should've replied, "Then why don't you ever apologize to me?" but the thought didn't enter my mind at that moment.

When we got home I had a little present for him. I gave him an ashtray that was shaped like a Spade (as on a gambling card), and it was made out of clear crystal and then inside was a joint. It was cool. We got stoned and watched another of our favorite movies, *Kingpin*. Ace loved the part in the movie where Bill Murray sees Woody's cut-off hand for the first time and says, "... Creepy." We laughed our heads off over that part. Whenever he calls me on the phone that's what he says to me. He said that he put it into his cell phone that way, so that other girls wouldn't know who he was calling, or who I was, when I was calling him. They would always assume that Creepy was a man. Ace also loved the part in the movie, where the guy got burned in the face with coffee and jumped out the window like a girl! We must have rewound that part a million times over.

The next night, Ace wanted to see *James Brown* at The House Of Blues. So I called Ace's management and got us on the guest list. That was one of the neat things about being a rock star. You can go to any show you want for free and always go backstage. I experienced what it felt like to be a rock star because of Ace. Whenever he went out of town, I would still be able to get into nightclubs with my friends for free. The people who worked the doors would always remember me and say, "that's Ace Frehley's girlfriend, let her in." If I went to the Rainbow without him I heard people whisper as I would pass by, "Hey, there goes Ace Frehley's girlfriend!"

We had a lot of fun at *James Brown*. We didn't go backstage or anything. We just stayed in the V.I.P. section and had dinner while we enjoyed the show. Kate Hudson sat in the same section that we were in. I had hoped to see Goldie Hawn with her but she wasn't. I found *James Brown* to be a bit contrived, with all of his sequined capes that were constantly being put on him during his show that said "King" on the back of them. But I guess it was all right. He's in his seventies for crying out loud. Ace had a good time. He sort of caused a scene though. He got so drunk he leaned on a tall round table and tipped it over. Luckily my brother was there to catch it! My brother was tagging along with us a lot and Ace began to like him. You could say they became very good friends.

I enjoyed doing the simple things for Ace, like his laundry. Like most men, you have to empty all of their pockets in their pants before you throw them into the load, otherwise you never know what you could be washing. My guitar pick collection grew and grew with every load I did. One time I was surprised to find a personalized Gene Simmons guitar pick. That was a nice surprise as I didn't have one yet. The only thing that I never found in Ace's pockets was money!

As I washed Ace's socks and underwear I would think about some of the things that make him different than the rest of the band. You see, Ace really lives as the "Space Man" on and off stage. He is true to form, which is something that I always admired about my favorite performers. For example, Stevie Nicks isn't putting on a costume to perform. She dresses like a gypsy all of the time. I appreciate that in an artist. I think that Ace's fans would really appreciate to know that

the same applies for him. For example, his underwear and socks all have little pictures of rockets, spaceships, glow-in-the-dark alien heads, and Ace cards, etc... It's really cute. He told me that Gene calls him,

Left to right: Ace Frehley, Wendy Moore, Gene Simmons, Peter Criss, Shannon Tweed and Gina Criss

"Socks Frehley." He also wears cute pajamas that have the same sort of space themes all over them. Ace also enjoys wearing clothes with pictures of celebrities that he is in awe of, like Marilyn Monroe and Jimi Hendrix. He has lots of silver and metallic colored shirts and jackets. He even has a pair of metallic blue high-top tennis shoes! I found a really cool dark green button-up shirt with Ace cards all over it from the 70's at a store on Melrose called, Wasteland (They specialize in vintage rags). It's one of the only stores that I love to shop in. I surprised him with the shirt when he returned from one of his short trips to New York. It was perfect for him.

Ace also keeps the gifts from fans. His room is filled with space-alien key chains that light up, alien figurines, rocket ship toys, and lots of silver jewelry. He personally receives all of his fan mail but he doesn't have time to respond to any of them. He said that whenever his girlfriend in New York went through his fan mail for him she would get too jealous and angry about the girls that were writing to him. He says he doesn't have time to read them but he'll usually open the ones that have more than just a letter in the envelope. He loves pictures and jokes. I laughed at the girls that would send their photos. Some of them looked so cheesey, wearing these awful silver 80's clothes. But Ace thought it was cute. If he really

Graffito found on a public bathroom wall

liked the way the girl looked he would actually call them! He doesn't like depressing mail. I remember one fan letter from a girl who also sent a photo of herself. She was blond and over-weight and wrote about how she was dying. He couldn't continue reading it. Then there were the letters from little kids that were so cute. I remember one in particular from a little boy named Melvin. Ace thought that his name was cute and kept repeating the way that Melvin signed his letter in a little boy's voice. Instead, Ace sounded more like Marvin the Martian in the Bugs Bunny cartoon. You know the one, "Where's the KABOOM? There was supposed to be an earth shattering KABOOM!!"

Ace used to wear this one chain that had a lightning bolt on the end of it. The reason he doesn't wear it anymore is because he said that it used to stab girls in the chest when he was having sex with them. He also said that he only had sex one time while he was wearing his *KISS* makeup. One girl begged him. So he did. It ended up getting all over the place, all over the girl, all over the bed. That was the last time.

To get back to the point that I was first making - you never see Gene Simmons running around town wearing T-shirts with demons on them, do you? That's what separates Ace from Gene and Paul. Ace never made up a fake name

Ace Frehley and Wendy Moore

like they did. I know what you're thinking… Ace is a made up name. Ace got that nickname way before *KISS*. He was called Ace in high school. I don't know why Stanley Eisen (Paul Stanley) would want to name himself Paul. Especially when there was already another real "Paul" in the band. Duh? (Ace's real name is Paul Frehley.) Paul has changed his makeup two times, indicating that he really doesn't know who he is. Peter is into his persona a little bit more than Gene and Paul are too. I also feel that he's a little more real, like Ace. That's maybe why they get along so well. Ace also told me that he used to be friends with Blackie Lawless, and he would watch him turn from Steve to "Blackie." He would become a totally different person. Ace is always the same, on and offstage. In fact, that's the best compliment that I have ever received about my own stage performances! What you see is what you get, all of the time!

CHAPTER 29
NO MORE MR. NICE GUY!

Michael Bruce (original guitarist from the Alice Cooper band) was playing a place in Clementon, NJ called Baron's. I had a chance to chat with him prior to his show. We went down memory lane a bit. I asked him how he felt about Alice's snakes.

Michael Bruce: Actually, that was not his snake. It was drummer Neal Smith's snake. This girl gave Neal the snake when were down in Hollywood, Florida. Neal took it around on the road and as a general rule we made anybody that traveled with us part of the show. They had to work with us to earn their way. Neal's sister traveled with us and she was the nurse that put Alice in the straight-jacket. She also made our clothes. We got everybody into the act. I liked the snake.

We were staying in Knoxville, Tennessee when the snake got loose and we couldn't find it anywhere. We even looked down the toilet. We had put it in the bathtub with water before it disappeared. We pretty much gave up looking for it and considered the snake officially M.I.A.. About two or three months later, the people that lived there started smelling this smell. It had climbed up in the back of a big radio (this was still back when they had tubes in radios). It had climbed up in there to get warm around the tubes and it just starved to death. Neal was really upset but Alice just kept getting them because they had become so popular. Even after the band broke up in 1975 Alice kept using them as part of his act.

As a rule "we" didn't really trash too many hotel rooms... there isn't that many tour bus stories because we used a jet to get around back then. I did meet this girl once and I kinda kidnapped her for three days (laughter). We got into the "Mile High Club" before there was a Mile High Club at the time. The plane that we had was called "The Starship" and it had a bed on it. It was really neat. We had it before *Led Zeppelin*.

One of my most memorable concerts was in Brazil. We had the largest indoor audience ever, 125,000 people. It was really interesting. By the time we got to the third song the people started standing and pushing towards the front. It was obvious they hadn't had a lot of rock shows there. It looked like a wave breaking. The stage was fifteen feet high and the bodies just kept piling up and up. The military came out and

Michael Bruce

shot off a machine gun and took us off the stage. We found out how the military government worked down there. They picked us up from the airport and led us towards the concert down the wrong way of a freeway with jeeps armed with machine guns. They made the cars pull over as we were going the opposite direction. It was crazy! I felt like *The Beatles*! At the time, they hadn't had many rock stars down there.

Website: www.MichaelBruce.com

After Lynn's interview with Michael Bruce I did some follow-up research and I found a lot of people had many problems with Michael. Here is a letter I received from one former manager, Dan Tuttle.

To Whom It May Concern:

I am here today telling everybody what's been going on, since everybody can tell that I am not Michael Bruce's manager anymore. I was working without a contract, but Michael had specifically asked me to be his manager. At first, I really didn't want to do the managing, but both Michael's former band and Michael really wanted me in, so I decided to take the job. Michael didn't have anything going for him other than fan conventions, etc... My partner and I were helping him to get back into the music where he wants to be - or where we thought he wanted to be; it certainly doesn't seem as if he wants to be a reputable musician after all. We created a music scene for him by coming up with the idea and putting together the U.K. tour, getting interviews for him, all kinds of things. If it had not been for my ideas, there wouldn't have been anything to manage.

At the time, my partner and I were also doing his new website, www.michaelbruceofalicecooper.com. I came up with the idea to use the two names "Alice and Michael" together for an address so people can find it better on the net. I bought the address and we built the site up from scratch, which took a lot of my partner's and my time. A lot of money went into that site straight out of our pockets. Michael never paid a dime to us for ANY of our actual money put into the site nor our time for building and maintaining the site. Nor did we ever make enough money selling his products to even cover the simple hosting fee per month.

Michael has a really big drug problem. He is into smoking crack, doing Methedrine, and some other drugs. I cannot stop him from doing it; he loves his drug habits and even brags about it. Michael drops everything for the drugs. That's what happened in L.A. at the GBMW (Glen Buxton Memorial Weekend). He hid from everybody because he was on a drug binge. He showed up at the Whisky without even a soundcheck, no rehearsal, no nothing. Even there, he was doing drugs; he and the girl that he brought there were sniffing coke backstage.

While he and his girlfriend were doing drugs, he blew off his U.K. band (big-time Cooper idols) that came there all the way from overseas (paid their own way) SPECIFICALLY to play at the Whisky with him. They were horribly let down; it really hurt them real bad-it was so bad that their wives were crying about it. I really think Michael did it on purpose, because they are a much better band than his band from Texas and he resented the fact that the band I got together in the U.K. was better than his Texas band. Don't get me wrong: Michael's Texas band is very good as individual musicians, but they had not been able to practice because of Michael's blowing them off time after time all the time, so of course they weren't as good together as the U.K. band at the Whisky. I feel really bad that they didn't get to practice enough before the GBMW, but that's how Michael is: just throw it together, go on stage, and HOPE it sounds alright.

An acquaintance of mine recently told me that Michael told him that his big "career goal", "plan for life", is to use fans and good people that he comes across-use them and milk them for all it's worth and then dump them. Unfortunately, I found that out too late. I was trying to get something going so we could get some kind of money flow coming in, but that was nothing but a pipe dream. Michael has no drive to make money and live respectably. All he wants to do is sponge off other good people that are willing to help him out; then he'll use them until they're drained and after that, he'll trash them out like he did Jeff Jatras, various people, and even Alice, himself. Some of these people are really nice people.

As for me, I got a lot of money invested in him; I didn't count on getting all of that initial investment back; I didn't think that would be possible. I wanted to help him out and get him back on the road and at least eventually make enough money off of that to make things turn around and make a profit. The website was not making any money either. When I started the website there were a lot of orders that got mailed to Michael. He kept the money, but never sent out the stuff they paid for. By the time I found that out, some of the stuff was months old. I had to use my own money to package and ship it out. A lot of time went to e-mailing people about it just to get everybody happy and keep the website from looking like a rip-off. I even found out about people that paid for stuff, BEFORE I took over being Michael's manager, that never got their products and I had to take care of those and pay for it out of my own pocket, too.

I wanted to change the bad image that Michael has. I wanted to start a new up-beat look and wanted to stop all the bad stuff that was going on at the time on all the e-groups, but, as I've finally realized, he did a lot of bad things to people and most of them are good people that he shit on. One of the things that Michael does to people after he uses them up is to trash them out on e-groups and tell people lies about them so he looks like he was a victim. That's what's going on right now with me and my partner.

Michael lost his apartment-didn't pay the rent-and ended up staying with me. He was just only supposed to stay here when he was in town doing rehearsals with his band. I had no problem with that but that was the door for him to take advantage of the situation. He ended up staying permanently for about a year. That really put things into a nosedive-he'd make overseas phone calls constantly. I got bills that were over a $1000.00 in long distance charges and sky-high electric bills, etc...

I've never been able to catch up on the bills he created and the only way out for me is to file bankruptcy or lose everything I've got, including my house.

Just to show what kind of person he is: I am a very sick person; I got kidney failure, lost 85% of my kidneys. I've been in and out of the hospital all year long, got real problems with my heart and almost died once already from it. Michael didn't even care about it; he never helped out. He was too busy watching the Simpsons and cleaning my refrigerator out. That took all of his time every day. He couldn't even sign autographs for fans or products we wanted to sell on the website. NO, that was too hard to do; it took too much of his effort and time.

Michael does come across like a good person and he is a fun person to be around when he's not doing drugs. But his bad side is what you have to look out

Michael Bruce hard at work.

192

for and everybody's got to know he is out for himself-nobody else. He will get you to spend lots of money on him and you will be run into the ground and he won't care about it; that's what he did to us and he has no plans of paying anybody back. That's how he works.

As for the website, that's the only thing I got left to sell off to try to get some of the money back we put into it. Michael didn't want us doing it anymore, because I got a girl as a partner and he has a problem with women getting involved in his business. She works with me as a partner taking care of things that I don't have time for and she does a good job of it; she worked very hard and long hours on the site and she didn't do anything wrong, but Michael hates her guts for no reason. I was about to update the site with new graphics and stuff to try to make it work one more time for the new CD that was coming out. But when I talked to a friend of mine, I found out that he was told by Michael that Michael didn't like the site, that Michael said it was all screwed up. Then Michael said he did like the site, but he didn't want a girl working on it because, like I said before, he hates businesswomen's guts. There was nothing wrong with the site itself. She did a lot for him and she didn't get anything from him-nothing but bad things and hurting her feelings.

Now that Michael is about to move on to the next person to use - he's used me all up now since I have no money and I'm filing bankruptcy, he thinks he can just simply demand me to hand the site over to somebody else for free like he doesn't owe anything for it. I own the domain name; I built the site up from scratch; I paid for everything. I'm not going to hand the site over for nothing.

All the stuff you are seeing going on at the e-groups, etc... is all about the website; that started everything that you see. Michael is mad that I will not hand over the site to him for free. I e-mailed him what I want from him for it. The answer I got was that he was going to come over and kick my door in, do bodily harm to me and my partner and take our computers and all the stuff that he claimed I stole from him.

Well, on January 6, 2002, he did come over and busted my door up and he didn't finish it, because my neighbors, who came out of their houses to see what was going on, saw him. So he ran back to the truck that he borrowed to do this and drove off. But what he didn't know was that I was at home and I did see him going to his truck after he tried to break in. Now my partner is having a nervous breakdown; she is walking around the house and office with a butcher knife in her hand and her cell phone ready for a 911 call all the time when I am at work or not at home. We pressed charges for a breaking and entering; there is a warrant out for his arrest, but apparently he is on the run since the cops can't find him. We will not drop charges, so anyone that has any contact with him: please know that he is wanted by the law.

I am also being affected with my kidneys and heart problems; it's been very hard on me. I didn't sleep for two days, always on the watch. Can't sleep knowing he will return-which he did that same night, watching my place to see if anybody was home but he saw me looking out the window so he drove off. Anyway I ended up getting very sick over it; now I'm at home sick again and running out of sick time at work. This is all I need from him right now.

I am writing this to let everybody know what really is going on; I am not the person that he is trying to make me out to be. I really don't care what he says about me, but I don't like to be treated badly by everybody like I'm the second Jeff Jatras. I do not want to have anything to do with him anymore. I do have a real job that is the most important thing in the world to me and another thing is that Michael is trying to get me fired from my job. And if he did manage that, I will lose my health insurance; the insurance is the only thing that is keeping me alive. If I lose it, I will die within a year or so, since no other insurance will take me and most jobs will not take somebody that is sick. Michael doesn't care; he only worries about himself and how much harm he can do to people he's used up.

I do not like putting him down; I really did look up to him at one time and still do in some ways. But he will never change. Once a druggie, always a druggie.

That's all he is, but there is some good in him. He is a very nice person when he's off the drugs for awhile. I know he was drug-free when we did the U.K. tour and that was the best I saw him on stage since the Cooper breakup. He sounded really good and he was playing good.

His life would be a lot better for him if he would just quit taking drugs. I just wish he could see that. The 70's are over but he still thinks he's a teenage idol and living in that era. There's nothing we can do to help him; I know this now. All I want to do now is to get some of the money that he owes me and move on...

If anyone has any questions, you can email me at dtuttle@houston.rr.com or my partner, Torah Bontrager, at tbontrager@houston.rr.com.

Dan Tuttle / Torah Bontrager

{I would love to find out how that turns out!}

194

CHAPTER 30
TULSA

This rock star requested to remain anonymous.

Hey Gordon, I loved your book *KISS & Tell*. I've read it over and over. I kept your book with me on the road whenever I needed a great laugh. It was hard to keep my copy because the band and the road crew were constantly stealing it. An investigation would start every other night on the bus, "Alright, Who's got *KISS & Tell*? If you're not reading it at this moment please cough it up." I got so fed up we finally stopped by a Barnes and Noble and I actually bought the three remaining copies the store had so I could finally keep mine in peace.

My absolute favorite story was "Cow Cunt" (Chapter 40 - ironically entitled War Stories). I actually read that one out loud to the guys. I almost pissed in my pants when I first read it. It reminded us of when we played in New Jersey. The Meadowlands is one of the coolest venues. Jersey girls are the sluttiest in the country. Must be the water... or the stench! It reminds me of the old joke... "While making out with a hot babe, she got carried away and whispered to me - 'kiss me where it smells.' So I took her to New Jersey." Ohhhhhh - rimshot please. I love the other one by Andrew Dice Clay. "If I drop a dime on a broad, I'm gonna cum in her presence even if I have to jerk off chasing her up her driveway." Cracks me up every time I hear that.

We had a great system worked out with our crew when it came to groupies. We would actually have the crew secretly rate the girls on their willingness to participate in wild sex. Most girls will hook up with us for the old boring in-out-in-out, but only a few would do something really wild - as in "blow a donkey" wild! Our crew would question hot girls, "how bad do you want to meet the band?" Of course, all the girls would say they would do "ANYTHING" to meet us, but our crew could take the place of any lie detector machine. They knew when a chick was full of shit. The lying chicks would get an ordinary backstage "ass pass." They would think they're all hot shit as they strutted backstage to meet us. But meanwhile we had the "real" passes for the real wild ones. We called them TULSA passes. They were ass passes but with the word TULSA printed on the pass. Little did these girls know what the word "tulsa" meant. Even when they looked in the mirror to primp themselves before the band arrived they couldn't figure it out. Some of them would ask and we would tell them the passes were extras from an Oklahoma show.

This particular show in Jersey had a slew of Tulsa chicks backstage. As I scoped them all out, I spotted one that looked very familiar. I couldn't place where

I had seen her before. She was fucking hellacious! Her face was an ultra-beautiful version of Cher, gorgeous long dark hair, big Cheshire cat smile like Cameron Diaz, and a fucking body that was straight out of Penthouse... incredible tits and ass! As the Tulsa chicks were proving their Tulsa labeling by getting it on with each other, it dawned on me where I had seen this chick before. A friend of mine started dating her and e-mailed me several pictures of them together. I knew she looked familiar.

She was in a loose mood, making out with a gorgeous Pamela Anderson look-alike. They were both feeling each other's tits when I walked over to her and asked her name. My suspicions were confirmed. It was the same fucking girl. I was freaking. What should I do? Should I tell her? Should I call my friend on his cell phone? Should I shut my mouth? I wanted to bang this girl but the guilt factor was setting in. I said screw it. Whatever happens, happens!

Her tits were stunningly beautiful and they had a good shot at being real. So, being the straightforward asshole that I am, I asked her if her tits were real.

She replied, emphasizing the point by sexually caressing her breasts, "Yes, REAL nice and REAL expensive." I started stammering like Ralph Kramden.

Before she could assess my personality as non-fuckable, I quickly grabbed her, and my drummer grabbed the Pam Anderson blond. We brought them on to the tour bus and escorted them to the back where we had one big round bed. It was all whored out with disco lights, bar, TV (with our favorite porn constantly on) and mirrors. We encouraged them to lez out on each other while we were getting primed. We asked them what their limits were. They both looked at each other and laughed.

Well we had our way with both of them. We ended up back at the hotel and continued the party. As all four of us were partaking in carnal pleasure I spotted a brand new blue Sharpie on my nightstand (a Sharpie, for those who do not know, is a permanent marker pen used for signing autographs, permanent being the key word). As my friend's girlfriend was expertly eating the blond Pamela Anderson look-alike chick, I grabbed the Sharpie and started to write messages on her ass. I wrote real small and right near her asshole so the other chick wouldn't see it. First I wrote "SLUT". She didn't feel me writing on her ass. Then I got daring and wrote "WOW" (in tribute to Opie and Anthony) or "MOM" (depending on which way you were banging her) I used her asshole for the "O." I didn't push my luck beyond that.

My drummer shot one last load on the blond's back. She got up and went into the bathroom while we were still kissing the Cher girl's tits and ass. I spread her ass cheeks for my drummer to check out. He almost blew it because he started laughing out loud. I gave him dagger eyes.

She kept saying, "Whaaat?"

Finally he said he was laughing 'cause he had to fart the whole time he was banging the blond chick. Stupid alibi but it worked. She was definitely all beauty, no brains.

We woke up the next day with the sound of her beeper going off on the night-stand. She bolted out of bed into a two-minute shower and got dressed. She kissed me goodbye and out the door she went for her groupie "walk of shame" home. I knew that marker writing would not come off unless you knew it was there and scrubbed it off.

I got an e-mail from my friend a week later with the sad news that he broke up with the hot chick he fell in love with.

I e-mailed back, "What happened?"

His e-mail in return was, "I don't want to talk about it."

I actually felt good. My secret message made it's way through to my friend without finding out it was me. I didn't want him to get hurt falling in love with a TULSA.

By the way, Tulsa was a code meaning A SLUT! Read the word TULSA backwards. Tulsa girls were the best.

CHAPTER 31
CLASSIC ROCK & ROLL WAR STORIES, MYTHS AND URBAN LEGENDS

As long as there is the ol' in and out, libation, and illegal substances, rock and roll will have outrageous stories of debauchery. Some absolutely true, some exaggerated and some just complete myth.

Not necessarily the most notorious, but arguably the most retold of rock's urban legends, this one has been around for decades and has been attributed to just about every performer. However, the original legend, as heard back in the early 70s, involved Rod "The Mod" Stewart and most likely has been repeated even earlier than that by your great grandparents about a silent screen star.

Stewart reportedly collapsed at a party and was subsequently taken to the emergency room of a hospital, where upon pumping his stomach a gallon of semen was extracted. The amount varies from story to story. Some outlandish versions claim that whale sperm was discovered in his stomach.

Many others have been the focal point of this urban legend over the years, including Richard Gere, Mick Jagger, Elton John, David Bowie, members of New Kids on the Block, and most recently Alanis Morrisette (who is supposedly addicted to semen) and Hip-Hop'er Lil Kim. So, for the record, the Rod Stewart stomach pump is completely false!

Perhaps the most disgusting of all is the legend that rock satirist Frank Zappa once ate his own excrement on stage. Variations include Zappa partaking in a "gross-out contest" between himself and Captain Beefheart, where both dined on their respective feces. Another version has a contest between Zappa and Alice Cooper, where Zappa ate shit while Cooper stomped baby chickens. In his autobiography, *Real Frank Zappa Book*, he vehemently denies that any of the incidents ever took place.

Zappa wrote, "For the record, folks: I never took a shit on stage, and the closest I ever came to eating shit anywhere was at a Holiday Inn buffet in Fayetteville, North Carolina, in 1973." Again for the record, Frank Zappa never ate his own shit!

The Rolling Stones should advertise their countless farewell tours as "The Rolling Stones Live, plus Keith Richards".

Keith Richards' drug and alcohol addiction became fodder for a rock and roll legend. One outlandish rumor, which has been circulating for years, claims that in order to cure his heroin addiction, Richards flew to Switzerland for a blood transfusion to completely replace the heroin-laced blood in his body.

According to the Rolling Stones FAQ:

"It was a widely circulated rumor that to cure himself of an addiction to heroin, Keith Richards flew to the Swiss chalet of an exclusive physician who had a method for replacing all of a patient's nasty addicted blood with good clean blood." Great gossip. Bad science.

It became rumored in the early '90s that David Bowie and Mick Jagger had once been sexual partners. This particular legend gained credence when Bowie's ex-wife published a tell-all tome called, *Backstage Pass*, where she claimed to have come home one day to find Jagger and Bowie asleep in the same bed. She stated this seemingly shocking revelation on several talk shows. Fans drew their own conclusion, and Angie Bowie used the publicity to sell more copies of the book. It was only after the rumor became widespread that she recanted, stating that yes, she did find them in bed together, but "I never said they were having sex. They were just passed out drunk on the bed." Some have speculated that Angie Bowie withdrew her previous statements under threat of legal action by her ex-husband. The truth remains unclear, however Bowie's bisexuality in the 70's was common knowledge, and Jagger was also rumored to have occasionally had sexual encounters with men during that time. Bowie and Jagger lovers? Possibility but never confirmed!

"Mama" Cass Elliot's death has been reported over the years to have been caused by "choking on a ham sandwich." The true cause of death, a heart attack, was not determined until an autopsy was performed a week later, but by that time it was too late. Another of rock's urban legends was born.

At 5'5" and 238 lbs., Mama Cass was twice the normal weight for a woman her age and height. The effects of long-term obesity, drug abuse and crash diets had weakened her heart to the point of failure. Because she was a large woman, and there was a sandwich (it became a "ham" sandwich through legend) on the nightstand when her body was found, an irreversible connection was made. However, no traces of food were found blocking her trachea, and there was never any indication that food played a role in her death. Mama Cass and the killer ham sandwich makes a great story but it is a false story.

Jim Morrison allegedly exposed himself at a Miami gig, got arrested, and set a precedent for overexposure. The chain of events on March 1, 1969, which lead up to the infamous concert where the *Doors'* Jim Morrison allegedly exposed himself onstage, should have signaled impending trouble. First, Morrison missed his initial flight to Miami, where the band was scheduled to play that night. He spent his time drinking at the airport bar while waiting for the next plane, and continued to drink after boarding. During a stopover in New Orleans where he again missed the flight, Morrison drank even more while waiting for the next flight. By the time he reached the stage in Miami he was extremely drunk, almost to the point of falling down.

Morrison's behavior that night at the show has been described as abusive towards the audience and his performance was disjointed; he would sing a few lines, then stop the song.

At one point he asked the crowd, "Do you wanna see my cock?" before allegedly exposing himself, then continued with the concert. Four days later, the state attorney's office issued a warrant for Morrison's arrest, charging him with lewd and lascivious behavior, indecent exposure and open profanity. Morrison turned himself in to Miami authorities on April 4, then entered a plea of not guilty in November. The trial began almost a year later, during which contradictory accounts of that fateful night were given. It was never proven that anyone actually saw Morrison's genitals, or that he did, in fact, expose himself to the audience.

Morrison was ultimately found guilty on the misdemeanor charges of indecent exposure and profanity, but not guilty on the felony charge and misdemeanor for drunkenness. He died before his sentences could be carried out.

The most recent rumor to surface on the legendary dead singer revolved around his final resting-place. Reports indicated that Morrison's body was going to be "evicted" from Pere Lachaise cemetery in Paris when the 30-year lease on the gravesite expired at the end of July, 2001. Initial news stories claimed that cemetery officials were fed up with the beer bottles, graffiti and half-smoked joints left at the monument by well-meaning fans that make the pilgrimage to France. Relatives of those laid to rest near Morrison's grave had also petitioned the cemetery to remove Morrison's remains.

Speculation abounded on where Morrison would go, since he had a strained relationship with his parents. Some suggested that the remains be cremated and scattered, while one claimed that Morrison's family should auction his remains to attract bids by cities that need a tourism boost.

However, an official from Pere Lachaise ultimately confirmed that Morrison would stay put. "There are those who would like him to be [moved], but Morrison's grave is on a perpetual lease. His body is there, and it will stay there." In addition Ray Manzarek, the *Doors'* keyboard player, told fans at a reunion that the grave was the fourth most popular attraction in Paris, and was unlikely to be moved by the French government. He expected French officials "to supersede" any petition by disgruntled families. Jim Morrison - dead and not moving!

The most famous TRUE rock and roll war story of all time has to be *Led*

Zeppelin's fish story. How apropos that the story has mutated over time and it involves a fish. You've probably heard it in some form or other. Even Richard Cole (he and deceased John Bonham were the guilty parties involved) has told variations of the story.

In 1969 at Seattle's Edgewater Inn, John Bonham and Richard Cole were fishing directly out their hotel window (that was this hotel's selling point). While successfully fishing (they caught several small sharks) a redheaded, 17-year-old female fan came into the room. We can all assume it was not for tea and crumpets. The story continues that she was playfully tied to the bed and Richard Cole took one of the sharks and fucked her with the nose of the live shark.

Richard recants the story and says the shark was actually a red snapper and says he blurted out, "You'd like a bit of fucking, eh? Let's see how your red snapper likes this red snapper!" He says he fucked her with the nose of the fish and the girl loved it, as "she must've come 20 times. No one was ever hurt."

Variations on that story has the members of *Led Zeppelin* raping a groupie using a live shark repeatedly into her vagina and rectum, ignoring her screams and pleas for help. Another variation has a large bag of fish guts and entrails dumped on the girl, with various pieces being inserted into her vagina and anus.

Another story has Mark Stein (*Vanilla Fudge*'s Keyboardist) filming the incident with an 8mm movie camera with Robert Plant and Jimmy Page present. Further variations state that Plant's and Bonham's wives also silently witnessed the event.

The event has been described as a rape. Images of forcefully, brutally violating someone come to mind. The girl was seventeen. She complied. Technically it was statutory rape.

Countless legendary rock and roll war stories exist. Here are rock's most prominent and bears repeating.

Sid Vicious / *Sex Pistols*

Sid Vicious was instantly transformed from junkie punk icon in rapid decline to the most infamous celebrity in the world when, in 1978, he stabbed Nancy Spungen to death at Manhattan's Chelsea Hotel. Everyone from Sid's record company (Virgin) to his mother and fashion designer Vivienne Westwood were out to make a buck off his newfound notoriety.

Spungen had been Vicious' manager and with her out of the way, ex-manager Malcolm McLaren wormed his way back into the picture, paying the $50,000 bail and intending to record an album while he awaited trial for second degree murder. It gets worse. McLaren and partner Vivienne Westwood sold T-shirts showing a shot of Vicious in army fatigues with the assinine slogan: "I'M ALIVE, SHE'S DEAD, I'M YOURS."

"(Vicious is) going to approach this thing in a productive and optimistic manner," then Virgin PR chief Al Clark declared. Verging on suicide, not helped by harrowing heroin detox, Vicious was anything but a happy man. Everybody wanted a piece of the action: even Vicious' mom, Anne Beverley, sold her side of the story to the press for $10,000!

After a bar brawl with Patti Smith's brother, Vicious was sent back to jail but was released a few months later, only to suffer a fatal drug overdose. His single *Sid Sings* became a huge hit after his death.

W.A.S.P.

In their early days, *W.A.S.P.* would throw raw meat into the crowd. Fans of the band started bringing their own raw meat to the shows to throw back at the band. During a concert at the Troubadour in Los Angeles guitarist Chris Holmes was hit in the head and knocked out cold by a fan who threw a rump roast.

Van Halen

Everybody has heard of the famous clause in *Van Halen*'s contract stating that they were to have a bowl of M&M's candy backstage after each show with all brown M&M's removed. One night when the brown M&M's were not removed the band destroyed their dressing rooms. *Van Halen* claims that this was in their tour rider to see if the promoters were reading the rider or not.

After throwing TV sets out of open windows seven stories high, soaking hotel room carpets with water and discharging fire extinguishers at each other in the hallways, *Van Halen* have been banned for life from the entire Holiday Inn Hotel chain.

Diamond Dave's Bonus Program

During the band's 1979 tour, *Van Halen* frontman David Lee Roth instituted an "incentive program" to keep the roadies on schedule. Crew members were given backstage passes to dole out to the ladies of their choice. The Roadie who gave out the pass pinned to the chosen girl's clothes on the floor of Diamond Dave's hotel-room floor was given $100 and a commendation at the next pre-show dinner.

Black Sabbath

During a concert on the *Black Sabbath Heaven and Hell* tour in 1980, the band would have buckets of water filled with dry ice to create fog for the bands stage show. One night the buckets of dry ice exploded because one of the roadies put too much dry ice in the buckets causing water and dry ice to fall onto drummer Vinnie Appice during the song *Black Sabbath*. A few minutes later Appice felt a burning sensation in the rear of his pants and ran to the backstage area. A piece of dry ice had fallen into Appice's pants and a nurse had to pry the dry ice off his "butt crack". Appice returned to the stage behind his drum kit but had to sit on a pillow for the rest of the show.

Frank Zappa and *Deep Purple*

The lyrics for the *Deep Purple* classic song *Smoke on the Water* were based on a *Frank Zappa and Mothers of Invention* concert the band attended in 1971. *Deep Purple* traveled to Montreaux, Switzerland to record their album *Machine Head*. They were going to use the Casino in Montreaux the day after the Frank Zappa concert.

During the concert someone fired a flare gun and the flare hit the ceiling causing the electrical wiring that was lining the ceiling to catch fire. This set off a string of events that caused the entire building to catch fire within minutes. The building filled with smoke causing fans to panic and jump through windows to escape. Luckily, there were no fatalities. The smoke from the fire descended over Lake Geneva and hovered over the water for hours as the casino burned to the ground. *Deep Purple* bassist Roger Glover then penned the song that night in his hotel room after the experience.

"We all came out to Montreux. On the Lake Geneva shoreline. To make records with a mobile. We didn't have much time. Frank Zappa and the Mothers. Were at the best place around. But some stupid with a flare gun. Burned the place to the ground. Smoke on the water, fire in the sky."

The famous casino has since been rebuilt.

Black Sabbath and Ozzy

In the early years *Black Sabbath* were having trouble getting gigs and were known as a band not very high on hygiene. They landed a gig at the Marquee Club in London and a condition of the agreement to play the club was that the *Sabbath* (Ozzy Osbourne, Tony Iommi, Geezer Butler, and Bill Ward) would not be allowed to take the stage unless they bathed first.

Guns 'n Roses

Lafayette, Indiana native Axl Rose left his hometown for Los Angeles to catch up with high school buddy, Izzy Stradlin, who moved out there the year before. Axl hopped on a Greyhound bus and ran out of money in St. Louis and ended up hitch hiking the rest of the way. Once he got there and not knowing how big Los Angeles was, it took Axl a month to find where Izzy had been living.

The power of MTV… In 1987 the music television cable channel was turning its back on airing hard rock and heavy metal videos, which was the form of music that made the channel a huge success in the early years. A new band from L.A. called *Guns 'N Roses* had just done a video for the song *Welcome to the Jungle* off the album *Appetite for Destruction*. When album sales stalled at about 200,000 copies, executives from Geffen Records pleaded with MTV's program director to air the video in which MTV continually rejected. MTV gave in to Geffen's wishes and cut a deal to air the video three times in the later hours of the day. After the third running which was at 3:00 in the morning MTV executives called the record company to congratulate them on having the most requested video of the week. MTV then began to air commercials for the song stating "You heard 'em here first" and the album went on to sell millions and make it one of the all-time best selling albums.

Rolling Stones

See if you can figure all the possibilities and confusion. First, you must play the *Deliverance* theme song. In 1989 Bill Wyman of the *Rolling Stones* married a 19-year-old model, Mandy Smith, whom he had dated for six years. Wyman's son (from a previous relationship) later dated the girl's mother.

Now, if Wyman's son married his wife's mother and had children, what would all their relations be? Great Mensa question!

Elvis

On December 21, 1970, Elvis Presley paid a visit to President Richard M. Nixon at the White House in Washington, D.C. The meeting was initiated by Presley, who wrote Nixon a six-page letter requesting a visit with the President and suggesting that he be made a "Federal Agent-at-Large" in the Bureau of Narcotics and Dangerous Drugs. Nixon made Elvis an "honorary" DEA Agent and Presley gave Nixon a Colt 45 pistol in the Oval Office. Elvis died seven years later of a drug overdose.

Ramones

I want to be fellated! Dee Dee Ramone, of the Ramones, moonlighted as a bisexual street hustler.

The Go-Go's

The *Go-Go's* film a raunchy video that included their sex confessions. The highlight (or lowlight - depending on which end of the spectrum you are coming from) has a fucked up male Roadie encouraged to handle his own equipment by the seemingly, squeaky clean all-girl band. At one point, the band shoved carrots up the bottom of the naked, unconscious, uncomplaining roadie. It is a hard-to-find bootleg video called The Bathroom Tapes.

Ol' Dirty Bastard

How stupid can you get? Ol' Dirty Bastard took a limo to cash his welfare check with MTV cameras in tow. Heyyy nowww!

Bay City Rollers

In the early 70's we had our share of crap commercial music and "bubblegum" bands. The *Bay City Rollers* were the cream of the crop of crap.

In 1976, guitarist Eric Faulkner almost died after a drug overdose of seconal and valium at manager Tam Paton's house. Tam, the nice manager that he was, called the press before he called for an ambulance. Scandals involving their manager got him jailed for three years on a charge of gross indecency. More recently, drummer Derek Longmuir also found himself on the wrong end of the long arm of the law for alleged kiddie-fondling.

Speaking of kiddie-fondling, Gary Glitter (real name: Paull Gadd), famous for *Rock and Roll, Part Two* wave starter was accused by ex-girlfriend Allison Brown, now 35, of befriending her as an 11-year-old fan and forcibly taking her virginity when she was 14 and he 39. Gadd denied the charges saying he waited until Brown was 16, the British age of consent and he was let off. Despite escaping the court's wrath - and very public romances with Roald Dahl's (one of the world's greatest children's authors) daughter Tessa (aged 17) and nubile TV presenter Denise Van Outen (aged 16) - Gadd was convicted of possessing more than 4,000 child-porn images downloaded from the internet in 1999. Now 60 and prone to wearing eight-inch heels and a ridiculous wig, Gadd reportedly lives with his 27-year-old fiancée in Cuba. Other rumors say tha he was deported from Vietnam.

Malcolm McLaren (manager of *Sex Pistols*, *Adam and the Ants*, and *Bow Wow Wow*) picked up a 14-year-old Annabella Lwin, put her in a band (*Bow Wow Wow*), wrote suggestive lyrics for her to sing, and had her pose naked for the band's album cover.

The Runaways

In 1975, *Runaways* Manager, Scott Anderson impregnated the band's singer, Cherie Currie. He also tried (or accomplished - depending on who you ask) to sleep with the other member's of the band, Lita Ford and Joan Jett.

"When the Runaways burst onto the stage in their tight little tube tops in 1975, rocking songs like *Cherry Bomb* and *I Love Playin' With Fire*, everyone imagined these five teenage girls fully living up to the reckless jailbait image manufactured by their producer-cum-Svengali, Kim Fowley. But Fowley, along with manager Scott Anderson, kept a tight lid on the offstage sleaze," writes Spin's Jaan

Uhelszki. No wonder: As reported recently in Mojo, Anderson attempted to sleep his way through the band's lineup, eventually getting 16-year-old singer Cherie Currie pregnant while the band were on their first European Tour. In Germany, Currie kept a bucket onstage unaware it was due to morning sickness.

Cherie Currie states, "I came back from Europe pregnant, though I was unaware of it by our 'manager' Scott Anderson, who I think was a horrific human being. He was the first one to try and plant the idea that I was better than the band, the real star of the show, all that nonsense. But the whole time I was with him, I didn't know that he was also with Lita and with Joan. This was one manipulative son of a @#%$. He thought he could have anyone of the band members to take to bed whenever he wanted. He really, really played on my heartstrings, and it was devastating. I was totally unaware of the pregnancy because I was so young. At 16 I'd never even had a normal period, so missing it was nothing unusual. I was sick throughout the entire European tour and didn't know why I had to go into Cedars-Sinai Hospital to have an abortion. Scott never even offered to pay for it, let alone be there to hold my hand. My father, who was then working as a bartender, had to take care of it."

Lita Ford's take on the situation, "That @#%$! Scott Anderson came on to me, but I didn't want it. I doubt Joan went for it either, though she might have watched. We got him drunk once, and after he passed out we stripped him and painted obscenities all over him with nail polish and make-up. He deserved worse, believe me. We could be rough on managers. We handcuffed one of our later geniuses to the wheel of his daddy's Mercedes and left him in New York City traffic somewhere. I hated our managers; hated all of' em. In retrospect my favourite one was probably Kim. Although he spoke to us like we were piles of @#%$ at least he 'spoke to us.'" Currie's upcoming book *Neon Angel: The Cherrie Currie Story - Expanded Edition* promises to blow the lid off the band's history with bags more dirt.

Great Balls of Fire singer Jerry Lee Lewis beat out Scott Anderson by a few years when he married his 13-year-old cousin in 1958. The marriage lasted 13 years.

Cynthia Plastercaster
30 years ago, a very clever groupie found a way to hold on to her favorite part of a conquered rock star. She would make a plaster cast of their appendage in hopefully, full mast. The list of stars is immense and quite a few are long gone but she has preserved a piece of HIStory, so to speak. Successful castings include Jimi Hendrix, Noel Redding, Richard Cole, Anthony Newley, Eddie Brigati, Aynsley

Dunbar, Jello Biafra, and a plethora of others. Some molds were not successful, maybe they literally broke the mold in the process. Proud mold breakers include Eric Burdon of the Animals and Pete Shelley of the Buzzcocks.

In the year 2000, Cynthia became an equal opportunist and began casting celebrity females such as Suzi Gardner of L7.

A "Cockumentary" has been filmed entitled *Plaster Caster* and a DVD will be released. She also started doing art exhibits and is currently writing an autobiography. Cynthia has a very clever website and you should check it out. www.cynthiaplastercaster.com

The Who

On January 4th, 1970 Keith Moon was invited to open a disco in Hatfield. Afterwards, as he was being driven away, a crowd of skinheads attacked his Bentley Limo. According to Larry Smith of the Bonzo Dog Doodah Band, who was there, Moon's personal chauffeur Neil Boland got out to try to protect the car, but left it in gear, and it started moving towards the main road. Moon (a non-driver) climbed into the driver's seat, while Larry Smith desperately tried to grab the wheel from behind. One hundred yards down the road, he realized he was dragging something along under the car. Getting out he found what was left of Boland who had fallen under the car when it sped off. Though the inquest absolved Moon of blame, Neil's family didn't, and neither did Moon himself. The accident was to stay with him for the rest of his life. According to famed groupie Pamela Des Barres, with whom Moon had an on/off affair, after this he 'didn't feel worthy to live'.

L7

Girl band *L7* raffled off drummer, Dee Plakas, for a one-night stand with an audience member during a live show at the Garage Club in London. Breakfast waas not included. They arrived onstage and announced, "this is my pussy, eat it and you shall live." The band has been known to throw used tampons into festival crowds, and their guitarist famously exposed herself on a British music program called The Word. The winner of the raffle, some guy named Jim, was treated to a "one night stand" with Dee. Apparently, Jim was a gentleman and didn't talk to the press about what happened in the back lounge of *L7*'s tour bus. Dee didn't say a word either.

Iron Butterfly

In-A-Gadda-Da-Vida was written by the *Iron Butterfly*'s lead singer and keyboard player Doug Ingle, and the name was actually a misinterpretation.

"Doug had been up for a day and a half," Dorman said, "plus he had been drinking some wine."

Dorman and Bushy went to his house late one night and Ingle played the song for him. They liked what they heard and asked Ingle what the title was.

"He said 'In the Garden of Eden' but it sounded like '*In-A-Gadda-Da-Vida*,'" Dorman said, "Bushy wrote it down phonetically."

In July of 1968, *Iron Butterfly* released the monumental LP, In-A-Gadda-Da-Vida, featuring the 17:05 minute sidelong track that shook the entire music industry with its phenomenal reception. '*Vida* outsold every record in the history of recorded music within the first year of its release (over eight million copies sold) and therefore outgrew and outsold the standard of the music industry's "Gold Album" award. For this achievement, *Iron Butterfly* was subsequently awarded the industry's very first "Platinum Album"! This historic award was created and presented by then-president of ATCO Records Ahmet Ertegun. Most recently, '*Vida* received the "Multi-Platinum" award.

In-A-Gadda-Da-Vida, stayed on the charts for 140 weeks, with 81 weeks in the Top Ten. To date the album has sold in excess of 25 million copies and remains an undisputed classic in the archives of rock with DJ's and audiophiles worldwide.

Gram Parsons

Gram Parsons sang and worked with 60's and 70's acts such as the *Byrds*, *Flying Burrito Brothers* and Emmylou Harris. Most of you probably never heard of him but this is one of the most bizarre deaths and funerals of a, then, rock icon.

Gram Parsons frequented the Joshua Tree National Monument (located in the Mojave Desert in southern California) for several years -- he went there regularly, with friends like Keith Richards, to get high, commune with the cactus, and watch the sky for UFOs. He reserved two rooms at the nearby Joshua Tree Inn. Along with Parsons on this trip were his buddy, Michael Martin; Martin's girlfriend Dale McElroy (no fan of Gram Parsons); and an old friend from his high school days in Florida named Margaret Fisher.

The foursome arrived Monday, September 17, 1973. The next night, Parsons scored some heroin in town and then topped it off with morphine he acquired from a drug connection, who was staying at the Inn. Several hours later, a wasted Fisher showed up at McElroy's door in a frantic state. Parsons had overdosed, she said. They grabbed some ice and went to his room, where he was passed out on the floor, blue. There Fisher revived him with an ice cube suppository -- an old street remedy for overdoses. When McElroy left the two alone again, Parsons was walking around the room, seemingly recovered.

After another hour or so, Fisher returned to McElroy's room and asked her to sit with the sleeping Parsons while she went out to get some dinner. McElroy grabbed a book and went to Parsons's room. After a few minutes, she realized that his breathing had gone from normal to labored. McElroy had no experience with drug overdoses and no training in CPR. Believing (incorrectly) that there were no other people in the hotel, she never called out for help. Instead she tried to get him breathing again by pumping his back and his chest and giving him mouth-to-mouth. "I tried to figure out whether to stay and keep him breathing or leave and get some help.... I figured if I left, he might die."

After about a half hour of futile pumping and pushing, McElroy realized that Parsons was probably beyond help. At this point Margaret Fisher returned, then left to call an ambulance. The rescue crew arrived quickly, but concluded that CPR would not be successful. They got Parsons to the nearby Hi-Desert Memorial Hospital in Yucca Valley by 12:15 AM. The doctors there found no pulse and, after trying unsuccessfully to restart his heart, declared him dead at 12:30 AM, Wednesday, September 19, 1973 at the young age of 26 years.

Both Margaret Fisher and Alan Barbary (the son of the hotel owners) told conflicting versions of that night's events, which added to the confusion and exaggeration that soon surrounded the death of Gram Parsons.

Here's where it got really wacky. Gram's father died when Gram was very young and his mother remarried Bob Parsons. When the news of his stepson's death reached Bob Parsons, he immediately realized that his own interests would be best served by having the body buried in Louisiana, where the senior Parsons lived. Parsons knew that under Louisiana's Napoleonic code, his adopted son's estate would pass in its entirety to the nearest living male -- Bob Parsons -- notwithstanding any will provisions to the contrary. But the code would only apply if Bob Parsons could prove that Gram Parsons had been a resident of Louisiana. Burying the younger Parsons in New Orleans would bolster the tenuous arguments for Louisiana residency. Bob Parsons booked a flight to Los Angeles to claim the body. At stake was his stepson's share of the dwindling but still substantial Snively fortune. (Parsons natural mother, Avis, came from the prosperous Snively family, whose orange groves made them millions by the mid '50s, when Snively Groves was the largest shipper of fresh fruit in Florida. The Snivelys later owned an interest in Cypress Gardens, the popular tourist attraction built on part of the Snivelys' land in Winter Haven, Florida.)

When Gram's road manager and best friend, Phil Kaufman, learned of the plan to bury his buddy in New Orleans, he became distraught. He knew that Gram had no connection whatsoever to that city, had little use for his stepfather, and would not have wanted any of his estate to pass on to him. He knew that Parsons had not wanted a long, depressing, religious service with family and friends. Most of all he knew he had made a pact with Parsons, at the funeral of Clarence White: whoever died first, "the survivor would take the other guy's body out to Joshua Tree, have a few drinks and burn it."

After a day of vodka-enhanced self-recriminations, Kaufman decided he had to try to make good on his promise. Thus began one of the most unforgettable episodes of what hackers call "social engineering." For the full story, check out Kaufman's biography, *Road Mangler Deluxe*, which describes the whole episode in Kaufman's own inimitable fashion. What follows is only a taste of Kaufman's tale.

Kaufman called the funeral parlor in the town of Joshua Tree and managed to learn that the body would be driven to LAX and then flown on Continental Airlines to New Orleans. He called the airline's mortuary service and found out that the body would arrive that evening. Kaufman recruited Michael Martin, who knew about the pact, and commandeered a hearse of Dale McElroy's, which she and Martin used for camping trips. It had no license plates and several broken windows, but it would do. They tried on suits, but decided they looked so ridiculous that they changed into their tour clothes -- Levi's, cowboy boots, cowboy hats, and jackets with the legend "Sin City" stitched on the back. They loaded the hearse up with beer and Jack Daniels and headed for LAX.

Kaufman and Martin arrived at the loading dock just as a flatbed truck rolled up with the Parsons casket. A drunken Kaufman somehow persuaded an airline employee that the Parsons family had changed their plans and wanted to ship the body privately on a chartered flight.

While Kaufman was in the hangar office, signing the paperwork with a phony name, a policeman pulled up, blocking the hangar door. Kaufman was sure his operation would be shut down, but the officer didn't do anything -- he just sat there. So Kaufman walked out to him, waved his copies of the paperwork, and said, "Hey, can you move that car?" The officer apologized, moved the car, and then, remarkably, helped Kaufman load the casket onto a gurney and into the back of the unlicensed, liquor-filled hearse.

Martin, also liquor-filled, got in the hearse and headed out of the hangar, only to run into the wall on his way out. The officer observed all this, and commented ruefully, "I wouldn't want to be in your shoes now." Then he left, and the two drunk bodysnatchers departed the airport with the body of their friend. They stopped at a gas station and filled a gas can with high test ("I didn't want him to ping," Kaufman is quoted as saying.) Then they headed back for Joshua Tree.

They reached the Monument and drove until they were too drunk to drive any farther. There, near the Cap Rock, a landmark geological formation, they unloaded their friend's coffin. Then Kaufman saw car lights in the distance and concluded the police were coming. He quickly doused his friend with fuel and lit him. The two watched as a giant fireball rose from the coffin, sucking his ashes into the desert night. Then they abandoned the charred remains and headed for LA.

The trip back to L.A. after burning the body of Gram Parsons was every bit as weird as the trip out had been for Phil Kaufman and Michael Martin. Part way home, the drunken pair decided they'd better pull off the road and sleep for a few hours. When they woke up, the hearse wouldn't start. They were stuck in the middle of the desert. Martin went for help and came back with a tow truck; after a few hours, they left with a fresh supply of cold beer.

They were nearly home when they got into a multi-car pile-up on an L.A. freeway, rear-ending another car. A highway patrolman approached and opened the door to the hearse. When beer bottles fell out, he handcuffed Kaufman and Martin together and told them to stay put. Then he left to attend to other drivers. Before he could return and take their licenses, the very thin Martin had slipped his hand from the cuff. Kaufman started up the hearse and fled the scene. When they got back to chez Kaufman, they sawed off the other cuff, stashed the hearse, and went into hiding.

After the trip home, Kaufman and Martin laid low. The morning after their return, the papers were full of the story of the rock star's hijacked and burnt corpse, playing up baseless speculation by local police that the amateur cremation may have been "ritualistic."

Kaufman knew the police were looking for him, so after a few weeks, he and Martin just turned themselves in. They appeared in West L.A. Municipal Court on Parsons's 27th birthday -- November 5, 1973. Since a corpse has no intrinsic value, the two were charged with misdemeanor theft for stealing the coffin and given a slap on the wrist: $708 in damages for the coffin, and a $300 fine for each of the bodysnatchers. Kaufman has surely made that amount back just dining out on the story -- his misadventures have been legendary in rock and country music circles ever since.

The aftermath of the court's sentence was as unlikely as the events leading up to it. Kaufman threw himself a party to raise the fine money -- Kaufman's Koffin Kaper Koncert. They pasted beer bottles with some homemade labels featuring a bad likeness of Parsons and the legend, "Gram Pilsner: A stiff drink for what ales you." Dr. Demento served as deejay, and live music was provided by Bobby "Boris" Pickett and the Crypt Kickers of "Monster Mash" fame and a young band being managed by Tickner and Kaufman at the time, Jonathan Richman and the Modern Lovers. Despite the gruesome streak running through the party, it was a memorable wake for their friend.

Bob Parsons had the charred remains of his stepson shipped to New Orleans, where, after a small service with family only, he was buried in The Garden of Memories, an unimpressive cemetery on a highway near the airport. A bronze plaque marks the gravesite; it reads "God's Own Singer." Although Bob Parsons succeeded in getting the body to Louisiana, his scheme to seize control of the Snively fortune was nevertheless thwarted by a Florida court. About a year later, Bob Parsons died of an alcohol-related illness. He never made a dime off of Gram Parsons.

When Parsons left for Joshua Tree, he believed he had initiated divorce proceedings against wife, Gretchen. As it turned out, this was not the case. Kaufman had the papers to serve on her but hadn't yet done so by the time Parsons died. Along with Gretchen Parsons, his daughter Polly, his sister Avis, and his half-sister Diane all received some money from his estate as well.

Check out the Gram Parsons website at www.GramParsons.com

CHAPTER 32
ROCK & ROLL WAR STORIES CONTINUE

The rock and roll war stories continue for me as a member of several bands. I have also been recording many upcoming CDs (most recently Keri Shore and Vick LeCar).

There weren't many "progressive" rock bands that I totally liked growing up, but bands like *Genesis, Yes, UK, Vangelis, Asia, Crack the Sky, King Crimson, Focus, Triumvirat, Jethro Tull, Eddie Jobson, Kansas, Mahavishnu Orchestra, Moody Blues, Pink Floyd, Rush, Tangerine Dream, Frank Zappa* all had their moments.

In 1975 a friend bought an album by an unknown band named *Angel*. From the first synthesizer intro of *The Tower* I was hooked. A band with very cool keyboards mixed into regular rock. *Angel* quickly became a band I listened to regularly and finally got to see perform live on April 16th, 1977 at the Palladium in New York City with Piper (Billy Squier's band) and Legs Diamond. *Angel* hit the stage at precisely midnight, "magically" appearing onstage. They had a David Copperfield-like opening bit. The mixture of presentation and great music was impressive. I got to see them again almost a year later on March 10th, 1978 with *The Godz* and *Judas Priest*.

If anyone came up to me at those concerts and said, "Someday you will be playing with those guys," I would've said, "Oh yeah! How come not right now? I need the money!" Actually, I couldn't imagine back then that I would be playing with them today.

On September 26, 1999 *Angel* officially announced me as their new

Gordon G. G. Gebert on keyboards performing with
Angel at the Sweden Rock Festival

Keyboard Player for the band and we performed at the New England *KISS* Expo - Boston, MA. We played a 40 minute set that included: *The Tower, Can You Feel It, Under Suspicion, Paradise, Bad Time, Hero, Goodbye* and the classics *Don't Leave Me Lonely*, and *White Lightning*.

Whenever I say I'm playing with *Angel* I get one of two reactions. I get, "Who?" or I get, "Is that the same *Angel* as in the 70's band *Angel* (Frank DiMino, Punky Meadows, Gregg Giuffria, Barry Brandt, and Mickey Jones)?" Yes, it is the same band from the 70's.

In May of 2000 we went to Miami, Florida (with the help of Steve Altman) to record in a studio, ironically named, Heaven Studio. We recorded four cuts; *Hero, Set Me Free, Wake of the Storm*, and *The Crow*.

Our biggest shows to date were performed in St. Louis (two shows) and the first European show ever for *Angel* at the Sweden Rock Festival, June 9, 2001.

My next book, tentatively titled, *On a Wing and a Prayer with Angel* will be released in 2004. Till then, keep safe. See you next time.

I would like to thank everyone that contributed a part of their embarrassing lives to this book. I really appreciate it. I wish you all continued success.

"Didn't you notice a change in Jani Lane? I mean, it couldn't have been us that got weird. I was a friend of theirs, and the time. I mean, just walking off a tour like this is so unprofessional. There's no excuse, really." - C.C. DeVille, Poison, Rip Mag August 1991

"They got booed in Europe. (David Lee) Roth's office called ours and said they had a really tough time with Warrant. They said, 'This character has a real attitude. He thinks Dave should be opening for them.' I said, 'Well, that was sort of the attitude we got. I mean, what was the fucking problem? I guess it was the best thing. They left." - Bret Michaels, Poison, Rip Magazine, August 1991

"C.C. and Bobby (Dall) really wanted us on the tour. It was between us and Winger. A couple people in Poison's management firm didn't want Warrant on the tour. They were totally against it. We went through hell getting that tour, and then we finally get it, someone from the Poison camp called Jani or our manager - I think it was our manager - and said, 'Do you think that Jani would dye his hair dark? Would he consider that? Because he does look a lot like Bret. We were like, 'Are you fucking out of your mind?'" - Erik Turner, Warrant, Rip Magazine, October 1991

"I'm twenty-four years old in ten days, and I am NOT fucking Kip Winger, okay? You want to talk about rock & roll; I'll sit there all day, as long as someone's buying the drinks. But don't expect me to be like everybody else. If you want an amusing anecdote, talk to Mark Slaughter. I'm sure he'll say something like, 'Yeah, we had a couple of lite beers and ran down the hall in our underwear. Whooooooo.'" - Chris Robinson, Black Crowes, Rolling Stone, January 24, 1991

"You know what's funny, Chris Robinson doesn't use real good information in the way he slags people. He lumped us together with Winger and Warrant. Winger is very much like what their record is, and Warrant is a good hard-rock band who do this coordinated trip of their own in concert. Slaughter borders on a heavier metal sound. Then he makes a comment like; we don't wear hairspray and eyeliner like Slaughter and Winger. In fact, he does wear eyeliner! Shit, he wears more eyeliner than Dana or I ever did in our previous band. And I might add that Mr. Robinson's clothing is definitely far and above what I can afford. Hey, man, be a bigmouth, that's cool, just know what you're talking about." - Mark Slaughter, Slaughter, Rip Magazine, November 1991

"I like Extreme but this guitarist - who's a serious guitar player, mind you-dumped on us. I remember the exact quote, 'I turned on MTV and saw Slaughter at Number One for nine weeks and figured I should think about retiring', something like that. I mean, what an angry, arrogant motherfucker." - Dana Strum, Slaughter, Rip Magazine, May 1991. (Metal-Sludge: Like Dana never talks shit! We salute Nuno for that comment.)

Here's a question that was asked to Mick Mars in the February 6th, 1988 issue of Kerrang! It was about a month after Nikki Sixx OD and died and their European tour was cancelled. What about the Nikki Sixx drugs OD story? It's said that it occurred right after that (The Japan Girls Girls Girls tour) ended.
"I heard about that too, and I just started laughing! It's total shit...just another one of those dumb stories that get put out about us. Honestly, man, stories like that about us go out all the time...did you hear the latest one about how I'm supposed to be getting married? I mean, COME ON! No way..."
So Nikki Sixx definitely did not suffer a drugs overdose?
"No! None of that happened! Nikki didn't die either...I heard that one, too! It's just dumb shit." - Mick Mars, Kerrang, February 6, 1988.

"We're better than they are. We're better musicians than they are. We're better players than they are. Put it this way, they can TRY and walk onstage after an Iron Maiden show if they want." - Bruce Dickinson talking about Metallica, Metal Hammer, May 1999

"KoRn are a fashion statement. The only fashion statement Iron Maiden make is fuck fashion. There's an eternal quality to great rock 'n roll; listen to the first Black Sabbath album - that album has never dated. Now play's KoRn's record - in 20 year's time I wonder what people will think of it. Will they truly be the future of rock 'n' roll or are they the Cinderella of the year 2000?" - Bruce Dickinson, Iron Maiden, Metal Hammer. May 1999

"Oh, fuck no. I saw that thing from Australia. It was so God-awful. I was so embarrassed. I couldn't stand it. It was just not what people want from Van Halen, obviously. The poor guy's singing Roth tunes, Sammy tunes, and it just doesn't sound right. Some of them sound flat fucking stupid. The band looked stupid. I was just wondering if we looked that stupid sometimes." - Sammy Hagar when asked if he was tempted to see the current Van Halen lineup live, from Rolling Stone Network, March 24, 1999

"Well, I've heard it...it's sad actually." - Sammy Hagar when asked his opinion on Van Halen 3, on the Howard Stern show March 9, 1999

"I'm pretty tired of hearing Billy Corgan from The Smashing Pumpkins whine about his fans and how they've turned their backs on him. Someone needs to smack that kid upside the head and tell him to shut the fuck up! He's always complaining." - Rob Zombie, Kerrang, February 13, 1999.

"I'm living the life of a rock star and that's more than 99% of all aspiring musicians can say." - Bruno Ravel, Danger Danger, Metal Edge, April 1996

es for still doing it." - Dana Strum, Slaughter, Las Vegas Review Journal, August 26,
cause it sure as hell ain't this one.)

rather tour with the Ramones or Iggy or Manson or KoRn. It's not about a period of time;
ey Crue, Express News, San Antonio, TX., March 4, 1999

ant to become (Motorhead frontman) Lemmy and be an overweight, wrinkled alcoholic.
besides you looking at me wrong." - Nikki Sixx, Motley Crue, Express News, San

ir name, you gotta look out for: 311, Third Eye Blind, Matchbox 20 - these are all bands
up to. I'm very concerned." - Marilyn Manson, Alternative Press, April 1999.

g to be rehabilitated from drugs and alcohol in order to be a more appropriate father for his
bastard child and his family ... ver, I see it's just a matter of hours now before I drag him down into my crystal-meth hell."
- Marilyn Manson on Jonathan Davis from KoRn, Alternative Press, April 1999.

"I use to get Slurpees for Dana Strum, the bass player in Slaughter." - Ross Robinson, Producer for KoRn, Limp Bizkit, Soulfly, Machine Head, etc..., Alternative Press, April 1999

"I still love being in Motley Crue, but it's becoming very trying. I find myself becoming more of a recluse. I'm the reluctant rock star. I don't want all this stuff that comes with it. The older I get, the more I hate it." - Nikki Sixx, Motley Crue, Metal Edge, May 1994

"I ain't some pretty boy glam fag." - Sebastian Bach, Metal Edge, March 1990

"Girls you don't hang on a tour bus and talk about the ozone layers, YOU SUCK DICK! THAT'S YOUR JOB." - Stefan Adika, L.A. Guns, From Metal-Sludge Gossip Board, 2/28/99

"I'm gonna spare you the usual 'We really matured as people and we've really grown up, the songwriting is so much more mature' crap. The day I become mature is the day I get out of what I'm doing because there's no room for maturity in this business. If anything, we've digressed. If people thought we were 19 on the last record, we're pushing eight or nine on this one." - Sebastian Bach, Metal Edge, October 1991.

"I'm not surprised that you think nothing of expecting me to drop everything and join... When we spoke about it six months ago I was a little interested in doing a live album but you fucked me then, and that's fine. Ralph deserved a break. But I've heard nothing but shit talked about me from you guys. I'd look pretty foolish jumping in now, don't you think? I have a band and a CD coming out soon. And knowing our chemistry the whole thing would last maybe a week... and I feel to get involved would be a step back. It would never work. It's like getting back with an old girlfriend. It's never the same. Bury LAG with a little dignity." - Phil Lewis, An open letter to Tracii Guns, released July 1998 after Ralph left L.A. Guns.

"Ya know what a lot of bands don't do? They don't age gracefully." - Nikki Sixx, Motley Crue, Decade Of Decadence Home Video, 1992

"If you want to find Nikki Sixx when he's not onstage, go look for him on the streets, hanging with the kids, sharing a beer and a sandwich 'cause that's where I'll be, man...on the streets where I belong." - Nikki Sixx, Motley Crue, Rock Shots '88

"Marilyn Manson is a completely different thing than Slaughter." - Dana Strum, Slaughter, Metal Edge, May 1999. Thanks for clearing that up Dana.

"I mean, hey, the guy's creative, okay? But he's a lousy human." - Eddie Van Halen on David Lee Roth, Guitar World, July 1985

"I fuck my brains out. I fuck everything that moves. And if it doesn't move, we work something out." - Gene $immon$, KISS, Playboy, March 1999

"Two days ago we saw this guy who had his whole back tattooed with our portraits. Stupid." - Peter Criss, KISS, Playboy March 1999

"The best gimmick I've seen is bands with multi-platinum albums going on-stage in ripped-up clothes making believe they're poor. That's a great gimmick." - Paul Stanley, KISS, Playboy March 1999

"The most bizarre thing was seeing my face wrapped around the gateway to hell. A tattoo. If you can imagine my mouth wide open-her lips at that point were not shut either. You know the phrase, Go fuck yourself?" - Gene $immon$, KISS, Playboy, March 1999

"I think my guitar playing is probably average. It's overrated." - Ace Frehley (in a sober, self-realization moment), KISS, Playboy, March 1999

"Oh, yeah, because he's (Billy Corgan) probably one of the few citizens of the alternative nation, or whatever you want to call it, that admits Van Halen was an influence. Everyone else says Kiss. I mean, give me a fuckin' break. If they play guitar, they must have heard Van Halen somewhere down the line. I just don't see Kiss being a guitar-inspiring type of thing. I mean, I'm not putting Kiss down at all. I love Gene, he helped us out in the beginning, and without him we probably wouldn't be where we are. But to say Ace Frehley was the reason you picked up a guitar?" - Eddie Van Halen, Guitar World, September 1996

"It reminded me of overdue dentist appointments."
"It sounded like hot water on a sick cat."
"You want me to sit here and salute the sinking of the Titanic?" - David Lee Roth on Howard Stern, when listening to the Van Halen song "How Many Say I", which is sung by Eddie.

"Eddie Van Halen's a weakling and his brother is a triple weakling." - David Lee Roth, October 18, 1997

"I don't understand U2's music. It's too serious. They bum me out." - Nikki Sixx, Motley Crue, Rolling Stone, August 13, 1987

"He looked like a pair of panty hose stuffed with cottage cheese." - David Lee Roth on Eddie Van Halen, October 18, 1997

"He's [Eddie Van Halen] got the spiritual spine of a chocolate eclair." - David Lee Roth, October 18, 1997

"I'm sorry I didn't do heroin when I was pregnant" - Sebastian Bach, Spin Magazine, February 1996

"If I hadn't made it in rock and roll I'd probably have become a hooker. You know, one of those high-class call girls who get paid for having sex with millionaires in exotic places. I think I could get off on that. But I've got to admit that I'd trade all the sex and all the partying in the world for a platinum album." - Lita Ford, Hit Parader Magazine, August 1988

"I was known as the metal guy, which I wasn't. I got labeled. I never picked one video the whole time I was at MTV! I never said I was metal." - Riki Rachtman, former Headbanger's Ball Host and former owner of the L.A. metal club the Cathouse, Spin Magazine, February 1996

"There's certain interviews I like. I hate Metal Edge and Hit Parader. I hate cheesey magazines. I think RIP's a really cool magazine, but I have to admit I don't really like doing interviews. I feel safe talking to you, but I've been burned by so many people. One person asked me, 'So Nikki, what's your favorite color?' Doug (Thaler, Motley's manager) couldn't get me to do an interview for a month after that. I don't like the bubblegum imagery of some magazines. It's a real catch 22-not wanting to talk to certain people, wanting to talk to others, not coming off as a snob" - Nikki Sixx, Motley Crue, Rip Magazine, March 1994

"The new record is so lame, and I'm not just saying that because of the way they look now. I don't care what they look like. I just hate the record because it has no attitude, no fire, no nothing. It sucks." - Kerry King, Slayer, on Metallica's 'Load' album, Kerrang, July 6, 1996

"There's also very little femininity in what Metallica do. Their gigs are like big wank sessions. All these geezers, virgin little boys, praying to this big willy." - Ian Astbury, The Cult, Vox, October 1991

"To me, Metallica is a shitty band. I mean I fucking hate Metallica. I think their music is crap. It's just garbage, and they won't be here in a few years. And I don't care if I get hassled for that. There is nothing in that music, lyrically, musically, rhythmically. I mean what's their fucking purpose? To me that's crap and I don't mind if I get shit for that." - Nikki Sixx, Motley Crue, Creem Metal, April 1990

"Dear, Sweet, Fat, Balding, Larz (love the make-up babe!)
Taking your ever-moronic soapbox position on a subject that's NONE of your fucking business has made you out to be an asshole as usual. Considering that me and Tommy know that your live tapes have been re-recorded. And ALL your instruments were repaired in Pro Tools (and had the balls to lie to your fans and call it a 'live' album)...People in glass houses should NOT throw rocks!! considering your bullshit to the press, we feel it's only fair to return the punch!!...You're such a poseur... Thanks for releasing that 'load' of shit CD of yours...you made more room for us!!" - Nikki Sixx & Tommy Lee on AOL, regarding Lars Ulrich's allegations that Motley performed to a tape at the American Music Awards in January of '97. (Motley did by the way.)

"Now that Poison's out of the way, we can go right to the top." - James Hetfield, Metallica, Rip Magazine, November 1991

"Ride The Wind? What the fuck is riding the fucking wind? How the fuck do you ride the wind?" I don't blame this song on Poison. I blame it totally on (producer) Bruce Fairbairn (R.I.P.). The tempo of the song, the happiness of the guitar sound-that's not fair to the band. Maybe there's some rock on here somewhere." - Nikki Sixx, Motley Crue, Rip Magazine, December 1990, when Nikki was listening to Poison's 'Flesh & Blood' Album.

"Poison is not a trendy band, because there's really no one that really does want to look like us or be like us." - Bret Michaels, Poison, Rip Magazine, December 1990

"I have no anger towards them (Poison). It's not like I'm talking about Phil Lewis of L.A. Guns, who time and time again has badmouthed us. Yeah, it's true that we used to open for you, and you ended up opening for us. But why get pissed off about it? Hey Phil, come over to my house, we'll sit down and talk about it. Otherwise you're gonna come off as the Kevin DuBrow of the '90s." - Jani Lane, Warrant, Hit Parader, November 1992

"If you've ever listened to Motley Crue you can't really say we're heavy metal. To me, heavy metal is Slayer or Anthrax, stuff that gives you a headache. It's boring noise! If you can't stomp your feet to it and it does not make you smile, I don't want to listen to it." - Nikki Sixx, Motley Crue, Metallix Sp. 2

"I'd cringe to see Motley Crue have that kind of success (referring to Bon Jovi). We're the largest cult band. We sell consistently three or four million records every year, sold out 15 to 20,000 seaters every night (two nights in the same city a lot of times). We're not going to ever be a pop band." - Nikki Sixx, Motley Crue, Metallix Sp. 2

"You know, the Feelgood thing got so big and so out of control. Only my friends who really know me understand this, but it was really a disappointing time in my career, because it was so big, with the jets, and limos and everything, it was just gross, man. It got so fucking big-four or five sold out arenas and stadiums, and four or five celebrities every night, I felt too far away from the fans, it was bumming me out, man. I remember Vince had this thing where he just really loved the jets and the limos. And me, Mick and Tommy were like, 'Can't we just ride in a van and a bus, so we can meet people?'" - Nikki Sixx, Motley Crue, Livewire Magazine, Volume 4 Number 11, Fall 1994.

"Well, they've disavowed drugs which I find a lie. Because at that age, if you're not doing drugs there is no reason to even be involved in rock 'n' roll. So if they don't start admitting to doing drugs, I'm gonna insult them. And I will plant drugs on them and call the police. Everyone's better when they're on drugs, undoubtedly. Rock 'n' roll is about drugs. - Marilyn Manson on Aerosmith, Kerrang

"A band like Aerosmith, one of my all-time favorite bands, they just made an album worse than Foreigner. Come on guys, you're fuckin' Aerosmith. You guys have got the balls to do. Fuckin' make a record that'll blow everyone's mind. Take a chance. Get rid of these bubblegum songwriters. The guys who wrote "Walk This Way" and "Dream On" do not need songwriters. It breaks my heart to hear a song like their first single "Falling Down Is Hard On Your Knees" or whatever it's called ("Falling In Love (Is Hard On The Knees"). I just go 'Nooooo, man. Come on guys, you're fuckin' Aerosmith. You're the bad ass motherfuckers! You hear the song they did for that "Sergeant Peppers" movie and the music they're doing now and you just have to hang your head. I'm not going to be that band. We're going to keep pushin' and pushin'. We may lose some people." - Nikki Sixx, Motley Crue, Q & A from Nikki's Car Phone by Sheila Rene', 1997.

"I'd like to see celebrity deaths from KoRn. I'd like to see several members of that band die, so that that Adidas rock would stop making young kids have a terrible sense of fashion and a terrible sense of what rock 'n' roll should be." - Marilyn Manson, Kerrang

Tommy Lee, Nikki Sixx, and Mick Mars were on MTV's Week In Rock back in 1994. They were asked how they felt about Vince Neil's jet ski accident when he hit a coral reef.
Tommy: "How's the coral reef?"
Nikki: "What do you expect when 300 pounds of blubber hits a coral reef?"
Mick: "You're invited but you weigh a ton."

"I don't drink and drive, I might spill it." - Eddie Van Halen, Rip Magazine, February 1992

"Puking is the second best release to orgasm. I dig it. When I puke, it's totally righteous. It's so great. It's like a total release of heaviness. It's like an orgasm coming out of your mouth. It's sexual." - Sebastian Bach, Rip Magazine, January 1991

"Bands get pissed off at us for having to do meet-and-greets. Because it's part of our tour, they now feel pressure by their fans to do the same. And many aren't happy about it." - Dana Strum, Slaughter, Screamer Magazine, September 1992

"There's an emotional commitment but you can never commit everything, and the person that commits everything has nothing for themselves. The only kind of relationship you can have in my opinion is a realistic one, which is you cannot control another human being, period. Expect nothing from another human being...It's too bad if they get hurt. Your happiness comes first. How can a person you've only known a year, two, five, ten, whatever, expect anything more than nothing? If someone takes a dollar from me I'll scream bloody murder but if I give somebody a dollar, I give it gladly. It's freedom of choice." - Gene $immon$ on relationships, Kiss Alive Worldwide 96/97 Tour Magazine

"It's fucking GREAT to be filthy rich, unbelievably famous, and able to fuck whoever I goddam please. It's too bad you'll never be able to experience anything close to the happiness I experience on my shittiest day, you live-in-a-snowbank-work-at-the-donut-shop piece of hoser shit." - Sebastian Bach, Replying to someone in Metal-Sludge Mailbag who was talking shit about him, November 28, 1998

"Well, the guys in Alice In Chains have bad-mouthed us over and over and over again too. We're on the same label, and we were asked to let them open for us. We did it, and I actually liked those guys. Then they sell half a million records, and they turn into a bunch of whiners who think they're the coolest thing since sliced bread. It just makes me want to say, 'Hey, grow up!'" - Jani Lane, Warrant, Hit Parader, November 1992

"Def Leppard? That's such a strange comparison. I guess I'll have to hack off my arm and beat my wife with my good one." - Marilyn Manson, when asked if he thought the song 'I Don't Like The Drugs' sounded like it could be a Def Leppard hit from 1984, Kerrang, September 19, 1998

"Chicken McNuggets don't die any easier than baby fur seals" - Ted Nugent, Rip Magazine, July 1991

"Too many fags on that stage for me, dude." - Tommy Lee on Madonna's back-up Dancers during the Blonde Ambition Tour

"God knows Guns 'N' Roses wore more makeup than Warrant ever did" - Jerry Dixon, Warrant, Rip Magazine, December 1992

"I've seen so many Glam bands get bounced from labels, and it makes me ecstatic." - Glenn Danzig, Rip Magazine, November 1992

"It's not commercial metal, it's not real heavy, it's comfortable like an old sneaker" - Peter Loran, Trixter, 1992, (Metal-Sludge: on the sound of their 'Hear' album that was a bigger bomb than the bombs dropped over Hiroshima. How can he say Trixter wasn't commercial metal? That's like saying Vince Neil can sing.)

"I think the Doors suck. The Doors blew! I went out and got the Jim Morrison lyric book and threw it in the trash! It's garbage! The guy couldn't write to save his ass!" - Nikki Sixx, Motley Crue, Rip Magazine, December 1991

"I don't understand why it's worse for a man to pose naked in a magazine than a woman" - Jesse James Dupree, Jackyl, Rip Magazine

"I hate coke, though. It sucks! If there's any kid out there doing it, just quit. You don't control it, it controls you. It's fucking horrible." - Sebastian Bach, Kerrang, April 8, 1995

"Ozzy is not paying the bands enough money. He asked us and we said no. Ten thousand dollars a night is chickenshit. It costs more than that for us to get from town to town, it costs more than that for us to have an entourage! You try and tell Dave, Nick, Marty and myself that we're gonna be able to split a fiver for playing the show tonight-fuck you, Ozzy." - Dave Mustaine, Megadeth, on why Megadeth didn't do Ozz Fest in 1997, Metal Hammer, September 1997 (I guess Ozzy paid them more the next year, 'cause they then went out with Ozzy)

"My contemporaries are Garth Brooks and the Spice Girls. They're not doing anything rock, but they're doing things on the same grand scale that I like to do things on" - Marilyn Manson, Kerrang, September 19, 1998

" I never met an asshole in the record business I didn't like." - Irving Azoff

"We live in an age of music for people who don't like music. The record industry discovered some time ago that there aren't that many people who actually like music. For a lot of people, music's annoying, or at the very least they don't need it. They discovered if they could sell music to a lot of those people, they could sell a lot more records." - T Bone Burnett

"The whole music business in the United States is based on numbers, based on unit sales and not on quality. It's not based on beauty, it's based on hype and it's based on cocaine. It's based on giving presents of large packages of dollars to play records on the air." - Frank Zappa

"Modern music is people who can't think, signing artists who can't write songs, to make records for people who can't hear." - Frank Zappa

"Just because it happened to you, doesn't mean it's interesting" - Dennis Hopper (Search and Destroy)

"Just because you can record, doesn't mean you should." - Christopher Knab, FourFront Media and Music

"Independent labels take nothing and make something out of it. Major labels buy that something, and try to make more out of it." - Tom Silverman, Tommy Boy Records CEO

"When you hear my records today...you hear a vanilla sounding artist with no black inflection, although I was trying to imitate what I heard." - Pat Boone

"You go through stages where you wonder whether you are Christ, or just looking for him." - David Bowie

"Actually I don't know if honesty is a strength or some kind of weakness." - Ani DeFranco

"That's not easy to find in a corporate world, somebody who cares about music." - Michael Penn, musician

"I'm a snake oil salesman as much as anyone else, but I try to keep something for myself...I don't kiss the world's ass." - Freedy Johnston

"Anybody that forms a group, writes songs and releases records and says they don't care if people like them are complete liars."

- James Dean Bradfield, Manic St. Preachers

"I mean the Cranberries could go on and take a shit and the people would probably love it." - Jon Spencer

"Music is a big machine that would go on with or without me." - Rob Thomas, Matchbox 20

"Music should be about bastardization." - John McCrae, Cake

"Rap fans are quick to forget what they appreciated just last year." - Trugoy, De La Soul

"In this business, the first rule is, never act out of desperation, because there is always someone out there looking to sucker you." - Kevin Czinger, Volcano Entertainment Founder

"The problem with alternative radio is that it has no fiber at all, and is giving itself it's own enema." - Mike Halloran, former KUPR PD

"The hardest thing in the world to do in this business is start a band nobody's heard of." - Tom Whalley, Interscope Records

"If we do our job...Music's not black or white, it's green." - Jim Caparro, PGD

"Going to radio with a rap record prior to going to the consumer is like having no foreplay with your girlfriend." - Lyor Cohen, Def Jam/RAL

"There would be no new school without the old school." - Vivian Scott, Epic Records

"Money had never been the main thing for me. It's the legacy that was important." - Barry Gordy, Motown Records

"Our whole preconception will be what's going to make the kid push our button and not someone else's." - Bruce Kirland, Capitol Records

"We'll take advantage of the changes going on in the music business because we're lean and mean." - Miles Copeland, IRS Records

"That's the shame about Miles Copeland; he's evil, but he's got a heart of gold." - Dave Wakeling, General Public

"We're starting to climb. I've got my fingers crossed, my toes crossed, my testicles crossed...And it's painful too I might add." - Rick Michaels, WENZ Radio

" People don't buy plastic and paper, they buy emotions." - Scott Young, Wherehouse Entertainment

"You can't control the public from itself. If they get good tickets, they scalp them. If they get bad tickets, they bitch." - Fred Rosen, Ticketmaster

"American music is something the rest of the world wants to listen to. Our job is to make sure they pay for it." - Jason Berman, RIAA

"You've got to feel comfortable with people telling you your shit stinks." - Andre Harrell, Uptown Entertainment

"I'm a survivor in a business that constantly rejects you." - Dick Clark

"I hate to say this, but at the time, (late 70's) it was like the smart people liked punk and the dumb people liked Journey." - Howie Klein, President Reprise Records

"Kill all the major record company presidents." - Howie Klein, 1978... KSAN Radio Show-the Outcaste Hour

"I've made hundreds of legendary records that people talk about that didn't sell." - Jerry Wexler

"Without freedom of expression, good taste means nothing." - Neil Young

"I think anyone with less than 10 years experience in this business starting his own label is looking to create a disaster." - Russ Regan, Quality Records

"Listen, the easiest way to get laid by a girl, or get rid of her, is to write a song about her." - David Crosby

"Without music, the greatest marketing plans in the whole world don't mean shit." - Eddie Rosenblatt, Geffen Records

"Without marketing plans, the greatest music in the whole world don't mean shit." - Christopher Knab, FourFront Media and Marketing

"Who could have dreamed in 1965 that the alternative society would eventually multiply to such extraordinary proportions that it becomes our mainstream." - Bill Graham

"I want to hear the word 'cherish' about 5 times." - Clive Davis, Arista Record (listening back to an Air Supply song during a mixdown in the studio)

"If the milk industry can make their product seem sexy and increase consumer demand, there must be hope for music." - Gary Arnold, Merchandising Manager, Best Buy

"I think the second you feel you've gotten somewhere, you're nowhere." - Michael Goldstone, VP A&R, Epic Records

"You're a local band until you get a record contract, then all of a sudden Bruce Springsteen is your competition." - Sammy Llana, The Bodeans

"I don't listen to music, I hate all music." - Johnny Rotten

"I don't think anybody steals anything; all of us borrow." - BB King

"He took my music, but he gave me my name." - Muddy Waters on Mick Jagger

"If KISS is a dinosaur, damn straight I'd rather be that than a mouse." - Gene $immon$, KISS

"We're the McDonald's of rock. We're always there to satisfy, and a billion served." - Paul Stanley, KISS

"Don't try to explain it, just sell it." - Colonel Tom Parker

"The way I see it, rock n' roll is folk music." - Robert Plant

"I wish there had been a music business 101 course I could have taken." - Kurt Cobain

"Rock n' roll does for music what a motorcycle club at full throttle does for a quiet afternoon. The results bear passing resemblance to Hitler mass meetings." - Time Magazine, 1956

"Rock n' roll is poison put to sound." - Pablo Casals

"In Los Angeles, they don't want you to fail, they want you to die." - David Geffen

"I sent a demo of the band Confederate Fagg to an A&R friend at Sony. I asked him what he thought. He said, "Don't know yet. Let me see what my boss thinks." - Dave Kathoyd

"There are more letters in the word 'business' than there are in the word 'music'." - Anonymous

"Consumers have musical choice? What musical choice? In our society we choose only from what we are given to choose from, and that choice is determined by 5 major media corporations who control the exposure outlets that consumers depend on for their entertainment." - Christopher Knab, FourFront Media and Music

"Music executives need to start thinking less like men and more like women. As men, we tend to believe more in selling someone something for $15 and transferring it to their possession without ever learning their names. Women understand the value of starting a relationship that never ends. There's too many men in our business." - Anonymous

"If you are still at the same point you were after six albums, and all of them came out on a major label, I don't want to hear about how 'the label didn't understand us,' or 'our management didn't make us a priority.' If after that time you are still at the same level, either you suck, or people do not like you." - Anonymous

"I told my dad, 'When I grow up I want to be a (rock star),' and he said, 'I don't think you can do both.'" - STEVEN TYLER

"There is nothing interesting to me about seeing a 50 year-old man with a guitar onstage." - GENE $IMMON$ - 1987

""The only way I could ever see doing any shows with makeup is if they're the last ones of our career. That's not about to happen for a long, long time." - GENE $IMMON$ - 1988

"God gives you a choice in life, you can have MORE money, or LESS money... pick one!" - GENE $IMMON$ - Metal Edge Magazine

"My family is no different than any other family." - JANET JACKSON

"I want to embrace a certain stupidity." - BECK

"I just want to come out with a party record with dumb songs and dumb lyrics." - BECK

"Dumbness rocks." - BECK

"Destiny's Child are here to stay." - DESTINY'S CHILD

"We think if you start as a group, you should end as a group. And we are together!" - FORMER DESTINY'S CHILD SINGER LATAVIA 1998

"My reputation as a tyrant, Svengali, asshole. There's truth in that." - BILLY CORGAN

"For a six foot three guy with no hair and a whiny voice, I've done alright." - BILLY CORGAN

"We have a rule in our band. You can't have sex on a show day." - BILLY CORGAN

"Call me what you like... there's a method to my madness." - BILLY CORGAN

"I must resign today due to medical reasons. Billy Corgan was making me sick." - SHARON OSBORNE - Former Smashing Pumpkins Manager

"He's a control freak." - SHARON OSBORNE on Billy Corgan

"Me and Malmsteen had broken up over religious reasons. He thought he was God and I didn't agree." - JOE LYNN TURNER

"Do I think I'm normal? Yes, I do." - PRINCE

"If people think I'm insane, fine. I want people to think I'm insane." - PRINCE

"Sometimes I stand in awe of what I do myself." - PRINCE

You've had a lot of rock stars over at your ranch to go hunting. Tell us who is the most natural at it and who was the biggest pussy about it?
"Joe Perry is a natural predator. Ace Frehley was funnier than Richard Pryor on fire."
"He (Ace Frehley) probably would've made a better welder than a guitar player." - TED NUGENT

ACE FREHLEY - "I'd like to toast all of my fans in Holland..."
PAUL STANLEY - "You'll toast anything!"

"Whenever I watch TV and see those poor starving kids all over the world, I can't help but cry. I mean I'd love to be skinny like that but not with all those flies and death and stuff." - MARIAH CAREY

"Researchers have discovered that chocolate produces some of the same reactions in the brain as marijuana...The researchers also discovered other similarities between the two, but can't remember what they are." - MATT LAUER on NBC's Today show, August 2

"The music business is a cruel and shallow money trench, a long plastic hallway where thieves and pimps run free, and good men die like dogs. There's also a negative side." - HUNTER S. THOMPSON

"I didn't know I liked the way you play guitar that much." - A prominent record executive

"Try to look at the big picture ... we're all in it and you're not!" - Industry executive to a stubborn engineer

"Show me a 'good loser' and I'll show you a friggin' LOSER!" - Bruce Allen (Bryan Adams' and Martina McBride's manager)

"It sounds a lot more like it does now than it did ten minutes ago." - unknown A&R guy

"Could you put that up an octave just a little?" - unknown producer

"I just want the vibe of the strings to be on the tape." - unknown producer after telling the engineer to erase the string tracks he just spent the entire day recording

"So let's run an instrumental version, and then one without any vocals." - Steve Lindsey

"Bruce just listened to all the songs on the greatest hits LP. He wants to speed them all up, except for 'Thunder Road', which speeds up all by itself." - John Landau

"He's not stupid. He just has emerging skills." - Diplomatic engineer referring to producer who spilled coffee on the mixing board.

"Does the noise in my head bother you?" - Highly caffeinated engineer up for 36 hours.

"I've never liked backwards ideas. It always sounds like you've run out of forwards ideas." - Gilson Lavis, former drummer with Squeeze

"Well, that's the dilemma. It's supposed to be a solo and the backing vocals aren't very good, so I'd turn up the hand claps and make it a party sort-of vibe." - Paul Westerberg in response to Bob's question "Is that a solo?"

"I make records so I can buy art." - Jimmy Iovine to Jim Kerr after hearing lyrics to a new Simple Minds song.

"And now he's flanging the VU meters" - A&R guy trying to impress an attractive woman in the studio by showing her how much recording experience he has.

Joe Pine (60's talk show host who sported a wooden leg) to Frank Zappa - "So, with your long hair, I guess that makes you a woman." Frank Zappa's response - "So, with your wooden leg, I guess that makes you a table."

"That's not a bug, that's a feature." - Phil Cork, SSL software engineer

"You don't actually have to be able to understand the lyrics, you've just got to feel like you could if you wanted to" - Chuck Plotkin (Producer for Bruce Springsteen)

"What do I care about lyrics... I'm a bass player!" - John Pierce

"Why the hell would I make up a name like 'Froom'?" - Mitchell Froom, upon being asked if 'Froom' was his real name.

"I can't wait to hear it with a real mix instead of a douche mix." - John Kalodner

Industry Executive - "So why didn't the trade show literature get edited?"
Marketing Assistant - "I guess nobody thought of it."
Exec - "OK then, who's the 'nobody' who didn't think of it?"

Richard - "I heard an Olivia Newton-John album that was mixed using an 'Aural Exciter.'"
Engineer - "Oh yeah? Did it sound good?"
Richard - "Nah, but she looked great!" - Richard Moakes (assistant eng. at Air Studios in 1987)

"He's not the same player he used to be - but even more so." - Unknown producer referring to recording artist who'd seen better days.

"The only thing worse than kicking a dead horse is saddling one." - Unknown engineer referring to a bad mix getting worse.

"No brain, no headache." - Unknown engineer referring to guitarist who accidentally swallowed his guitar pick.

"When you get to Hell will you save me a seat?" - Female vocalist to irreverent engineer.

"You play it now, I'll skip it for you later." - Producer asking for a part from a violinist after the violinist suggested skipping that section.

Glen Matlock, 45, told Reuters backstage the Sex Pistols would be "daft" not to capitalize on their momentum and play more shows. Additionally, he said it would take only a week to make an album. "It's just finding the right week." Even though the band members are hardly friends, Matlock said the musical chemistry was unmistakable. "It's like an old comfortable shoe -- with a nail coming through it," he said.

"What's that sound?" - A 14 year old visitor on hearing a two inch tape machine rewind.

INDEX, ACKNOWLEDGEMENTS AND CREDITS

PITBULL PUBLISHING CATALOG

Title: KISS & Tell
ISBN # 0-9658794-0-2
228 Pages
5 1/2" x 8 1/2"
Price: $19.95

Title: Rock & Roll War Stories
ISBN # 0-9658794-2-9
240 Pages
7" x 9"
Price: $19.95

Title: KISS & Tell MORE!
ISBN # 0-9658794-1-0
300 Pages
5 1/2" x 8 1/2"
Price: $19.95

Coming Soon!
Release Date
To Be Announced

**On a Wing and
a Prayer With Angel**

by Gordon G. G. Gebert

ISBN # 0-9658794-5-3

Title: Into The Void...
With Ace Frehley
Author: Wendy Moore
ISBN # 0-9658794-4-5
Price: TBA

Title: Still Wicked CD
UPC # 6 69510 00012 4
Price: $11.95

Release Date
To Be Announced

Stand-Up Guy

by Frank D'Amico

ISBN # 0-9658794-6-1

Release Date
To Be Announced

**ANGEL DVD
with
Gordon G. G. Gebert**

Release Date
To Be Announced

KISS & Tell - THE DVD

Pitbull Publishing ORDER FORM

Qty.	ISBN Number	Description	Price	Subtotal
	0-9658794-0-2	KISS & Tell Book	$19.95	
	0-9658794-1-0	KISS & Tell More! Book	$19.95	
	0-9658794-2-9	Rock and Roll War Stories	$19.95	
	0-9658794-4-5	Into The Void... With Ace Frehley	TBA	
	0-9658794-5-3	On a Wing and a Prayer With Angel	TBA	
	0-9658794-6-1	Stand-Up Guy	TBA	
	6 69510 00012 4	Still Wicked CD	$11.95	
	TBA	KISS & Tell - The DVD	$29.95	
	TBA	Angel with Gordon G. G. Gebert DVD	TBA	

Shipping (check one) Additional items add $3.00 per item (Foreign orders add $5.00 per item)

☐ U.S. Basic $4.00   ☐ Foreign Basic $10.00   ☐ Canada and Mexico Basic $7.00

☐ U.S. Priority $7.00   ☐ Foreign Priority $17.00

☐ U.S. Overnight $15.00   ☐ Foreign Overnight $30.00

Total $_____

Please print extremely clearly and legibly

LAST NAME_____ FIRST_____

STREET_____

CITY_____ STATE_____ ZIP_____

COUNTRY _____

PHONE: (_____) _____ E-MAIL_____

Method of payment: ☐ VISA ☐ MASTERCARD ☐ DISCOVER

☐ CHECK ☐ MONEY ORDER

NAME ON CARD_____

CARD NUMBER_____

EXP. DATE_____Auth. Code (Office Use Only)_____

MAIL Check, Money Order or Credit Card order (U.S. funds only) to:

Pitbull Publishing LLC
PO Box 350
Fleetwood NY 10552-0350

* AUTOGRAPHED COPY - $5 extra each item. (1 signature of one author's authentic signature at distributor's random discretion when available)
ALL SALES ARE FINAL.
United States currency, check, credit card or money order only.